FREEDOM ISN'T FREE

FREEDOM ISN'T FREE

THE PRICE OF WORLD ORDER

MARKOS KOUNALAKIS

ANTHEM PRESS

Anthem Press
An imprint of Wimbledon Publishing Company
www.anthempress.com

This edition first published in UK and USA 2022
by ANTHEM PRESS
75–76 Blackfriars Road, London SE1 8HA, UK
or PO Box 9779, London SW19 7ZG, UK
and
244 Madison Ave #116, New York, NY 10016, USA

British Library Cataloguing-in-Publication Data
A catalogue record for this book is available from the British Library.

Library of Congress Control Number: 2021951240

ISBN-13: 978-1-83998-128-9 (Hbk)
ISBN-10: 1-83998-128-8 (Hbk)
ISBN-13: 978-1-83998-190-6 (Pbk)
ISBN-10: 1-83998-190-3 (Pbk)

Cover credit: Price Tag icon vector illustration logo template for many purpose.
Isolated on white background. By Free Production/Shutterstock.com

This title is also available as an e-book.

CONTENTS

FOREWORD

By Nancy Ancrum
Editorial Page Editor
Miami Herald

I leapt at the chance to edit Markos Kounalakis' weekly column when the opportunity first arose. Not because I thought he would be an easy edit—though he was. Not because he was a dream to deal with personally—though he was that, too.

No, I looked forward to reading his columns—both before and after becoming his editor—because they always left me saying to myself: "I didn't know that!" I learned so much each time—even from the tidbits in his taglines (always rigorously relevant to the column):

- "Markos Kounalakis is considering vegetarianism. He's a visiting fellow at the Hoover Institution," following a column on African Swine Fever decimating China's pork production.
- "Markos Kounalakis no longer has a Christmas Club account. He is a visiting fellow at the Hoover Institution," highlighting China's banking misbehavior.
- "Markos Kounalakis hopes Greek Kalamata olives still get shipped to America. He is a visiting fellow at the Hoover Institution," on how our food choices can hurt the environment.

No, Markos's columns are not all about Markos. Then again, maybe they are, because he so aptly connects the personal to the global. His astute op-eds about the world and our place in it, are the best sort of opinion essays: informed, rooted in fact, experience and compassion. Published and avidly read in the Miami Herald—where I have been editorial page editor since 2013—and on other McClatchy news sites, they represent Markos's non-negotiables.

Readers never need to guess what he holds dear: our personal freedoms, the social compacts that guarantee those freedoms—and what we all must do to ensure that those guarantees never expire. And where they don't exist? Then, people have some hard work to do. Markos clearly elucidates "the price of world order in the pursuit of national interest."

Which means that Markos's collection of columns comes at just the right time in this current historical juncture, no matter where we reside. Given the guiding principles by which they were produced—preserving and defending our freedoms—they remain ever relevant, no matter when they were initially published.

His columns resonated especially with readers in South Florida, a region rich in refugees from the world's most enduring dictators and autocrats—often dressed in progressives' clothing—who sold their hopeful people a bill of goods.

"The Castro successors in Havana and the endless Ortega family business in Nicaragua govern with an iron fist. Political change threatens their power, and they avoid it at all costs." That's characteristic of Markos's cautionary précis.

"People are on the move from Syria and Libya, desperate humans trying their hardest to escape civil wars. In both countries, civilians are Russian and Turkish pawns caught in punishing proxy wars."

"On Israel, the Paris Climate Accord, and the Iran nuclear deal, [presidential candidate Pete Buttigieg] argued for no more than a restorationist policy. Rejoining deals Donald Trump famously 'tore up' is not a plan to renegotiate terms or reformulate conditions. It's safe, easy, and not exactly bold to tape together and add a new signature to these previous deals." Ouch!

Markos doesn't waste his words, which are clear-eyed, honest, and relevant. This book delivers. Oh, and Markos also regularly burns popcorn on the stove.

INTRODUCTION

AN EXPENSIVE GOOD

What is the price of freedom? It seems like a straightforward question. The answer is anything but simple. This edited collection of my newspaper columns explores our various types of freedom and the ways in which we pay for them.

The desire for freedom has deep historical roots. Philosophers have opined about free will and the nature of freedom since time immemorial. In the modern era, American colonists fought a revolution to be free from oppressive "taxation without representation" levied by the British Crown.

Throughout the twentieth century, freedom has been the battle cry of democracies and would-be democracies at home and around the globe. In his first campaign for the White House, Woodrow Wilson successfully ran on a "New Freedom" platform. During his State of the Union address on January 6, 1941, President Franklin D. Roosevelt famously advocated for four freedoms:

1. Freedom of speech
2. Freedom of worship
3. Freedom from want
4. Freedom from fear

But what is freedom's price tag?

The cost is borne by individuals, institutions, and society. People sacrifice blood and treasure to achieve independence as well as to maintain and defend it. For some, the cost may be perceived as too high. Sadly, some freedoms are lost, frittered away, or taken away.

Although we pay lip service (and are bound by international treaty) to respect universal human rights, freedom's details differ from one country or culture to another. In the United States, we hold freedom of speech, assembly, and belief as fundamental to our national identity. They are enshrined in the documents that established America as independent and sovereign. They are constitutionally codified and traditionally cherished.

Those fundamental freedoms have been hard won in the Anglophone world. They are also unavailable or, at best, exclusively limited privileges to the majority of the planet's population.

While democracy is a desired state and freedom a desired condition, state-sponsored regime change in the name of democracy promotion has become a disfavored—and often failed—policy option. Achieving democratic ideals at the point of a gun has proven a misguided approach, whether in Vietnam in the 1970s, or in Libya and Iraq in the twenty-first century. The means to achieve rooted, lasting, and successful democracy and individual freedoms is for these ideals to permeate society and appeal to a majority of a populace based on its merits, not on its foreign power promoters.

In these compiled columns, you will read arguments and advocacy for universal freedoms. They echo the fundamental belief that every person on earth should have the right to life, liberty, and the pursuit of happiness. At the moment, this is not a universal view. In fact, it is not even a consistently held aspiration in countries enjoying or seeking to achieve those rights.

Many in the United States believe that America should promote democratic rights and liberal freedoms everywhere. Others argue that the costs of doing so are too high.

Even guaranteeing freedom domestically—for example, to ensure universal suffrage—comes with a cost that is politically high and is often highly partisan. We witness frequent efforts to manage, marginalize, or entirely disenfranchise large swaths of the electorate. Meanwhile, the price of promoting democracy in places like Afghanistan and Iraq has been enormous with marked consequences at the ballot box back home.

Those wars, initially fought in unilateral retribution and with imperial hubris, have humbled America's greater global ambitions. The failed policy, lost war, and squandered allocation of precious national resources created a dissonance on the home front, and the space and time necessary for America's most menacing competitor, the People's Republic of China, to act more aggressively and prominently on the world stage.

This book lays out in some disturbing detail the price tag for those seeking assorted liberties.

- Freedom of speech cost the life of dissident Saudi Arabian journalist Jamal Khashoggi. His October 2018 murder and dismemberment at the kingdom's consulate in Istanbul shocked the world. The horrific crime and subsequent denial of responsibility by Saudi government officials underscored, among other things, the difference in values between the United States and its close ally.

- Freedom of religion cost the killing and beheading of French school teacher Samuel Paty in October 2020. As President Emmanuel Macron put it after that death, the gruesome homicide contradicts everything that the French Revolution fought to achieve—*liberté, egalité, fraternité*—as well as "the freedom to believe and the freedom not to believe."

- Freedom of assembly and protest has had a very high cost in Ukraine and Belarus, Hong Kong and Venezuela. For decades, these places erupted in unprecedented democratic uprisings followed by brutal, dictatorial suppression.

- Freedom to a clean environment. For centuries, experts have warned about an existential threat to our ecosystem from reckless human activity. The entire planet is already paying a heavy cost for anthropogenic climate change. Less developed nations also pay a disproportionately high price for mitigating a whole range of other ecological hazards, from air and water pollution to drought, flooding, erosion, and the like.

- Freedom to life. There might be none greater than the right to live and to thrive as a fully actuated human being, in dignity, without fear, and to achieve one's God-given potential. That basic freedom to breath and a heartbeat has been wantonly taken by dictators and authoritarian states.

As of this writing, good health has been increasingly fragile during a global pandemic managed better by some governments than others. In light of the highly varied responses to and management of the novel coronavirus, authoritarian states want liberal-minded people to reassess their systems and the failed responses to contain the virus and protect its citizens.

Bizarrely, some individuals in democratic societies assess the value of their freedom so highly that they are willing to risk the lives of others as they express their freedom to protest public health directives. This is just one contemporary issue where the price of freedom is actively being reconsidered—and the costs may ultimately be seen as too high.

Although I originally wrote these columns as commentary on current events, the larger issues transcend politics and news headlines. Taken together in this context, they provide additional insights into the human spirit. My conclusions trend toward an optimistic view of ourselves and the world around us.

CHAPTER 1

FREEDOM OF SPEECH

SILENCING "THE CANNON"

Introduction

Americans traditionally (and constitutionally) hate censorship. The U.S. government has rarely even tried to silence its critics. Instead, that power is exercised by privately-owned media companies which have muzzled some of the most notorious voices. By contrast, China has shut down several pro-democracy activists including a highly prominent one online.

Originally published: March 2, 2016

Social media made him a star. He is a real estate mogul whose followers believe he speaks truth to power. As a result of his outspoken anti-establishment political posture and popularity, his party wants to shut him down.

He is, of course, "The Cannon." Never heard of him? He is the man with 37 million social media followers on Sina Weibo—China's top microblogging site—and the country's ruling Communist Party just took him on by taking him offline.

The Cannon is Ren Zhiqiang's nickname and what happens to him next is uncertain, but with such a big and passionate following, it will be difficult to disappear him either quickly or quietly. He is known as The Cannon because of the straight-talk missives he fires at the authorities. Cannon is not alone, however, in finding that speech in China is not free.

Two weeks ago, Premier Xi Jinping, who has refashioned himself in short order as the "core" leader[1] of the Chinese people and has begun the makings of a

---

1 Shi, "Xi's New Title Highlights China's Power Struggle."

new cult of personality,[2] declared what most people already understood: China's media exists solely to serve the party. End of conversation.

Well, almost. Cannon expressed his opinion that, in fact, the media should instead serve the public, not the party! In liberal democracies, the 21st century is characterized by the cacophony of voices and opinions that flow freely in Western societies and on the Internet. But in places where authoritarian control is still firmly in place, free speech and assembly are seen as subversive and potentially revolutionary acts.

Enter the dragon: Jiang Jian of China's Cyberspace Administration forced the social media site to delete Cannon's posts. Jiang said, "Cyberspace is not a lawless field, and no one should use it to spread illegal information."

Think about that for a moment: What would qualify as "illegal information" in the West? Yelling "fire" in a crowded theater?[3] Divulging troop movements[4] during time of war? The bar for banned speech is set high in the United States and most of America's allied nations—though Turkey is a notable exception.

What did Cannon say? "When did the people's government change into the party's government? Is their money the party's? [...] Don't use taxpayers' money for things that don't provide them with services." That post and Cannon's voice have been deleted, now existing only in screenshots and the servers of San Francisco's Internet Archive.[5]

China is flexing its muscle and silencing its critics with more intensity and focused intent. It builds a higher Great Firewall[6] to keep ideas out, kidnaps book publishers[7] across borders, intimidates and arrests peaceful protesters carrying yellow umbrellas,[8] religious practitioners,[9] religious practitioners and artists like Ai Weiwei.[10] The rising voices of a burgeoning, bustling Beijing are being tamped to sound a monotonous pro-party thrum.

---

2 "The Power of Xi Jinping."

3 Volokh, "'Shouting Fire in a Crowded Theater.'"

4 Goldfarb, "State Secrets?"

5 "Internet Archive: Digital Library of Free & Borrowable Books, Movies, Music & Wayback Machine."

6 AFP & SCMP, "Great Firewall 'upgrade' Hits Internet Users as China Prepares Crackdown."

7 Beijing, "Gui Minhai."

8 Yuen, "Yellow Umbrella Protesters in Tense Standoff with Police in Mong Kok."

9 Dyer, "Is China Afraid of the Next Miss World?"

10 Yeung, "Ai Weiwei."

Free speech must feel very threatening to a leadership that wants only one story told, only one idea promoted, only one party to stay in perpetual power.

Secure nations and leaders are less worried about speech and more concerned with the health and well-being of their people. They look to increase people's liberties because those freedoms are not threatening to a healthy, self-renewing, innovative and confident system. Silencing a blogger is an admission that the party is feeling fear and insecurity.

Clamping down on dissent is usually the first stage of how an insecure nation reacts to challenges to its ruling structure. The United States and others must work to make sure China feels secure and successful enough within her borders to neither threaten her people nor the world.

In the meantime, America faces its own challenges from a network and social media phenom.

Unlike China, however, the Republican Party will not shut down the Twitter accounts of its front-running real estate mogul—despite the number of people Donald Trump would personally like to shut up or punch out. Like it or not, this is a world of courageous Cannons and bombastic blowhards.

Coda: Social media companies finally did what the GOP would not: They pulled the plug on the former 45th U.S. president. In September 2020, A Chinese court sentenced Ren Zhiqiang to 18 years in prison.

BOOKS AND IDEAS

Introduction

The ultimate threat to oppression is free expression. Just ask China. Or pro-democracy demonstrators no longer free to protest on the streets and in the shopping malls of Hong Kong. But long before Beijing implemented its "national security" law to silence those seeking autonomy, the central government arrested critical writers and banned their books.

Originally published: July 14, 2016

Book publishers are an endangered species. Amazon.com may be the most immediate worry[11] for anyone in the book publishing business, where fear of the internet retail giant's power over content and distribution is pervasive. As a former publisher, I understand the economic challenges of today's marketplace.

---

11 Gessen, "How Did Amazon End Up as Literary Enemy No. 1?"

Global publishing industry fears, however, go beyond the mere concern surrounding profit margins and shelf placement. In Hong Kong, publishers and booksellers have a deeper, more immediate worry. They get kidnapped.[12]

The Mighty Current book publishers in Hong Kong put out juicy books that likely provoked mainland China's leadership. Kidnapping the messenger has become an effective way to stop the presses and kill the message. Such brazen actions are a clear warning to regime critics—the Chinese state's long arm can easily reach across borders.

In the Mighty Current case, five Chinese nationals disappeared last year from Hong Kong and Thailand right around the planned release of a critical book on China's leader, Xi Jinping. The result? No publishers, no book.

One of the booksellers, Lam Wing-kee, was recently released,[13] one awaits Chinese sentencing on unrelated charges this fall, and all of them got the message. The book remains in limbo.

While bookseller rendition is the latest form of literary censorship, it is by no means the only form of book banning in a world where societies and political leaders increasingly want to dictate what is "good" or "bad" speech.

Salman Rushdie wrote "The Satanic Verses" and had a global "fatwa" declared on him during Ayatollah Khomeini's reign. In Florida, pastor Terry Jones barbecued Qurans in a book burning that singed Americans' First Amendment sensibilities and challenged their understanding of protected speech. Is book burning a free speech "right"?

Supreme Court Justice Sandra Day O'Connor put it best:[14] "The hallmark of the protection of free speech is to allow 'free trade in ideas'—even ideas that the overwhelming majority of people might find distasteful or discomforting."

"Good" speech seldom needs protection; not so edgy literature or writing that challenges authority. Trickiest of all are books that delve in societal taboo. "Bad" speech is what often gets challenged.

Books are banned[15] and writers condemned for the ideas inside them. They deliver condensed knowledge that incite us and make our thoughts burn with visions of places and circumstances never before seen or experienced. New concepts are created out of thin air.

---

12 Joseph and Hunt, "Missing Hong Kong Bookseller: I Was Kidnapped."
13 Cheung, "Returned Bookseller Says He Believes Others Will Be Released after Colleague's Sentencing Later This Year."
14 O'Connor, *Virginia v. Black*, 538 U.S.
15 EDIAZ, "Banned Book FAQ."

They can take us to the outer reaches of the universe or down the gutter. And the ideas stick. You can never unlearn something once exposed to it. The only remedy for the mental itch is to scratch it.

Ideas can be revolutionary or reactive. They have no mass but are far from weightless. The only way to contain ideas is to kill them in the crib, before they spread their truth, myth or lie. Ideas are a threat like no other and can reveal that any emperor has no clothes.

The Nazis burned books. Romans and Christians destroyed the greatest library[16] in the ancient world. The Taliban are "students"[17] of nothing other than the Quran.

Nigeria's Boko Haram are just plain opposed to new knowledge and ideas. Boko hates books. It burns them [...] and children, too.[18]

In liberal democratic societies, we mostly celebrate the book for its role as a repository of ideas. We revere the book—whether a physical paper product or on a digital device. That is why one of the greatest democratic salutations given is: "Read any good books lately?"

Books are a greater threat to illiberal systems. China may sense that it is losing its confidence or party control and that kidnapping booksellers is an effective way to maintain national security and stability. Such indirect book banning, however, is a desperate act unworthy of any great nation.

In the meantime, the unpublished Xi Jinping biography will not be on Amazon's website.

Coda: Amazon does list several other biographies of the Chinese leader including *Inside the Mind of Xi Jinping*[19] by French journalist François Bougon.

BET ON BEYONCÉ

Introduction

In Cold War 2.0 between the United States and China, put your money on the nation of diversity and creativity. Beyond our military and diplomatic corps, America steadily leads the world through the entertainment industry and creative enterprises.

Originally published: October 4, 2018

---

16 Chesser, "The Burning of the Library of Alexandria."
17 "Taliban."
18 Williamson, "Burning Books and Children."
19 Bougon, "Inside the Mind of Xi Jinping."

Beyoncé and Jay Z are proving that America has the diversity and creativity to survive the new China challenge. The musical duo inspires a new generation, shows America's cultural strength, resilience and power—and just may help lead the world out of the new Cold War.

American culture and free commerce proved an attractive model during the first Cold War against the Soviets. "Lemonade" and the Carter couple's just-finished five-month "On the Run II" tour[20] are just two recent American cultural products that will help check China's 21st century rise and prove America's creative pre-eminence.

China may be stealing American technologies, draining U.S. trade coffers and interfering in the 2018 midterm elections, but it will always struggle to replicate America's creative dynamism born of unbridled social and cultural expression and experimentation. The passion and energy of a row of Beyoncé dancers, legs flying—plus lights flashing, fireworks popping, bodies cavorting, *plus* the thumping, driving message of emancipation, inspiration and starkly sexy imagination—beats a bunch of stiff leadership dudes at the microphone any day.

Under President Xi Jinping's increasingly authoritarian rule, China's party-state is oppressive, dogmatic and punishing. It's not much fun, either. It's a place that won't show Disney's new movie, "Christopher Robin,"[21] for example, because Winnie the Pooh is considered subversive and is banned.[22] Visa policies and the Great Firewall of China keep creative chaos and politically challenging messages at bay.

Innovation does not tend to thrive in a sterile and controlled social environment and managed economy. It can go far, but it can't go forever. That was true during the Soviet Union's existence, and it's true today for China. The appeal of Western rock music, for example, with its protest spirit, represented freedom propelled by a fresh youth culture. It was a dizzying and appealing tonic for students and strivers locked up behind the Iron Curtain. I saw it first-hand in Czechoslovakia and the USSR and, while living in Hungary, gave a TEDx talk[23] titled "How Rock & Roll Saved the World." I argued that Western music and culture helped bring down Soviet Communism.

---

20 Beyoncé, "Beyoncé: Tours."
21 "China Snubs Release of 'Christopher Robin.'"
22 Kounalakis, "Goodnight Mao."
23 TEDx Talks, "TEDxDanubia 2011—Simonyi & Kounalakis—How Rock&Roll Saved the World."

Western culture and democratic chaos appealed to youth throughout the Soviet Union and its East European captive states. The same is true for China today. The absence of a healthy and active artistic feedback loop leads to stagnation, even in the face of today's rapidly growing Chinese economy. Poets, painters and non-conforming potential pop stars quickly find themselves in official disfavor, exiled or jailed. They don't get record contracts and they don't fill stadiums.

An artist as popular and independent as Beyoncé, who also challenges the status quo, would never arise or survive in contemporary China. There are no Uighur breakout bands. Instead, China's government is working "to strangle Uighur culture," says[24] Vice President Mike Pence, as it jails and "re-educates" around a million[25] members of this minority group.

China's state-sanctioned cultural diversity is celebrated in formal presentations of traditional dress, music and dance, on show as rarified, regional objects intended to serve a message of national unity and overt support for the Chinese Communist party-state. Performances are safely anodyne. In the meantime, Chinese pop culture is plainly derivative.[26] A recent music video and official song celebrating China's far-flung build-infrastructure-around-the-world initiative is based entirely on the old Coca-Cola song,[27] "I'd like to buy the world a Coke." Really?

African-American artists such as Beyoncé and her husband, the producer-rapper Jay Z, incorporate into their work their racial identity and black America's collective struggle. They melodically and percussively present a mix of boasting and barbed lyrics as the soundtrack to provocative video images that strike both at America's greatest aspirations and its deepest social ills. It is raw and it is real.

One moment, Beyoncé will be singing "I just may be a black Bill Gates in the making" from the "Formation"[28] mix and the next thing you know Jay Z is onstage reminding black America—and all America—that racism is real and present in "The Story of OJ."[29] Last week, in the San Francisco Bay area, packed and pumped audiences swayed to and sang with the music's both

---

24 Hudson Institute, "Vice President Mike Pence's Remarks on the Administration's Policy Towards China."

25 Nebehay, "U.N. Calls on China to Free Uighurs from Alleged Re-Education Camps."

26 Daly, "A Rise without Shine."

27 Steger, "China Ripped Off an Iconic Coke Ad for Its Belt and Road Theme Song."

28 Beyoncé, *Beyoncé—Formation (Official Video)*.

29 JAY-Z, *JAY-Z—The Story of O.J.*

hopeful and doleful meanings at Levi's Stadium—the same stadium where Colin Kaepernick played his last professional season as a 49ers quarterback.

Protest is necessary for a healthy, creative, liberal, and democratic society. It is a source of systemic self-correction, a means to audit institutions, check power, express displeasure, and register dissent. It is fundamentally American.

This country was founded in political protest. Some of the most effective is rooted in musical traditions that today are amplified, distributed, and are able to go globally viral—even when officially censored in other countries.

Democracy is messy, but it is preferable to a stifling and staid Sino-socialist system of command-and-control. Chaotic creativity thrives in America's bubbling social, racial, ethnic, and religious cauldron. To quote[30] Jay Z, China needs to "Show me what you got."

In a straight-out fair competition between an unimaginative and controlling regime and an irrepressible creative democratic system, my money is on America's dragon-slaying beast.

Coda: Beyoncé and Jay Z continue supporting progressive social causes. The couple have donated millions of dollars to fund various programs in the United States and abroad.

CHINA SUBVERTS FREE PRESS IN THE U.S.

Introduction

Beijing uses its news organizations in America to undermine independent journalism through espionage. China also punishes Western foreign correspondents for telling stories that offend the ruling Communist Party. All this can mimic the tit-for-tat targeting of diplomats accused of illegal intelligence gathering.

Originally published: February 28, 2020

A decade ago, I first saw signs that Chinese news organizations were operating as global spy dens and diplomatic outposts. Last week, America decided not only to call them out for what they do, but to punish[31] them further for this activity within the United States.

It's about time.

---

30 JAY-Z, *JAY-Z—Show Me What You Got*.

31 Jakes and Myers, "U.S. Designates China's Official Media as Operatives of the Communist State."

It's also time to counter China and help American journalism survive.

My 2018 book[32] "Spin Wars & Spy Games: Global Media and Intelligence Gathering" detailed how China's global news organizations are used to advance its national interests. China—and also Russia—uses its foreign news bureaus as fronts for editors and journalists to work as both witting and unwitting spies. My research over the years shows that these news bureaus' primary responsibility is to report to their countries' political leadership in Beijing.

Chinese state-run news organizations task their correspondents with actively taking advantage of America's open society. That means exploiting First Amendment journalism rights and the relative naivete of unsuspecting subjects and institutions.

China's reporter-agents collect and analyze critical information about the United States and other countries. Bureaus then package and deliver it to their masters back home. In the process, they also repurpose it as a quasi-journalistic propagandistic product for a mass foreign audience in their newspapers and broadcasts. To audiences, it looks and feels like real news, but it's really just a by-product of intelligence gathering.

For this reason, the State Department recently led the charge against five Chinese news organizations: Xinhua, CGTN, China Radio, China Daily and The People's Daily. As a result, the United States has further downgraded[33] their status. Last year, CGTN and Xinhua fell under the Foreign Agents Registration Act (FARA),[34] requiring them to report to the U.S. Justice Department. The DOJ did not explain why, but the reason is that these seemingly benign institutions really are just extensions of the state, delivering a slanted, Beijing-approved, often heavy-handed propaganda message. They were also operating surreptitiously as intelligence gathering shops.

China's state-run bodies must serve the state. They live or die by the authority and funding they receive from the country's leadership and, in this case, the Chinese Communist Party. Whether Xinhua or China Global Television Network (CGTN),[35] these Chinese information-gathering institutions do the Party's bidding and coordinate the priorities of its United Front Work Department propaganda. China is willing to spend billions of dollars[36] to

32 Kounalakis, *Spin Wars and Spy Games.*

33 Kounalakis, "Chinese Agents Posed as Journalists in US. And the US Just Did Something about It."

34 Viswanatha, "Chinese State Media Giant CGTN Registers as Foreign Agent in U.S."

35 "CGTN (TV Channel)."

36 Lim and Bergin, "Inside China's Audacious Global Propaganda Campaign."

promote its United Front work and support the growing network of Xinhua and CGTN bureaus around the world.

However, the advertising-based business model for American and other Western news organizations has collapsed, diminishing not only the frequency of publication—goodbye Saturday editions—but also dramatically reducing the number of journalists, researchers and editors at nearly every single news source. This is bad news for everyone. It is bad news for democracy.

Not only is the Chinese government outspending the West's traditional news organizations, it is hiring some of its former reporters and editors. These freshly unemployed or underemployed Western professionals bring with them their Rolodexes, networks and access. In the process, they become unwitting foreign agents. Further, readers and audiences feel comfortable with the deceptive news product delivered by these familiar and credible journalists. We accept familiar faces appearing on China's television networks.

The goal of China's relatively new entry into the global news and information marketplace is a troubling development around the world. Western open societies welcome and protect traditional news organizations as important components of society. They have traditionally been bulwarks of democracy[37] and an integral part of a system of checks and balances.

China has taken advantage of America's openness, not merely with unfair foreign trade in its commodity and consumer markets, but now in the marketplace of ideas. It is right that the government has called out China for this behavior and activity.

But it's also time for American society and government to invest in traditional American news institutions to help them not only to survive but to thrive in this newly competitive global information environment. Both the government and the public need to recognize and support American news organizations for the sake of maintaining democracy's infrastructure.

Washington's targeting Chinese news outlets has led to retaliation against American journalists in China. Three Wall Street Journal foreign correspondents were expelled[38] last week. That's rough, of course, but for years China has been using other means to limit the presence of undesired foreign correspondents in the country. The easiest, preferred method was to deny Western journalists visas.[39]

---

37 Chadwick, "Journalism Has a Vital Role in a Constitutional Democracy."

38 Feng and Neuman, "China Expels 3 'Wall Street Journal' Reporters, Citing 'Racist' Headline."

39 Staff, "China Denies Credentials to Wall Street Journal Reporter."

Expect more Chinese retaliation against Western journalists. Some will be accused of spying. The real retaliation, however, will be the further demise of the credibility, strength and economic viability of traditional American journalism.

Coda: In February 2021, Beijing banned BBC World News from broadcasting in China, saying the agency had "undermined China's national interests and ethnic solidarity." This followed BBC reports about the COVID-19 pandemic and genocide against the Uighurs.

TRUMP ALWAYS DISSED OBAMA

Introduction

Presidents routinely criticize predecessors from opposing parties. Donald Trump was certainly not the first. But mimicking one of FDR's pettiest and most pointless mistakes was a sad waste of president power.

Originally published: March 6, 2020

Presidential elections are on everyone's minds and TV sets these days because presidents matter. In America's democracy, presidents are its singular most important leaders. Heightened attention to their selection and performance reflects how critical they are to the nation's strength and survival.

In February, five living presidents were celebrated—Jimmy Carter, Bill Clinton, George W. Bush, Barack Obama and Donald Trump. It is a remarkable democratic achievement and a testament to America's confidence that the country transitions power peacefully from administration to administration regardless of political party. Republicans yield to Democrats who yield to Republicans.

Unlike other countries, America's previous presidents are neither hounded nor capriciously thrown in jail. Instead, our former commanders-in-chief live and travel freely.

Unfortunately, they are also currently being ignored and denigrated. That not only deprives America of potential power—it comes at a cost.

Presidents in the late 20th and early 21st centuries relied on their predecessors for counsel and collaboration. Ex-presidents have been previously used to free hostage[40] in hostile foreign lands, participate in humanitarian[41] endeavors or lobby[42]

40　CNN, "The Story behind Clinton's Trip to North Korea."

41　Phillips, "The Clinton Bush Haiti Fund."

42　Rodriguez, "Playing the Long Game."

for difficult bipartisan policies. It had become commonplace to deploy former presidents—regardless of party or personality clashes—to help administrations in power do hard things. This was true for nearly every modern president.

There are, however, two very notable exceptions: Franklin Delano Roosevelt and Donald John Trump.

Once in office, Roosevelt dissed Herbert Hoover at every opportunity. Trump remains allergic to all things Obama, making the African-American 44th president the 21st century's Herbert Hoover.

Ignoring a young Hoover in the past and vibrant Obama today has deprived the nation of opportunities both for greater domestic harmony and difficult foreign intermediation. America's once clear, sometimes singular, voice abroad is now processed and overamplified as a noisy global cacophony.

Disrupting the presidential continuum, comity, and collaboration can be blamed for some of today's international ills. Could Obama, for example, be quietly deployed to make diplomatic overtures today to a sanctioned, struggling and coronavirus-infected Iran? Where could Clinton, Carter or Bush be leveraged?

Trump may admire Andrew Jackson, but he is emulating Roosevelt by trying to stack the courts, open up state coffers and punish his perceived adversaries and enemies. It's hard to accept, but what FDR successfully did was erase Hoover. He never allowed Hoover's works be recognized. Hoover was roundly defeated in the 1932 election, persona non grata at the White House and exiled to the farthest end of the continental United States at Stanford University.

Where Hoover had the foresight to build the Hoover Dam, Roosevelt had the pettiness to rename it Boulder Dam. Policy after policy, person after person, if the scent of Hoover[43] lingered on a bill, banker, business, politician or pet project, it was regarded as the pervasive stink of someone who had defecated in the Oval Office.

When Roosevelt died, he left an unprepared Harry Truman to take over as his constitutionally mandated successor. Truman inherited an ongoing war, the overblown legacy of a four-term president and a decision to make about blowing up Japan with the world's newest weapon—the atomic bomb.

FDR never deeply briefed Truman, and 82 days into his vice presidency, Truman was thrust[44] into the role of 33rd president. He sought a lifeline from the only other person alive who knew the pressures he was facing and understood the presidency. He needed an ex-president, and the only one available was a

---

43 Lemann, "Hating on Herbert Hoover."
44 Franck, "How F.D.R.'s Death Changed the Vice-Presidency."

vilified California Republican: Herbert Hoover. Truman and Hoover joked[45] that this was the beginning of a "former presidents' club."

Hoover, desperately seeking rehabilitation and respect, hungrily accepted the role of hidden adviser, careful consultant, proven European post-war logistics master and savior.[46]

Trump has not only taken a page from FDR's playbook, he's writing a whole new chapter on political purges, with updated sections on baiting, backbiting and bullying former presidents. Barack Obama meet Herbert Hoover.

In the recent past and on solemn national occasions, group photos[47] of living presidents showed the world America's power and unity. It is remarkable to see pictures of Nixon, Ford, Carter, Bush and Clinton together. It is powerful to know that they relied on each other for insights into foreign leaders, difficult hostage negotiations, secret two-track discussions with adversaries, joint humanitarian missions and general counsel on thorny issues.

Today, those photos seem like relics of a bygone era. Instead of former U.S. presidents posing for Associated Press photos in the Oval Office, spying foreign journalists are now welcomed into the White House to shoot Russian Foreign Minister Sergei Lavrov and Ambassador Sergey Kislyak who yuk it up[48] near Andrew Jackson's portrait.

American presidents past and present are a national asset and should be welcomed into the White House—whether ushered in the front door or snuck in the back. Unfortunately, the only president with an open invitation[49] today is Vladimir Putin.

Coda: Unlike the man from Mar-a-Lago, President Joe Biden was not publicly obsessed with his predecessor. After taking office, Biden refrained from daily condemnation of Trump, and even avoided mentioning the name.

---

45 Maslin, "The Knotty Ties Binding America's Ex-Leaders."
46 Braswell, "How Herbert Hoover Saved Belgium."
47 Jacobs, "Photos of Former US Presidents Hanging out Together."
48 Chappell, "Trump Hosts Russian Foreign Minister Lavrov and Ambassador Kislyak at White House."
49 Hayes, "Donald Trump Invites Russian President Vladimir Putin to Washington."

CHAPTER 2

FREEDOM OF THOUGHT

GOODNIGHT, MAO—THE GREAT FIREWALL OF CHINA

Introduction

To the monitors of China's "Great Firewall," even storybook characters can be subversive. Chinese strongman Xi Jinping put up a digital barrier to neuter internet dissent. That, coupled with a change in the country's constitution, enables him to govern for life.

Originally published: March 8, 2018

Dictators hate a challenge to their rule. That's why China uses its vast policing and advanced technological resources both to arrest individuals and to disappear from public view any protest words, phrases, images or symbols that might be seen as threatening the state. The kinds of things that, if unchecked, can potentially overthrow a regime.

One of the high-priority targets of China's security systems today? Winnie the Pooh.

Yes, Pooh Bear is a danger to the Chinese Communist Party, the Chinese state, and, most importantly, President Xi Jinping.

Xi should be feeling pretty confident these days, as China prepares to change its constitution to rid it of presidential term limits. Not since Chairman Mao Zedong will China have had a more powerful and unchallenged leader. But the power of Pooh must not be underestimated.

Why Pooh and his media parent company, Disney? Popular protest in countries where speech is controlled often finds expression in seemingly innocent ways as well as through symbols loaded with hidden or ironic meaning.

From blue Smurfs in Poland[1] in the late 1980s to yellow rubber duckies[2] in contemporary Russia, Serbia, and Brazil.

The absurd directly challenges the entrenched.

In China, an inspired citizen saw a resemblance between Xi Jinping and the cuddly, befuddled Pooh and posted it on Weibo[3]—a Chinese version of Twitter. The picture of an oversized Pooh benevolently sitting in a car instantly ricocheted around People's Republic of China social media. It was quickly interpreted by the Chinese public as mocking an official image of Xi Jinping in a car reviewing a People's Liberation Army formation.

The Chinese state, communist party and President Xi—China's "core" leader—are now seen as the PRC's holy trinity. They must be considered one single solitary and infallible unit with perfectly aligned interests. Any attack or mockery of Xi is thus also considered an attack against the party and the state. Therefore, it is potentially punishable by all the tools and methods available to the state.

It's not officially declared policy that Pooh—or any Disney character—is an anti-China agitator. But the reality is that the Chinese state actively censors subversive words from being searched on the carefully controlled and firewall-protected internet. The China Digital Times[4] dynamically crowdsources phrases that are blocked online, an ever-changing list that recently included the following:

- Long live the emperor
- Disagree
- Personality cult
- The wheel of history
- Xi Zedong
- Incapable ruler
- Rule the world
- Great men sent from heaven
- Emigrate
- 1984

---

1 Doucette, "Mightier than the Sword: Polish Independent Publishing, 1976–1989."
2 Bershidsky, "The Yellow Rubber Duck Is a Potent Protest Symbol."
3 Lim, "China's Top 5 Censored Posts in 2015."
4 Rudolph, "Sensitive Words: Xi to Ascend His Throne."

Information sovereignty is China's goal. That means being able to decide and control what its population reads or sees. Chinese authorities have been astute students of the Soviet Union's demise and collapse. They have understood that free-flowing information and state counter-narratives are powerful and effective at undermining a state's legitimacy.

It may seem simplistic and naïve today, but in the pre-internet era, radio broadcasts with jazz music and alternative, credible news programming could infect the minds of an otherwise programmed people with visions of liberation and dreams of democratic governance. That's why the Soviets put so much effort and expense into jamming shortwave radio signals and programming—the kind I also once produced for Radio Sweden International[5] in the 1980s.

Total information control proved impossible. The populations of Eastern Europe and the USSR knew that there was an alternative to their political oppression and economic suffering. It took a good 74 years[6] before the Soviet Union dissolved, but the slow-drip of truth eventually helped corrode the Iron Curtain.

China is on an economic tear, boasting an astronomical annual growth rate with high future financial growth targets. It has successfully lifted hundreds of thousands of its people out of poverty, in part, as Donald Trump has rightly argued, thanks to huge American and European trade deficits.[7] As long as the country stays economically viable and financially underwritten by the West, the only thing the communist party and Xi need to stay in power is to control regime-challenging democratic messages and ideas.

The 21st century gives any state sophisticated tools for filtering information and finding malcontents. Monitoring IP addresses and social media accounts allows the Chinese state to track and control its population. Managing the message, and the messengers, prevents subversives from spreading revolutionary ideas or organizing anti-state protest. "The Great Firewall of China" effectively keeps out news, information, and ideas that challenge the State–Party–Xi triumvirate. While Americans protest for net neutrality to keep an anarchic flow of information moving freely within the USA, the Chinese state is practicing and preaching net neutering[8] of its citizens to insure China's domestic tranquility and maintain the state's legitimacy.

---

5 Radio, "Radio Sweden."
6 Schmemann, "END OF THE SOVIET UNION; The Soviet State, Born of a Dream, Dies."
7 Franck, "Trump Says White House Asked China for Plan to Reduce US Trade Deficit with Country by $1 Billion."
8 Denyer, "China's Scary Lesson to the World: Censoring the Internet Works."

President Trump has broken ranks with his predecessors and America's traditional values as he enviably looks[9] at totalitarian states' control of media, message, and manipulation. His benevolent attitude towards China's blind pursuit of its own interests makes it more difficult for China's global critics to pressure President Xi's regime.

Coda: In his first foreign policy speech as president, Joe Biden announced that his administration would confront China on defense, trade and human rights. But unlike his predecessor, the 46th president said the United States would work with allies on the world stage.

WATCH OUT FOR TURKEY

Introduction

Journalists are careful when covering wars, revolutions, gang crimes and natural disasters. But reporting in Turkey brings special risks. That danger was exacerbated by the Trump presidency which cozied up to—rather than standing up to—the anti-democratic Erdoğan regime. This column was written before the murder of journalist Jamal Khashoggi, which sparked more conversations about a free press. Ironically, Turkey eludes the very accountability that they demand for Saudi Arabia.

Originally published: April 12, 2018

Working as a Middle East correspondent can be hazardous to your health. Freelance journalist Austin Tice[10] is approaching the six-year mark since his kidnapping in Syria. Reporter Marie Colvin was tracked and targeted[11] for lethal attack by the Assad regime.

Things have certainly gotten hairier for foreign reporters, but even more so for local journalists as regional tensions rise, alliances become fluid, nationalism grows, and refugee populations are on the move.

It's not just Syria and Iraq, either. While the Trump administration weighs how further to respond to Damascus's latest chemical weapons attack, the whole neighborhood is in flux and rules are being actively rewritten. Slowly, surely, countries once considered welcoming and safe are turning more menacing for both citizens and strangers. Turkey is the latest to flip.

---

9 Moody, "Why Trump Can Envy, but Not Imitate, China."

10 Smith, "What Happened to Austin Tice?"

11 Krever, "Marie Colvin Was Deliberately Targeted by Assad Regime, Sister Says."

Not long ago, while reporting on the refugee crisis on the island of Lesbos in Greece, I sat at a modest seaside fish tavern and looked across the water at nearby Turkey, wondering whether I would go to jail if I stepped foot on Turkish territory. It was a week when journalists from the Turkish opposition newspaper Cumhuriyet were on trial[12] in a country that has imprisoned more journalists than anywhere else[13] on earth.

Since a failed 2016 coup attempt, some journalists have been labeled terrorists, gone to jail, and become jobless for no obvious reason. Recep Tayyip Erdoğan's dictatorial rule has used a state of emergency and a no-critic law to lock up over 50,000 people, rebuild Turkey's military with loyalists, and purge 150,000 employees from schools and the civil service. Erdoğan has also given free rein to Islamists[14] and bolstered the enemies of his sworn personal adversary, the Pennsylvania-residing Turkish cleric Fethullah Gülen,[15] accused by Erdoğan of orchestrating the unsuccessful 2016 overthrow.

Turkish journalists now unemployed or jailed are guilty of truth-telling about their regime. As an American, I have not felt compelled to moderate my speech or make it fit Ankara's politics. Instead, I have over the years called Erdoğan what he really is—an unreliable[16] American ally and an unsavory[17] and corrupt authoritarian living lavishly[18] in his 1,000-room Ankara palace as he plots to lead a new 21st century Caliphate while playing nice with anti-Nato countries Russia and Iran. A Turk saying these things would be in trouble. Big time.[19]

While safely reporting in Greece, I stared across the sea at the familiar Turkish coast and daydreamed about Hammam baths and visiting Istanbul friends. I wished to meander through Hagia Sofia's splendor and entertained nostalgic thoughts that the nearby country I saw was the same progressive, modern Turkey of a few years back—a Turkey that once had a female prime

---

12 Deutsche Welle, *Trial of Cumhuriyet Journalists Resumes in Turkey*.

13 "Record Number of Journalists Jailed as Turkey, China, Egypt Pay Scant Price for Repression."

14 Peterson, "In Turkey, Erdoğan Fans an Islamic Nationalism to Build Ottoman-Style Influence."

15 Sanderson, "From Ally to Scapegoat: Fethullah Gulen, the Man behind the Myth."

16 Kounalakis, "Opinion: Hostile Turkey Aims to Sideline Washington, the West."

17 Kounalakis, "Adding to America's Rogues' List of Unsavory but Friendly Leaders."

18 Kounalakis, "Home Sweet Palace."

19 Staff, "Turkey Detains 300 People over Criticism of Syrian Offensive."

minister[20] and a nation that outlawed the death penalty so it could unify with the European Union.

I recalled a time when Israel and Turkey were closely allied and the ruling Turkish political party's closest ideological organization was not the Muslim Brotherhood.[21] It's hard to believe today that Ankara once pursued peace negotiations[22] with Turkey's Kurdish minority. For years, this was the Turkey the United States was betting on. It is not the Turkey we got.

The Turkey we wanted was a tolerant, Western-looking, dynamic nation— the model of a secularized, democratic, Muslim-majority state that would lead the Middle East towards modern reforms, with a healthy press helping guide and chronicle a growingly multicultural, multiethnic future.

Turkey's historic tolerance for religious minorities made it possible for Spanish Jews to find refuge[23] there in 1492. Modern Turkey's 20th century founder Kemal Atatürk firmly placed the country on a Western modernization path, symbolically shunning the Pasha's dress to adopt the topcoat[24] and creating a state that codified constitutional secularism,[25] establishing a clear mosque– state separation. Along the way, there were serious abuses, mistakes, horrific human rights violations, the Armenian genocide.[26] Despite being on the wrong side of history during both World Wars, Turkey entered the 21st century as an imperfectly evolving modern state on a solid, steady path towards something better, greater and more democratic.

All that is now gone. That Turkey is a distant memory. Even worse, as the Trump administration devalued America's concern for human rights, Erdoğan increasingly and blatantly disregarded the rights of journalists and all citizens.

Teachers, business owners, reporters, students, and all Turks feel less secure in their opinions or daily jobs today. They can be carted away at a moment's notice as Turkey is a country now ruled by men, not laws. The legal system justifies and reinforces the power structure and supports the all-powerful Turkish president.

---

20 "Tansu Çiller."
21 Ant and Shennib, "Saudis Are After the Muslim Brotherhood, and Turkey's in the Way."
22 Aydintasbas, "It's Time for a New Peace Process between Turkey and the Kurds."
23 Montalbano, "For Jews, a 500-Year Turkish Haven: Sanctuary: In 1492, 60,000 of Them Driven from Spain Were Welcomed in Istanbul, Where They Have Flourished."
24 Genç, "Turkey's Glorious Hat Revolution."
25 Pierini, "The 2018 Turkey Regress Report."
26 Arango, "A Century After Armenian Genocide, Turkey's Denial Only Deepens."

Now Erdoğan has slowly exported his ruthlessness, as witnessed last yea. when his security henchmen[27] beat American protesters in Washington, D.C. Erdoğan's legal reach extended abroad to Germany, where he sued a German comedian[28] for reading an on-air poem ridiculing him. His military arm regularly stretches across Greek, Syrian, and Iraqi borders, challenging those nations' sovereignties and asserting national security claims. Can it be long before Erdoğan takes a page from Putin's playbook to punish his detractors, wherever they might be? Journalists beware.

Coda: Even before his inauguration, President Biden made it clear that the United States would change course from his predecessor, taking a tough stance against Turkey's human rights abuses and international misdeeds. One of Biden's first foreign policy acts as president was to demand the release of Osman Kavala, a jailed Turkish civil society leader.

DON'T LET THE SMILE FOOL YOU

Introduction

Kim Jong-un, Vladimir Putin and too many other dictators are not champions of democracy. Their easy, egalitarian-sounding words and images are no substitute for the heavy lifting required to govern "of the people, by the people, for the people."

Originally published: January 23, 2020

Democracy is a test. You can't just wing it and you can't just skip it. It requires study and it is strongest when everyone participates on test day, which is every day.

That makes democracy hard, too. You can't rely on others to take the test for you or to look over someone else's answers to figure out how to add your unique voice and perspective.

Democracy is in retreat globally. Only 5.7 percent of the world lives in a "full democracy," according to the Democracy Index. American democracy, too, is facing a stress test in the form of impeachment. It's time for all of us to cram around democracy's meaning.

---

27 Hermann, "D.C. Police Issue Warrant for 12 on Turkish Security Team in May Brawl."
28 Roxborough, "Germany, after Recep Tayyip Erdoğan Case, Drops Law against Insulting Foreign Leaders."

There are governments and systems claiming they are democratically legitimate. Some of the worst offenders use democratic tools to say that they are free and open societies.

Russia's Vladimir Putin, for example, uses elections, suggesting that mere voting makes his presidency valid and legitimate. Here's the rub: In Putin's Russia,[29] he disqualifies, sidelines, arrests or destroys any credible opposition to his one-man rule. The result? Those who go to the polls have the right to choose, but only from a winnowed-down list of survivors and sycophants. Is that democracy?

Freedom of speech is another democratic feature. But not all speech is created equal. A joke told in the Soviet Union when I lived there in 1991 was often repeated by Ronald Reagan:[30]

An American visiting Moscow crows about U.S. freedoms and tells a Soviet friend, "I can demonstrate in Washington, go into the White House, see President Reagan and tell him he's a lousy, no good president."

The Soviet tells him he has the exact same freedom of expression. "Really?" asks the dumbfounded American.

"Yes," says the Muscovite. "I can demonstrate at Lenin's tomb, walk into the Kremlin, find General Secretary Gorbachev's office, irately pound on his desk and tell him what a lousy, no good president Ronald Reagan is."

Democracy in name is not necessarily democracy in deed. That's why so many authoritarian and totalitarian states fondly flaunt "democracy" in their titles. North Korea, for example, is officially the Democratic People's Republic of Korea. Go figure. There is no truth in that advertising.

Voting is only part of the equation defining democracy. The other part requires an informed citizenry where everyone has the franchise.

Democracy relies on its participants knowing what they are voting for or against. There are all kinds of tricks to keep people from figuring out what they are really pulling a lever to achieve. Those include referendums that implore you to vote "No" for something while actually wording things to allow the very thing you believe you are voting to quash.

Brexit is a good example[31] of confusing the electorate. European "Leave" and "Remain" stories became misleadingly muddled by the time the referendum was

---

29 Agence France-Presse, "Anti-Putin Activist Ruslan Shaveddinov 'forcibly Conscripted' and Sent to Arctic."

30 Ramishvili, *Reagan Jokes.*

31 "Why Referendums Aren't as Democratic as They Seem."

help. Did Brits vote for greater sovereignty if they voted against the European Union? Would Scotland or Ireland agree that an independent Great Britain assured a stronger union at home? These are unanswered questions, but they exemplify how a plebiscite can be gamed and voters confounded.

Information is the key to giving individuals power and insight into the democratic process. Knowledge is power, after all. For this reason, we are often at sea in this new digitally driven, internet-dominated, social-media-sloshing information environment, where a tsunami of data is coming at hyperspeed. Given the data deluge, our ability to judge and value that information is severely diminished. How can we know if someone is telling the truth, an advocate is supporting our interests or a candidate represents our views? For every site or post that reinforces our opinions and beliefs, there is an equal or greater number of datapoints to counter our preferred narrative and understanding. And most seem real and credible. Yikes!

In a world where democracy is a test—and in an era where we have less and less time to study—a citizen's abilities and responsibilities are challenged. In fact, they may be at a breaking point.

This suits demagogues and dictators just fine. They are not friends of democracy. They just like to claim that they are. So they do whatever they can to add to the cacophony, contribute to the misinformation or prevent rational and reasonable voices from being heard and credible alternative narratives from being told.

Suppressing information is the favored tactic of these scoundrels. That's why strongman Nicolás Maduro[32] has forced AT&T's DirecTV to yank CNN and BBC from being broadcast in Venezuela. It's why Russia[33] and China[34] are experimenting with plans to cut off their countries from the internet. And it's why in the United States, with Facebook[35] allowing fake news sites and prevaricating political speech to be propagated, we have an information environment of competing false claims and equivocating candidates.

Democracy is a test, and we are less equipped than ever to pass it.

Coda: In February 2021, President Biden announced he would scrap changes to the United States' citizenship test implemented by his predecessor, which reportedly had made the exam less efficient and more difficult to pass.

---

32 Goodman, "AP Exclusive: AT&T under Pressure to Defy Maduro's Censors."
33 Newman, "Russia Takes a Big Step toward Internet Isolation."
34 Davis, "China's Internet Censorship Law Sets Out Content Rules."
35 Rodrigo, "Critics Fear Facebook Fact-Checkers Losing Misinformation Fight."

LOSERS TAKE THE HIT

Introduction

From Trump to Rouhani, the powerful commit many offenses, but the usual suspects keep getting rounded up. Even when evidence of culpability is openly and convincingly presented, the guilty often go unpunished.

Originally published: February 6, 2020

Murder took place as the airplane was lifting off the runway, a lethal shot taken in the Humphrey Bogart movie, "Casablanca." Rick Blaine pulled the trigger in front of the French police prefect Captain Renault. The Vichy official witnessed it. He allowed it. And then Renault uttered those infamous words[36] that said everything, but meant nothing: "Round up the usual suspects."

Murder also took place just as the airplane was taking off last month from Tehran's Imam Khomeini International Airport. Missiles were fired at the Ukraine International Airlines plane, killing all 176 passengers and crew on board. Iranian officials witnessed it. They may even have ordered it. The government then made a predictable and cowardly move by rounding up the usual suspects.

Iran's government is the latest authority preparing a show trial intended to bring peace to the streets and some justice to the murdered victims of Ukraine flight PS 752. Street protests were launched in Tehran shortly after the commercial Boeing 737 was felled from the sky by a land-based missile. Iranian authorities eventually suggested that errant, on-edge operators brought down the jet at a moment of high tension and an anticipated American attack. The shooters will go to jail. Or worse.

The real guilty parties, however, remain in power and escape both arrest or conviction. They inhabit the high offices and low politics of a theocratic regime. The Islamic Republic holds that the Supreme Leader can do no wrong. Its high-ranking military officers operate in an accountability-free chain of command.

The fall guys[37] carry out policy, follow orders or, frightened, mistakenly launch missiles. The result is dead innocents and a global call for justice that likely will result in unjust outcomes. President Hassan Rouhani and Ayatollah Ali Khamenei will not be held accountable. Iranian officials knew the truth for three days, but pretended[38] they had no idea.

---

36 Bill Kirk, *Casablanca Bogart Round Up the Usual Suspects.*
37 Karimi and Batrawy, "Iran Announces Arrests over Downing of Plane That Killed 176."
38 Euronews, "Iran Immediately Knew Its Missile Downed Ukrainian Plane—Leaked Recording."

On the other side of the Persian Gulf, in Saudi Arabia, five men have been sentenced to death[39] for the murder and dismemberment of American journalist Jamal Khashoggi. Pinning the death on these five is the kingdom's response to an international call for justice. U.S. intelligence agencies blame the death on one man and his orders. Since the man the CIA fingered[40] is the sovereign who exists above the law, Saudi officials instead arrested and convicted individuals who carried out the gruesome deed, not those who ordered it. The authorities went after the usual suspects.

In nearly every country, the usual suspects are the functionaries, intermediaries, fall guys and fools who are like the moths that get too close to a flame and get burned.

Michael Cohen is sitting in jail[41] while his boss sits prettily in the Oval Office. He turned on his master, but his credibility was shot. Cohen likely is serving his time in remorse, trying to salvage his self-respect and dignity. But his illegal acts weakened our democratic system and perverted our judicial system. He is one of America's usual suspects, along with Michael Flynn, George Papadopoulos, Roger Stone, Paul Manafort, Rick Gates and a host of others.[42]

The big guy gets acquitted.

Even prison has its own code of justice and pecking order. The convicted sex felon and fraudster, Jeffrey Epstein, was found strung up and dead in an unmonitored jail cell, taking with him his keen memory and his ken of contacts. Asphyxiated and alone, Epstein's suspicious death[43] reeks of supreme negligence and potential foul play. His countless, once-teenage female victims stumble along scarred in life while their famous johns strut scot-free along the streets of London, New York and Miami, and on private Caribbean islands.

Who gets caught? The usual suspects. A couple of prison guards with seemingly no motivation to see Epstein die. They were asleep or checking the internet while Epstein sipped his last breaths. No one truly powerful will suffer the consequences or be held accountable for this screw-up.

The usual suspects are a bunch of losers in every sense of the word. Sometimes they come from disadvantaged backgrounds, and their only shot

---

39 Hubbard, "Saudi Death Sentences in Khashoggi Killing Fail to Dispel Questions."

40 Labott, "CIA Concludes Saudi Crown Prince Ordered Jamal Khashoggi's Death, Sources Say."

41 Weiser, "Michael Cohen, Broken and Humiliated, Asks for Leniency from Prison."

42 Fernandez, "All the Trump Associates Convicted or Sentenced in the Mueller Investigation."

43 Zill de Granados, "Did Jeffrey Epstein Kill Himself? '60 Minutes' Investigates."

at escaping their conditions is to grab onto famous coattails. Others are just dimwitted and susceptible to the perks of power and privilege, behaving as sycophants have through the ages and jumping as high as they're told.

The usual suspects are everywhere, from America to Zimbabwe, and they will inevitably be charged, found guilty and imprisoned. The louder ones will be silenced. At a time when societies questioning their systems of justice and law enforcement, when body cams and social media are amplifying questionable practices that have gone on for generations, a call to change the status quo is inevitable.

Iran arrested the bystander[44] who took video of the missile downing the passenger jet. Arresting the messenger is always a bad sign. All the while, the powerful and privileged loudly hum the catchy tune of injustice while regularly asking their minions to learn the melody and to, "Play it. Play it again."

Coda: As of early 2021, no one had been held legally culpable for the deaths of those onboard Ukrainian International Airlines flight PS 752. Nor was anyone found responsible in the death of Jeffrey Epstein. Nor had there been any significant international repercussions for Crown Prince Mohamad bin Salman's role in the murder of Jamal Khashoggi. Meanwhile, Trump pardoned many of those previously convicted of crimes in his administration— except, notably, for his former attorney-turned-whistleblower, Michael Cohen.

HONORING HEROES OF THE WAR AGAINST COVID-19

Introduction

It's time to build a monument to the frontline fighters in PPE. The war might be metaphorical, but the casualties are just as real, the sacrifices just as heroic and the consequences just as existential.

Originally published: March 26, 2020

Vegas is surreal on any given day. A place of fake pharaonic pyramids, Imperial Roman palaces, Venetian canals, an Eiffel Tower.

Surreal.

In the middle of the Las Vegas Strip is the New York-New York Hotel and Casino complex,[45] with a faux cityscape—a scaled-down skyline. In

---

44 "Iran Plane Downing."
45 "Las Vegas Strip Hotel."

front of the Statue of Liberty, a faux harbor floats a replica of the New York Fire Department's fire boat #2 that was spontaneously turned into a living monument[46] to New York 9/11 firefighters.

First responders and citizens garlanded this model city with flowers, firefighter T-shirts, images of the fallen, loving notes. This makeshift 9/11 firefighter memorial told the world that we will never forget the bravery and sacrifice of the first responders who rushed through ash-choked streets and into burning buildings to save our souls.

At this moment, we have a new set of heroes putting down their lives to save us from an invisible viral scourge: doctors and nurses. They are on the front lines fighting the coronavirus, intubating patients and working against all odds without sufficient[47] protective gear and medical equipment.

Naturally, we voluntarily need to stave off the illness and protect our potential saviors—wash your hands!

We also need a way to honor these individuals for their bravery and sacrifice. It's time to design and fund a meaningful monument to the nation's medical practitioners.

Healthcare fights and the partisan politics of public health insurance have tarnished the medical profession. Sky-high prescription costs and hospital claims make doctors, and the entire medical field, sometimes seem like an exploitive class and industry. We have a weird love–hate relationship with those who lessen our suffering. Let's now focus on the love part of the equation and be both respectful and profoundly grateful for their work.

Many front-line healthcare workers took on steep student debt to serve this moment. These people are in the trenches, in danger of becoming coronavirus cannon fodder. Currently, 14 percent of Spain's 40,000 healthcare workers— 5,400 workers—are already infected[48] and unable to go to work. The numbers will likely go up from the time this was written. Medics' work may be valued during a crisis, but it's often underappreciated. The risks they are taking, often without the equipment they need, is like sending troops to war without guns and hardened[49] Humvees.

---

46 Brean, "Spontaneous New York-New York 9/11 Shrine Lives on at UNLV as Historical Collection."

47 Hopkins, "Coronavirus: Medical Workers Are 'Desperate' for Masks as Trump Fails to Act."

48 Minder and Pelitier, "Coronavirus in Europe: Thousands of Health Workers Out of Action."

49 Moran, "Frantically, the Army Tries to Armor Humvees."

During the current crisis, doctors nationwide give daily COVID-19 medical updates and advice. Some doctors practice activism. Dr. Neil Shah, at the University of California San Francisco, helped author a nonpartisan activist petition. In three days, more than 5,000 healthcare professionals joined this plea to federal authorities. Here's the petition he forwarded to me, which has been slightly edited:

"We are physicians and healthcare providers with views that span the political spectrum. We are committed to promoting the health and welfare of the people of the United States of America. We are gravely concerned about the potential national and global impacts of the novel coronavirus upon human life and well-being.

"To 'flatten the curve,' the most effective proven strategy of mitigation is coordinated, synchronized 'sheltering in place.' To be maximally effective, this effort must take place at the national, if not international, level. This will undoubtedly incur substantial economic hardship, but the expected burden of not taking such action over the coming months and years will likely be enormous.

"Time is of the essence, and immediate action is required. We hereby call upon our leaders in Washington, D.C., to uniformly and unequivocally mandate sheltering in place across our nation for a minimum of four to eight weeks."

Four to eight weeks. Not Passover. Not Easter.[50]

Are we willing to gamble our lives and further endanger the lives of those who will care for us by risking an abbreviated, unmandated sheltering period? It's not only doctors demanding a national shelter-in-place order. U.S. Rep. Ro Khanna, D-California, led 20 other[51] members of Congress in a similar call. Let's face reality and leave the gambling in Vegas.

Again, Vegas is surreal on any day. A vacated Vegas is even more so. The garish gambling houses are silenced, hawkers and hookers are off the streets. The ad hoc Vegas 9/11 memorial is now gone, too, its artifacts stored at the University of Nevada. The surviving 9/11 New York firefighters and first responders are not yet gone, but they are slowly being forgotten.

Today's frontlines are populated by selfless, triage-trained medical practitioners. Also on the front lines? Unsung delivery drivers, retail clerks and other "essential" personnel[52] risking their good health. They are all answering the call of duty. Let's honor them in life with the support, resources, materiel,

---

50 Nelson, "Trump Sticks to Easter Reopening despite Skepticism."
51 Coleman, "20 House Dems Call on Trump to Issue Two-Week, Nationwide Shelter-in-Place Order."
52 "Guidance on the Essential Critical Infrastructure Workforce."

political action, social behavior, appreciation and love they need to get us through this crisis.

Planning a future monument now could help focus an often-short-sighted federal leadership that is keenly sensitive to symbolic acts.

Coda: More than one year after the pandemic began, frontline workers continued to fall on the COVID-19 battlefield. Many remained unvaccinated and unappreciated. The next crisis is coming. Are we ready? And will we eventually recognize the grand sacrifices made by the previously unsung?

CHAPTER 3

FREEDOM TO WORSHIP

POPES AND PRESIDENTS CAN MAKE A POWERFUL TEAM

Introduction

The United States has long separated church and state. Nevertheless, religion and politics have many common characteristics as well as common interests.

Originally published: May 1, 2014

St. Peter's Square teemed last weekend with believers witnessing the extraordinary canonization of two contemporary popes, John XXIII and John Paul II.

Americans who are critical of the church, its failings and even the sanctification process focus on recent scandals and exclusionary practices. Without minimizing these criticisms, there should also be a secular recognition of these two past popes' international achievements, remembering that they both partnered with U.S. presidents to positively change the course of global events.

Whether helping to prevent a hot war or to end the Cold War, these two popes worked with Presidents John F. Kennedy and Ronald Reagan to achieve peaceful outcomes.

Pope Francis' ascension to St. Peter's throne creates unique opportunities for President Barack Obama to leverage a fresh, credible message of social justice and leadership aimed at Latin America. If pursued, it could be the latest collaboration between a president and a pope and potentially change the face of the Southern Hemisphere.

Rome and Washington, D.C., do not always see eye-to-eye, as during World War II or the two Vatican-opposed Iraq wars.

But ever since Woodrow Wilson's first meeting with Pope Benedict XV in 1919, shared foreign policy goals[1] between the White House and Vatican have often achieved success.

In October 1962, John XXIII played an effective intermediary role between Kennedy and then-Soviet leader Nikita Khrushchev in the heat of the Cuban missile crisis.[2] More recently, John Paul II[3] was the unelected, morally superior Polish opposition leader in absentia. He offered hope, peaceful resistance and a path to freedom from Soviet captivity.

I experienced the power of John Paul II's papacy as a reporter covering his Rome meeting with Mikhail Gorbachev[4] in 1989—the visit itself was recognition that the pope led vast spiritual divisions. Months later, I stood amidst reverent throngs at John Paul II's post-revolutionary victory tour to Czechoslovakia. A profound shift had taken place.

John Paul II did not act alone. As Carl Bernstein reported in "The Holy Alliance," a 1992 Time magazine cover story,[5] "Reagan and the pope agreed to undertake a clandestine campaign to hasten the dissolution of the communist empire." Together they succeeded.

It is easy to bristle at the idea of a religious leader conspiring with a U.S. president. Faith in the U.S. Constitution means for most a belief in the absolute separation of church and state.[6] But church and state sometimes need to work together to change big things.

Today, there is an opportunity for positive change in Latin America. The region is rife with corrupt and powerful populists. Exploiting the weak and preying on their passions, some of these leaders were criticized years ago for their "exhibitionism" by the man who is now Pope Francis. The first Latin American pope's influence amongst Catholics in the Americas is comparable to the first Polish pope's popularity behind the Iron Curtain.[7]

Where Francis is finding fertile ground, however, the heavy hand of past U.S. interventions is still felt throughout the continent. The 1973 CIA actions

---

1 Flatley, "The Convenient Alliance."
2 "Cuban Missile Crisis."
3 Editors, "John Paul II."
4 Lagunina, "Gorbachev Remembers Pope John Paul II."
5 Bernstein, "Cover Story."
6 "The Religion Clauses."
7 Institute of National Remembrance, "'The Pope from Behind the Iron Curtain'— Cracow-Budapest."

against Chile's Salvador Allende or the more recent Washington support for opponents of Venezuela's Hugo Chávez still whips people up down south.

Grenada, Cuba, Panama, Nicaragua, Guatemala, El Salvador, Mexico, Bolivia, Colombia—there's a long list of countries where the U.S. has engaged directly in war, supported authoritarian regimes, overthrown leaders, secretly armed groups or feigned ignorance of death squads.[8] Throughout the region, the U.S. propped up reprehensible military leaders and created long-lasting resentments. Uncle Sam became an easy target for anti-Yankee rhetoric and attitudes.

Today, despite wariness toward U.S. engagement, there is still an opportunity to confront and counter new challenges and foreign alliances being forged in Latin America. Both the passage of time and President Obama's light touch play a role in softening the Yank's image. During his recent Asia trip, the president characterized his foreign policy approach as hitting singles and doubles. "Every once in a while, we may be able to hit a home run," he said.

It may now be time to swing for the fences and for Washington to increase quiet coordination with the Vatican.

The president shares a passion and a purpose with Pope Francis. They are both committed to combating inequality. Francis offers a credible alternative voice to the loud populist leaders who trade on angry rhetoric to achieve authoritarian rule. A more prosperous and equitable Latin America would be a homer.

Coda: Joe Biden was the second Catholic to be elected president. His faith aligns with the Bishop of Rome's social justice views and offers new opportunities for popes and presidents to work together.

KANYE AND THE ARMENIAN GENOCIDE

Introduction

Not recognizing the Armenian genocide as a genocide by President Trump and Turkish President Erdoğan was disappointing and long overdue. While Kim Kardashian and Kanye West traveled to Armenia in 2015 to commemorate the 100th anniversary of the genocide, 100 American lawmakers wrote to Trump asking him to recognize the genocide.

Originally published: April 25, 2018

---

8 Schwarz, "Dirty Hands."

Armenia is not the first thing that comes to mind when you think about Kanye West and the Kardashians. Truth is, however, Kanye has always cared and sang about justice and his wife's Armenian-American family has always felt strongly about the need to recognize one of the world's greatest crimes and injustices—the Armenian genocide.

Kanye should leverage his newfound kinship[9] with President Trump to prod him towards doing what no other sitting American president has done: Use an executive order to declare that the murderous events of 1915 were the world's first modern genocide.

Genocide means a single group is targeted for systematic and premeditated death and extinction. Armenian families who survived the genocide await the world's recognition of this reprehensible event. America officially regards it as regrettable, unfortunate, and tragic, but does not recognize it as the event that spurred the word "genocide."[10] It is time.

Kim Kardashian and Kanye traveled to Armenia in 2015 to commemorate the 100th year[11] of the genocide. Kardashian publicly continues to memorialize the event every year, for good reason. The Armenian genocide was the 20th century's first mass crime against humanity, with 1.5 million Armenians either systemically butchered or forced onto death marches through the Syrian Desert by military regulars of Turkey's Ottoman government.

Modern Turkey does not like to be reminded of this historic fact. It prefers to look at the Christian Armenian deaths as unfortunate collateral damage during a World War, not a group targeted by Turks for ethnic and religious cleansing. Turkey's President Recep Tayyip Erdoğan threatens to exact punishment from countries recognizing that genocide. He made good on his threat when the French parliament passed a recognition bill in 2012. Erdoğan sanctioned France.[12]

President Trump does not take kindly to threats. Trump is always inclined to do things differently and buck tradition. American presidents have feared riling Ankara or challenging Turkey's revisionist history regarding events that the U.S. Ambassador at the time, Henry Morgenthau, called Turkey's acts

---

9 Ohlheiser, "How Kanye West Became a Hero of the Pro-Trump Internet: A Step-by-Step Guide."
10 Goldstein, "Review: 'Architects of Denial' a Powerful Look at the Armenian Genocide."
11 "Kanye West Hurls Himself into Lake on Armenian Genocide Anniversary Trip—Video | Music."
12 Jones, "Turkey Imposes Sanctions for French Genocide Bill."

"cold blooded, calculating state policy."[13] Those fears have to do with losing access to an important NATO air base or causing Turkey to reassess its strategic U.S. alliance.

The reality, however, is that President Erdoğan has already all but officially abandoned the relationship with America and the West in favor of building bridges to Putin's Russia and accommodating Iran.[14] In his worldview, America plays no role in his personal project to build a more Islamic Turkey. Erdoğan's self-perception as a rising caliph[15] means there is also not much of a role for human rights, a free press, independent judiciary, Israel, Christians, Kurds, or critics. Erdoğan not only effectively holds American personnel and military materiel hostage on Turkish bases, he holds millions of Syrian war refugees on his territory and threatens to expel them into Europe via Greece. He understands his real geographic and demographic leverage and is willing to use strategic assets and vulnerable populations as bargaining chips to get whatever he wants.

President Trump, on the other hand, is willing to trash treaties and renegotiate deals, making him the most likely and least hindered American politician able to recognize Armenia's genocide—a campaign promise on which President Obama reneged.[16] Trump recognized Jerusalem as Israel's capital, has prepared to drop out of the Iran nuclear deal, threatened "fire and fury" against North Korea, imposed tariffs on imported steel and aluminum, and even made enemies of the entire Mexican nation. He's not afraid to implement his foreign affairs policy instincts. It's his defining trait and it endears him to his loyal base.

But there are two things that he seems unwilling or unable to do. One is to criticize Vladimir Putin. The other is to hold Turkey accountable for its current domestic abuses and military adventures—even when they threaten American values and interests, as in Syria's political tinderbox. Erdoğan wants to make sure his own heroic narrative of a greater Turkey, rooted in empire and glory, is not sullied by American recriminations or real historic reckoning. Trump seems willing to accommodate him.

---

13 Adalian, "Ambassador Henry Morgenthau, Sr., and the Armenian Genocide."
14 Associated Press, "Turkey, Russia Ties Grow Stronger as U.S. Gets Elbowed out of the Middle East—Middle East News."
15 Taylor, "'The Caliph Is Coming, Get Ready,' Pro-Erdogan Turkish Politician Tweets."
16 Associated Press, "Despite Campaign Vow, Obama Declines to Call Massacre of Armenians 'Genocide.'"

From France to Pope Francis, 29 countries and 48 American states have recognized the genocide. 100 U.S. lawmakers recently wrote Trump a letter to seek the same.[17] Trump punted.[18] That was wrong.

Survivors of the Armenian genocide scattered around the globe, with large communities living in Moscow, Paris, New York, Fresno and Los Angeles after post-Ottoman Armenia wound up as part of the USSR. Since the dissolution of the Soviet Union, Armenia has been independent and rarely makes news. During this last week, however, young Armenians tired of logrolling autocratic national politics made the headlines with mass street protests forcing President Serzh Sarksyan to quit.[19] The modern country is alive and dynamic while the nearly wiped-out Armenia of a century ago is nearly forgotten by the world. Who remembers those Armenians? Does Trump?

If lawmakers can't convince Trump to recognize the genocide and his good friend Rep. Devin Nunes, whose political future hangs on the love of his Fresno Armenian-American electorate can't do it,[20] and if Kanye can't do it, then who's left? Maybe Hip Hop artists Kendrick Lamar[21] or Nazo Bravo[22] can find the right beat and lyrics to pull the president's heartstrings. It's time.

Coda: Just as every president before him, Donald Trump refused to recognize the Armenian genocide. Moreover, he failed to stop Turkish-backed attacks on ethnic Armenians in September 2020. Joe Biden became the first sitting president to explicitly recognize the mass killings of Armenians in the Turkish Ottoman Empire. In contrast to his predecessor, Biden also condemned Turkey's involvement in the Nagorno-Karabakh conflict.

RESPECTING THE RIGHTS AND RITES OF OUR ENEMIES

Introduction

The truth of Jamal Khashoggi's death is buried under a mountain of Saudi lies and religious hypocrisy. Governments, particularly our allies, must be held to certain minimal standards of decency, even regarding those we hate.

---

17 ANCA, "Over 100 U.S. Representatives Press President Trump to Properly Commemorate Armenian Genocide," 100.
18 Samuels, "Trump Again Declines to Describe Mass Killings of Armenians as Genocide."
19 Nemtsova, "A Bloodless Uprising in Armenia Just Forced the Leader to Resign: Will New Peaceful Revolutions Follow?"
20 "Armenian Genocide | Rep. Devin Nunes | President Trump | The Fresno Bee."
21 Editors, "*DAMN.*, by Kendrick Lamar."
22 Nozizwe, "Pulse."

Originally published: November 25, 2018

Osama bin Laden was killed by American special forces on foreign soil. His body was secreted off to a U.S. Navy ship and received ablutions, prayers. It was wrapped in a white sheet out of respect for the dead and following Islamic custom.[23] He was then given a sea burial and returned to his maker.

Jamal Khashoggi's body remains desecrated and his spirit despoiled. This is the sad tale of the death of two Saudis, one a targeted terrorist, the other an innocent journalist.

No matter how you feel about giving mass murderer bin Laden a proper and respectful burial, you have to credit the United States for giving a sworn enemy his last rites. It's only a small part of what makes America great. It's also what makes America big.

Under different circumstances, orders or regimes, American soldiers might have been less respectful of bin Laden's remains. But they knew they attacked bin Laden's compound not as vengeful, angry men. They were there on a mission:[24] to capture or kill America's enemy, not to create new ones.

This mission was, indeed, accomplished. The Obama war room photo revealed to the rest of us the heightened tension and drama of the moment. As a nation, we were both relieved by the outcome and repelled by what bin Laden represented and the lasting damage he did to our nation and the world.

We laid him and his ideology to rest. The respect we showed was not meant strictly for his dead corpse or his living faith. America would not make him a martyr.

Khashoggi was shown none of this decency. The Turkish account and audio recordings of what happened in the Saudi Arabian consulate reveal that Khashoggi's person was assaulted and his body defiled the moment he walked in the door.

Strangulation, torture, bone sawing. The purported acts and painful details slowly unfold, each more gruesome than the last. Turkey's President Erdoğan's insistent calls for the Saudis to present Khashoggi's body are made with the seeming knowledge that there is no body—only a dismembered bloody pile.

Erdoğan suggests this act was an assault on an innocent, a grave insult to Islam and a direct challenge to NATO. It may seem a little rich coming from a person who has jailed more journalists than any other leader, but it is a welcome message that shows Erdoğan can potentially evolve. Whether it's for reasons

---

23 Swaine, "Osama Bin Laden."
24 Research, "Death of Osama Bin Laden Fast Facts."

of personal affront, public relations or political expediency is unimportant. What matters is that Erdoğan has actually expressed outrage and called for an international inquiry,[25] setting a higher accountability standard to which he, too, should now be held.

Is this a new Erdoğan? That's a question only time will answer. As important, the world is asking if what we are seeing is a new Saudi Arabia? Or is this the same old kingdom suddenly revealed in a new, politically embarrassing light? Killing inconvenient journalists may seem like a good solution. It is, however, usually a gross miscalculation to believe that such brutal murders will go unnoticed or unanswered—even by an American president who takes a forgiving transactional approach to friends, if not always with allies.

President Trump feels the cranked-up heat of the moment as new Saudi consulate tapes are released to implicate a tightening circle of those who ordered the deed be done.[26] The more the lies, justifications, diversions and cover-ups come from defenders of the Saudi royals, the greater the resolve and calls for retributory action by the United States and others.

That doesn't mean the Trump administration will not try to create a binary choice between America's Saudi friends and Iranian foes. The current narrative favored by White House is that Iran is abjectly evil—an easy narrative to accept about Tehran's regime—while promoting the story that the Saudi kingdom is going through a hopeful generational leadership change being led by a youthful and progressive reformer. In a nutshell: Iran bad, Saudi good.

Things have gotten complicated, however. Iran is not yet globally seen as totally evil, and the Saudis are not seen as entirely trustworthy or even humane. The Saudi-conducted Yemen war has created the world's greatest humanitarian crisis, and the sheer butchery of a simple Washington Post columnist is beyond the pale.

In the film version of Homer's "The Iliad," Brad Pitt performed brilliantly the rage of Achilles[27]—a rage that led him not only to kill Hector at Troy's gates, but to further desecrate his body by tying it to his horse, dragging it and then leaving it on the open field in the greatest expression of disrespect and dishonor. This is an ancient story, but the deep and true nature of our species viscerally

---

25 Staff, "Turkey Calls for International Investigation into Khashoggi Murder."
26 Barnes, Schmitt, and Kirkpatrick, "'Tell Your Boss.'"
27 Desta, "Troy."

understands the importance we place not only on the living but also we demand for the dead.

Khashoggi's body was reportedly a beheaded and dismembered mound of pulp, strewn to the fields of dogs or swept by the unforgiving and unblessed winds. If the Saudi murderers have an Achilles' heel, it is their unbridled pride and the callousness of this cold-blooded killing.

The guilty may be able to bury the truth, but they cannot hide from time-tested fate.

Coda: The Biden administration announced that it would declassify an intelligence report into the Khashoggi murder. That could reveal the complicity, if any, of Saudi leaders including crown prince Mohammed bin Salman.

NOT WHAT PUTIN WANTED FOR CHRISTMAS

Introduction

Maybe the Kremlin boss found new Russian orthodoxy. Or perhaps he was just playing old Soviet sleight-of-hand. In the USSR, Christianity was replaced by communism. In today's Russia, communism has been replaced by Putinism. How well is that working for its namesake?

Originally published: December 20, 2018

Vladimir Putin won't find many great presents under the Christmas tree this year.

Orthodox Christian religious leaders worldwide are weakening an important institution that gave him outsize power and legitimacy.

The Russian Orthodox Church is being broken up, and an independent Ukraine Orthodox Church will be established. The Ukrainian flock soon will be led not by the Moscow-based church and Patriarchate, but rather by its own independent church and youthful leadership. Ukraine and its political class are suddenly freed from an influential Russian institution that has been fiercely loyal to Putin.

This was not on Putin's Christmas list. Instead, the news is like a lump of coal in his stocking.

Russia's wider designs on—and power over—Ukraine have included a wide hybrid war from the Donbass to the recent naval blockade in the Black Sea. Moscow has its fingerprints on the shoot-down of the Malaysian MH-17 passenger plane over Ukrainian territory and its paw prints on an annexed Crimea. Every step of the way, Putin has found legitimacy in his actions and the nation's military activity through reignited Russian nationalism and the silent acquiescence of Moscow's spiritual leadership and clergy.

Religion did not always play a central role in Russia. Not long ago, when Communism ruled the Soviet Union's people and territories, an officially encouraged atheism led to secularized churches and iconoclastic behavior. Marxist ideology did not support both a Communist system and religious beliefs. But people continued to worship, both privately and surreptitiously. Putin himself admitted to being a closeted Christian during those dark days.

By the end of the Soviet era, however, Mikhail Gorbachev was making overtures to the West and meeting with Pope John Paul II in Rome during a state visit. Gorbachev saw religion as a means to bridge a godless Soviet Union to a secularized West, that nevertheless respected religion and religious freedom. As a Newsweek reporter, I traveled to Sicily with Raisa Gorbachev and Russian Patriarch Alexey II for a symbolically important trip that highlighted a mutually beneficial Russian church–state relationship.

That relationship grew and strengthened after the Soviet Union collapsed— a relationship I observed while a Moscow correspondent living next door to Alexey II's Arbat residence. Putin now openly embraces the church, its power, and, seemingly, his faith.

For a while, it seemed that the Muscovite church was unstoppably ascendant. Tax-free revenues, powerful patrons and Putin-primed subsidies made it a rich realm. In a post-Soviet Russia, the enriched Moscow Patriarchate imagined a new, unique role and envisioned the glory and opportunity to take the spiritual crown from an Eastern Orthodox church, whose Ecumenical Patriarch lives and works in an increasingly inhospitable Turkey. Moscow's religious hierarchs and political leaders believed that Russia's time had come to fulfill its historic destiny: Moscow as the "Third Rome."

The Third Rome doctrine asserts that Moscow picks up the Christian mantle following the fall of Rome and after Constantinople (known as "New Rome") succumbed to Islam's Ottoman Empire. The updated version of the doctrine[28] continues to drive Moscow's belief that its time for ascendance is now.

Coda: Just as his predecessors had a hard time getting rid of Christianity in the USSR, former atheist-turned-Orthodox confessor Vladimir Putin struggled to eliminate his main political rival. Alexei Navalny inconveniently refused to die after being poisoned, perhaps prompting Putin to pray for a miracle.

---

28 Poe, "Moscow, the Third Rome."

HOW WOMEN AND CHILDREN BEAR
THE BRUNT OF WAR'S BRUTALITY

Introduction

In the Middle East, wars usually have a strong religious component. The victims of those conflicts are often preordained by the perpetrators' dogmatic views.

Originally published: November 8, 2019

Sex and gender decide our fate more than some like to admit. Men and money make the world go 'round, after all, and grown men are mostly responsible for society's most critical decisions surrounding war and peace. Children don't vote, and women often don't have a voice.

The latest military rout taking place in northern Syria is only the most recent installment of war's practice of disappearing the dead. Not because the killed are invisible, but because they are unseen. There are many victims in these conflicts, but the ones who suffer most and longest always seem to be the women and children.

ISIS remains a particularly vile scourge to both moms and kids.

Consider the Yazidi women who were raped, tortured, kidnapped and killed by Islamist fighters not long ago. Or the countless kids who were maimed in ISIS attacks and left orphans on the field of battle. Or all the noncombatants terrorized in the savage streets. Women and children are the ones whom we see the least—and who reflect war's inhumanity the most. ISIS may no longer have territory or a putative leader, but it continues to exist, and its ideology is not dead. Ask a grieving mother or orphaned child.

These suffering individuals are shuttled from refugee camp to detention camp, as when Saddam Hussein evilly used foreign women and children as human shields to surround his troop locations—pawns in a bloody chess game. ISIS' urban guerrilla fighters now hide among civilians in hospitals and hovels. It's always the women and children, mostly unarmed, regularly unfed, who take the brunt of warfare, who suffer loss of life and who inherit a failed future—if any future at all.

When a ship goes down, we are versed in the practice that women and children should be saved first, that a captain stays until the end and goes down with his ship. But somewhere along the line between sailing ship and ship of state, priorities changed. Kids and their mothers, once valued for procreation, legacy and honor, became merely tactical tools. In this dishonorably warring world, women are chattel and children uncherished.

Some of the world's most abominable atrocities against humanity are committed in Syria. The Turkish invasion[29] only made this grim situation worse. As always, the horror has visited women and children disproportionately. From Assad's chemical attacks[30] to Putin's hospital bombings,[31] they have turned the vulnerable into victims twice over.

Now and again, we see women and children fighting[32] either for their defense or liberation, taking up arms because they are forced to by overwhelming men or circumstance, so that they have some agency over their lives, so that they can die for a cause or with dignity. Abandoned Kurdish women fight because no one else would fight for them or with them. They have learned and relearned this lethal lesson. So, the women fight, their long hair or braids dangling from their headscarves as they bear arms with covered heads. The children, too, do what they can and endure what they must.

If a woman or child is injured or caught in battle by Turkish-aligned militias, as was recently reported,[33] they are enslaved, tortured or worse. Çiçek Kobane was hauled off the field of battle by bragging men who called her a pig and sought to "slaughter" her. Kobane's captors joked they would slit her throat and watch her bleed, but not before taking her last bit of dignity as the men's faces first promised the violence of rape.

Atrocities know no ideological boundaries or national purity. America committed them in Vietnam[34] and at Abu Ghraib.[35] Here's the difference: The United States punished the perpetrators and recognized the incivility of the violent actions against innocent civilians. America is not perfect, but it tries to be good.

This week I was again reminded of war's barbarity. I've seen my fair share of it over the years in the field. But though I am safely ensconced in my comfortable American home, far from the action and free from the trauma, I am not divorced from the lesson. In fact, this week's reminder came from home.

My son Eon, 17, reacted to news reports[36] calling the al Baghdadi operation and death "successful."

---

29 McDonnell, "Turkey's Invasion of Syria Worsens a Humanitarian Crisis."

30 Barnard and Gordon, "Worst Chemical Attack in Years in Syria; U.S. Blames Assad."

31 Triebert, "Russia 'Bombed Four Hospitals in Syria in Four Hours', Report Finds."

32 Lazarus, "Women. Life. Freedom. Female Fighters of Kurdistan."

33 Dri, "Kurdish Force Makes Appeal after Female Fighter..."

34 Editors, "Was My Lai Just One of Many Massacres in Vietnam War?"

35 Hersh, "Torture at Abu Ghraib."

36 Sanger, "Al-Baghdadi Raid Was a Victory Built on Factors Trump Derides."

He noted that 11 children were safe and saved in the raid. The ISIS terrorist's two wives and three children died, however, when he detonated an explosive vest in a tunnel, while running from American Special Forces troops, robots and dogs. Eon turned to me and said, "Dad, it's good they got him, but three kids died—that's not 'successful.' "

The last cowardly act of this menace was not only to commit suicide, but to take his family with him. The women and children. After all, it's a man's world.

Coda: ISIS reportedly chose Abu Ibrahim al-Hashimi al-Qurashi, a religious scholar, as its next leader. The U.S. government classified al-Qurashi as a "specially designated global terrorist" and offered up to $10 million in exchange for information leading to his capture.

CHAPTER 4

FREEDOM TO LEARN

IMPACT OF PANAMA PAPERS

Introduction

The effect of leaking an enormous cache of notorious documents depends on a nation's regime type. The long-term consequences might never be known. There is no doubt that it has shaken some beyond repair.

Originally published: April 16, 2016

Warren Buffett is known for his pithy sayings and homespun investment philosophy. One Buffettism states that "it takes 20 years to build a reputation and five seconds to destroy it."[1]

This is as true in business as it is in government. It requires less time to take down institutions and destroy public trust than it does to develop and strengthen them.

Enter Mossack Fonseca,[2] a Panamanian legal firm specializing in hiding offshore assets. Revelations regarding the firm's clients and capital flows are the latest salvo on government credibility and citizen credulity.

The recently leaked 11.5-million-document dump known as the Panama Papers[3]—a load of Mossack Fonseca's private internal documents—is roiling the waters for a handful of leaders who wanted or needed to cache their cash.

One minute a prime minister is a respected leader, then next he is judged a shady figure in the court of public opinion. In Iceland, Prime Minister

---

1 Berman, "The Three Essential Warren Buffett Quotes to Live By."
2 Fitzgibbon, "New Panama Papers Leak Reveals Mossack Fonseca's Chaotic Scramble."
3 Zeitung, "All You Need to Know about the Panama Papers."

Sigmundur Davíd Gunnlaugsson had to step aside while Britain's David Cameron faces media questions and public concern about his wealth, privilege and the economic patriotism of Britain's upper crust. Neither the British nor the Icelandic leader appear to have acted illegally.

The uniquely collaborative journalistic effort that brought to light the large and shadowy world of capital's global hiding places was impressive. While the Panama Papers' effect may be to force governments toward greater accountability and transparency, the likely effect on some governments is just the opposite. It just depends on what type of government rules; it depends on "regime type," whether a government is a democracy or authoritarian regime.

In liberal democracies like Iceland, there is an established democratic process that provides for the peaceful transition of a government and for increased oversight. Greater openness and responsiveness is likely to follow the recent leak.

In other countries, however, like Russia, an autocratic leader may be exposed, but his power is further cemented. President Vladimir Putin is not going anywhere soon, the leak likely reinforcing his tendency to crackdown on dissent.

Various news analysts—and Russia itself—suggest Putin was the target of the Panama Papers leak, showing he siphoned sovereign wealth and padded family accounts. They argue that these revelations put pressure on Putin's regime. But the opposite is true.

Putin is perversely strengthened. Russians had always believed the rumors of his $2 billion of personal stolen wealth and could clearly see his administration's deeply rooted and formal corruption. It reaches down to their daily lives.

Putin argues the Panama Papers are a targeted foreign conspiracy aimed at toppling him and weakening Russia, giving him greater latitude to defend its interests. The leak also gives him personal leverage over those he favors and from whom he demands fealty. Putin just got more power over his now publicly exposed ruling coterie. Their dependence on Putin's benevolence and favor has just grown exponentially.

For democrats and autocrats alike, there are many surprises yet to come from the Panama Papers leak. The public's trust in individuals and democratic institutions will be tested. It would be a mistake, however, if citizens' faith in liberal systems is questioned. It would only embolden those whose rule goes unchecked and strengthen systems that reward despots and demagogues.

Scandal serves cynicism and amplifies anger. Whether real or manufactured scandal, the results are often the same: A crisis of confidence in democratic political leadership and the questioning of individual's motivations for public service.

The world over, the drumbeat of derision and the calculated cry of corruption are a potent mix. Together they create the conditions for populists to steal the show and further sink—instead of save—institutions that took generations of hard-fought battles to build.

Government needs to be good enough—and resilient enough—not only for Warren Buffett and the rest of us to believe in, but in which free people worldwide are willing to invest.

Coda: In October 2020, German authorities reportedly issued international arrest warrants against the former owners of the law firm involved. Two dozen countries have recovered more than $1 billion in taxes, and countless reforms have been put into place around the world as a result of this scandalous revelation.

UGLY HISTORY OF FOOTBALL MASCOTS

Introduction

Super Bowl teams and their fans wrestle with ties to offensive imagery. Whether it's due to racism, cultural misappropriation or simply bad taste, corporate owners are bending over backwards to replace bad logos and bad names, while finding the right balance between good marketing and good citizenship.

Originally published: January 31, 2020

Super Bowl Sunday is a uniquely American celebration of guts and grit, cash and commercialism. It's our annual ritual and favored sport. Thanksgiving is the only other American holiday that Super Sunday rivals.

This year it's the San Francisco 49ers versus the Kansas City Chiefs in Miami for Super Bowl LIV, the 54th championship gladiator event.

But before there was the NFL, there were real 49ers who fought against actual chiefs. It was history's Version 1.0 of a non-gridiron battle where native sons fought Native Americans. This partly forgotten fight remains a shameful part of U.S. history. That long-ago chapter is relevant today, at a time when racism and foreign immigration remain hot-button political issues.

So let's take a minute, hit the TV remote and pause the action to think about the meaning and history of this Super Bowl's team names.

Most NFL and other sports teams have benevolent names and mascots: Giants, Titans, Marlins, Jets, Sox, Rays, Rockets. Some, however, are stuck with a dehumanizing naming tradition. Their stadiums feature[4] tomahawk-chopping costumed fans wearing war paint and feathered headdresses.

---

4 Bogage, "Chiefs' War Chant and Tomahawk Chop Hits the Super Bowl Stage."

Heated national debates about Native American mascots have occurred over many years and will continue as long as there are Redskins, Braves, Blackhawks and Chiefs. I went to San Francisco's Lowell High School,[5] where our 60-year-old mascot, the Indian, was reluctantly changed to a Cardinal in 1983. I currently work at Stanford University, where the Indian was retired in 1981 and the unofficial mascot became the uncontroversial Tree.[6]

But let's face it. It's time to dump dated and demeaning symbols. Keep any parts that might honor and elevate American Indian[7] history and culture and use the Seminole tribe's accommodation with Florida State University as a positive example of how to figure out workable solutions.

In contrast to the ongoing controversies surrounding Native American mascots, the 'Niners' mascot escapes scrutiny. They are represented by a seemingly benign, if ornery, gold prospector in well-worn clothes. The 19th century scruffy old coot in the turned-up hat represents the thousands upon thousands of Americans who flooded into California for the Gold Rush. Arriving in droves in 1849, they made up America's biggest[8] mass migration, which is why they are called 49ers.

Simultaneously, the rest of the world flocked to California, too. The Gold Rush also became the world's most diverse migration. Altogether, California saw 300,000 new arrivals from home and abroad during the Gold Rush.

It was a wild time, when gold fever ran hot, and gold was there for the taking in the nation's westernmost and least governed territory. Lawless, aggressive, criminal acts ruled the day. Those heading West brought few provisions and less understanding of non-Caucasians. Most Americans arriving at the mining fields and gold panning banks of the American River had never before encountered Chileans, Polynesians, Australians and Russians. It was the first time they had seen a Chinese person.

In 1852, more 20,000 Chinese came through San Francisco, a city they had called "Gold Mountain" in China. By the end of the 1850s, the Chinese who crossed the Pacific to seek their fortune made up one in five people[9] scouring California's rich Sierra foothills and fabled gold fields. Such a massive Asian presence fed prejudice. Racism ran rampant, and new California whites wanted native Indians gone and servile Chinese.

---

5 Miller, "S.F. Schools Boss Orders Lowell High Mascot Change."

6 Kieschnick, "Caroline Kushel '21 Chosen as New Stanford Tree."

7 Zotigh, "Introduction & 1st Question: American Indian or Native American?"

8 HistoryNet, "California Gold Rush."

9 Editors, "Chinese Immigrants and the Gold Rush."

An Indian genocide[10] that began in other parts of America followed the populations rapidly flowing West. In the end, Native Americans were decimated. As the San Francisco Bulletin newspaper put it[11] at the time: "It is a painful necessity of advancing civilization that the Indians should gradually disappear." And they nearly did. By the turn of the century, a population of tribal California natives went from 300,000 down to 16,000. The 49ers did their part to kill off Indian chiefs and their tribes.

Nowadays, when we think about the original 49ers, we imagine hardscrabble, risk-taking men expressing radical individualism, showing fortitude and pluck by braving travel west across rough and dangerous territory to hunt for gold nuggets and flakes of fortune. Today's football team is named after those romanticized 49ers of yore who fought tough odds and hard conditions to survive and, just maybe, hit the jackpot. That's an acceptable image for a team mascot.

When it came to Indians and Chinese, however, these very same 49ers were often a ruthless bunch of thieves, claim jumpers and race baiters. Their actions and beliefs led to the near extermination of California natives and stoked support for Congressional passage of the 1882 Chinese Exclusion Act—which is eerily reminiscent of today's Muslim ban.[12]

Super Bowl fans can appreciate the astounding athletic prowess and power of both remarkable teams, despite the fact that their mascots are bad marketing choices.

Coda: In a mighty gesture of exasperation, the U.S. capital city's NFL team jettisoned its former "Redskins" name in July 2020 and adopted the nondescript "Washington Football Team" as a placeholder until a permanent new name was selected. In December 2020, the Cleveland baseball team dropped its team name and mascot, the Indian.

CHINA'S AMERICAN DREAM

Introduction

Beijing appreciates America's higher education system, even if America sometimes takes it for granted. This column was written with a wink and a nod.

---

10 Blakemore, "California Slaughtered 16,000 Native Americans. The State Finally Apologized For the Genocide."

11 Oakland Museum of California, "Gold Fever Law, Order, and Justice for Some—Discrimination."

12 American Civil Liberties Union, "Living with the Muslim Ban."

Originally published: April 16, 2020

It's nearly graduation time around the country, which can only mean one thing: Boring commencement speeches to indifferent students.

The "Coronavirus Commencements" will be different, however, because graduates will not go through a public procession of pomp and circumstance. They also won't dine with grandparents who traveled great distances to get to the ceremony. Travel curtailed, campuses closed, bookstores stuck with unsold "Class of 2020" swag. Graduation speakers will stay home to deliver their laugh lines and sage advice as webcammed words of wisdom.

Into this breach, let's invite an atypical commencement speaker to give a universal graduation speech that can be simulcast to every U.S. institution of higher learning. Who should that person be? The guy who paid for more undergraduates' educations in America than any other single individual: China's "Core"[13] leader and Communist Party General Secretary Xi Jinping.

At the start of the 2020 academic year, approximately[14] 360,000 students from the People's Republic of China attended American colleges, most of them paying full freight for tuition, books, housing and food. The overall estimate of what the United States earns from all the foreign students coming to America for education comes to around[15] $39 billion a year. Not all of that is from China, but a lot of it is. So let's hear what their sugar daddy has to say.

In lieu of a CCP-vetted speech to the many Chinese students and other attendees, here's my best shot. I include both the text and subtext of a potential Zoomed speech to the graduating classes all across America next month:

"Graduates of the Class of 2020, congratulations! This is your time.

I am told that speeches in America should begin with a joke, but this is not a common practice in Beijing. In fact, we never joke. Not about how powerful we are or our plans for world domination.

We do not have William Shakespeare, "Will & Grace" or Will Ferrell. What we have is iron will.

China's cultural strength and fortitude are born from your parents' generation and sacrifice. They suffered through a century of humiliation,[16] living through extreme poverty and eating what little they had to eat out of an iron rice bowl.

---

13 Lim and Kang, "China's Xi Anointed 'core' Leader, on Par with Mao, Deng."
14 Reality Check Team, "Trade War."
15 Leiber, "Foreign Students Sour on America, Jeopardizing a $39 Billion Industry."
16 Schiavenza, "How Humiliation Drove Modern Chinese History."

Your generation, however, is a privileged one. For those of you watching who are Chinese nationals, you come from single-child homes. My generation's one-child policy[17] made you all privileged princelings who have never known want, always experienced economic growth and who had the extraordinary luck to go overseas to study. You got to learn, see and live in America.

Please bring back to China your technical training, especially your insights into artificial intelligence and quantum computing. Bring back our Middle Kingdom's power and help re-establish the privilege of a nation destined for greatness and global leadership.

You have a great number of gifts and learning that you must bring back to Beijing, Shanghai, Guangzhou, Shenzen and Wuhan.

But as you bring back your valuable knowledge, there are some things you must leave behind: Do *not* bring back your dangerous ideas of liberal democracy.

Leave behind whatever decadent thoughts you have appropriated. Muzzle any new instincts you have developed for free speech, religion or assembly. Purge from your hearts any passion or interest of the need for self-expression over the collective common good. Remember the primacy of the Communist Party.

Yes, we have reports from our student committees, consular corps and others unknown to you that some of your student comrades experimented with cannabinoids and studied anti-authoritarian theories. Some of you have toyed with direct democratic governance, participated on campus and in the classroom in discussions surrounding the Tiananmen Square events of 1989, Falun Gong, Winnie the Pooh,[18] Taiwan independence, Uighur detention or the Dalai Lama. Take these learnings and your newfound understanding of our adversary and apply them for the greater good. Take them with you to help achieve China's greatness.

This is our time.

We will use the Trump era as an opportunity to woo Western allies. We will confound[19] the conversation surrounding China's culpability in the coronavirus crisis. We will cry racism[20] whenever our national interests are threatened and wherever our newfound confidence and regional hegemony is questioned.

---

17 Neuman and Schmitz, "Despite the End of China's One-Child Policy, Births Are Still Lagging."

18 Kounalakis, "Goodnight Mao."

19 Knight, "China Flexes Its Soft Power with 'Covid Diplomacy.' "

20 Chugani, "Chinese Who Cry Racial Abuse amid the Coronavirus Epidemic Forget They Are as Bad as the Rest of Us."

You have all profited from an undeniably strong American higher-education program. In this, the United States continues to excel. The price of that education has been high and unattainable for many American students.

China has invested in you and in our nation's future. The return on that investment is the unarticulated understanding we established at the start of your foreign education journey. It is now your obligation and duty to help your nation become globally more productive, competitive and successful.

Your collective strength, wisdom and vision will assure that our party, state and future will remain inseparable. Together we will achieve the Chinese Dream.[21]

This is, after all, my time."

Coda: From coast to coast and at odd hours around the world, American college graduations in the age of COVID-19 have occurred virtually. As of this writing, no foreign dictator has given any pandemic-era commencement speeches in the United States.

COVID-19 PAUSE WON'T SHIELD AUTHORITARIAN LEADERS FOREVER

Introduction

Inept or authoritarian leaders caught a brief break when the novel coronavirus erupted into a pandemic. But even before vaccines rolled out, many protestors quickly started feeling emboldened and defiant, taking to the streets again.

Originally published: May 5, 2020

Teenagers around the country have a very specific plan for what they will do when they are released from COVID confinement: party!

Around the world, however, the decriminalization and return of mass gatherings likely will lead to something else: demonstrations!

Governments and regimes everywhere are going to face a greater test of their resilience and staying power once masses of people are freed from public-health fears and able to express their dissent. Demonstrators who were a prominent feature in the streets of Hong Kong or on France's highways have all been forced to curtail their collective protest activities. Instead of gathering in person, they are cowering from pestilence.

---

21 Deutsche Welle, "Xi Jinping and the 'Chinese Dream.'"

In country after country, concerns over public health are trumping the urge to amass in their outrage over social inequity, curtailed human rights, government corruption, resource scarcity, healthcare inadequacy, supply-chain failures, leader ineptitude, worker exploitation and citizen disempowerment. Some of this pent-up frustration is finding online[22] expression via virtual demonstrations. Internet-based organizing may provide some outlet for public expression, but is no substitute for real world assembled venting.

Public suffering and popular disenchantment with leaders who failed to serve citizens before this pandemic are building in a pressure cooker of protest that will surely blow its lid. This is as true in authoritarian regimes as it is in democratic states. Democracies, however, are more vulnerable and responsive to the mood and will of indignant people.

Democratic systems around the world have implemented stay-at-home orders or guidelines that keep people apart, whether in parks or in front of parliaments. The actions are deemed necessary and have unquestionably made a difference in containing viral spread and flattening the curve.[23] These measures have certainly succeeded in keeping the disgruntled far away from the accountable.

Strained governments currently struggling to manage reasonable pandemic responses should expect to face the music once it is safe for the disgruntled to organize and protest. Leaders everywhere will confront an angry, frustrated, aggrieved, unemployed electorate demanding justice and seeking political retribution for any mistakes or miscalculations currently being made.

In places where government legitimacy was already being challenged by public demonstrations against unpopular policies—places like Turkey[24] or Algeria[25]—the lockdown orders have provided regimes a reprieve. In fact, for authoritarians and illegitimate rulers, their enforceable orders demanding citizens to stay off the streets and inside their homes has been a godsend. Many of them are eyeing this current status as a preferred state and a permanent feature.

Surveillance states such as China are continually experimenting with new tech tools to control their people. Authoritarians are deploying both smartphone apps that read QR codes to manage movement and assembly. They are also

---

22 "In Russia, Anti-Putin Protests Thrive with a Little Help from the Internet."
23 Wilson, "The U.S. Has Flattened the Curve. Next Up Is 'Squashing' It."
24 Editors, "Environmentalists Cleared from Protest Camp in Turkey While Mining Operations Continue."
25 Ahmed, "Algeria Bans Street Marches Due to Virus; Some Protesters Unswayed."

relying on snooping police and neighborhood snitches to remind citizens that they are always being watched. Privacy falls by the wayside and, along with it, the anonymity of private thought and public movement.

In some parts of the world, people's deepest fears are realized. Lifesaving, convenient, politically empowering smartphones have turned into devices used 24/7 not only to monitor citizens' every move, conversation, financial transaction and medical interaction, but also to report it to a centralized and powerful government entity.

In the United States, people across the country have regularly opposed any government-run identification system, shunning[26] past attempts to create national ID cards. Smartphones, however, perform the same function. They possess within them a treasure trove of data that reveal the most intimate details of our lives. Citizens have voluntarily filled them with personal and private data in exchange for convenience or free services delivered by profit-seeking companies—whether Facebook or WeChat.

This pandemic makes every citizen more vulnerable to governments demanding this smartphone data, even if the reason is to protect communities. In authoritarian states, companies must hand over this private data to the government—often for good, but also for ill. While protesters are temporarily off the streets, they are still on their phones.

It may take a while before "Yellow Vest"[27] flash mobs reassemble to block France's highways or for the early return[28] to protest in Hong Kong's malls to gather steam. Malls[29] that are barely able to service shoppers, however, seem unlikely gathering places for multitudes opposed to Beijing's covetous designs over the former British colony.

Right now, Americans willing to protest in the streets feel strongly that the current lockdowns infringe on their rights of speech, assembly and religion. Some paranoid citizens believe that the federal government is using COVID-19 as an excuse[30] to impose armed authority over society and assert dictatorial powers. A few of the assembling folks are just cranks.

---

26 Harper, "The New National ID Systems."
27 De Clercq and Pennetier, "More French Protests See Roads Blocked, Trains Disrupted and Scuffles in Paris."
28 News, "As Virus Infections Dwindle, Hong Kong Protests Gain Steam."
29 Kounalakis, "Malls, Dying in America, Have Been Revived by Protesters in Hong Kong."
30 Ratner, "Liberty or Death?"

The ultimate protest in a democracy is expressed at the ballot box. For those currently in power and either flailing or failing, the verdict on their crisis management skills and actions will arrive in November.

Coda: The pandemic didn't stop most voters from turning out in record numbers on Election Day in November 2020. A group of protesters did briefly manage to disrupt one of the nation's largest COVID-19 testing and vaccination sites at Dodger Stadium in Los Angeles on January 31, 2021.

DEALING WITH OPPRESSORS' STATUES

Introduction

Statues of old Communist leaders are preserved in Eastern European countries' (Hungary, the Czech Republic, Estonia) parks or in designated, protected spots to serve as reminders of a country's past. America's politically incorrect monuments deserve the Soviet treatment.

Originally published: June 26, 2020

Statues and monuments—from Columbus to Confederates, presidents to priests—are heatedly being removed, defaced or destroyed. Police actions and popular protests have rekindled debates over American history that can be informed by how other countries have managed their tortured pasts and controversial memorials.

Ironically, lessons from former communist countries such as Hungary and Russia can be instructive.

Budapest's Freedom Square hosts a prominent and controversial Soviet war memorial. Hungarians regularly argue for its removal, but it remains unmoved and guarded. It is an exception.

The bulk of Soviet-era statues in Budapest and in countries once behind the Iron Curtain have been removed, relocated and reinterpreted. The idea is not to erase history, but to contextualize it.

In Budapest, Freedom Square's remaining monument is a fenced-off reminder of the Soviets' World War II liberating army. The obelisk sits next to the U.S. Embassy, just below[31] the American ambassador's window. Unlike other Soviet monuments in the city, a treaty guarantees this one's place, preservation and protection.

---

31 *Failed Architecture*, "Hungary's Identity Crisis Fought in Concrete and Bronze."

Other Communist monuments in Budapest, however, have been removed and relegated to a final resting place outside town in Memento Park.[32] The park boasts "the biggest statues of the Cold War" and shows how to reinterpret a nation's painful past. Supersized statues of Communist-era commissars stand quietly in the elements. Stalin's empty boots. A lunging Lenin. A modernist bust of Marx. A museum barracks full of educational material puts the era and objects into complete and nuanced context. School groups and tourists visit regularly.

Hungary's President Árpád Göncz at the time hailed Memento Park's creation for its measured approach. Göncz said it "utilizes politically neutral means of art to emphasize the dignity of democracy and the responsibility of historical thinking." America could use its own Memento Park to present and interpret Confederate symbols of a resoundingly defeated past. Historic context creates a cold understanding of the past, countering mythology and revisionism.

Countries throughout Eastern Europe have moved their monuments from prominent pedestals to out-of-the-way detoxified destinations. Tallinn, Estonia has an outdoor garden of bronze and stone sculptures strewn helter-skelter at the Maarjamäe Palace.[33] It's disarming to see a larger-than-life Stalin dumped on his back or Lenin's brutal bust resting its chin on overgrown lawns.

In Prague, a Soviet IS-2m heavy tank on a massive stone block was erected to honor the Soviet mechanized divisions who fought Nazi forces and helped free Czechoslovakia at the end of WWII. Soviet tanks, however, also reminded Czechoslovaks of a pernicious recent past—they were used to put down the 1968 Prague Spring uprising. Following the 1989 Velvet Revolution, a group of Czechoslovak artists took buckets of paint and visually disarmed the formerly ominous Soviet Tank Square memorial. It became known as the Pink Tank.[34]

Eastern European nations found it easier to remove the Soviet symbols and statues of their occupiers and oppressors, but even the Russians themselves put lots of their Soviet-era monuments out to pasture. Shortly after the 1991 Moscow coup that tried to overthrow President Mikhail Gorbachev and helped end the Soviet empire, statues of former heroes, ruthless functionaries and self-aggrandizing leaders were taken down. Soviet sculptural detritus was moved to Gorky Park's "Graveyard to Fallen Monuments."[35] In its stillness, the Fallen

---

32 "Memento Park Budapest | Communist Statues and Ghosts of Communist Dictatorship."
33 "Permanent Exhibitions."
34 Takac, "When David Černý Made a Tank Monument Interesting."
35 "The 'Graveyard to Fallen Monuments', Moscow."

Monuments park still arouses dread—infamous figures such as "Iron Felix" Dzerzhinsky, who founded the Soviet secret police, stir strong emotions.

Despite Eastern Europe and Russia's rapid monument removal following the upheavals at the end of the last century, there are now movements to resurrect the past, rehabilitate the rotten and re-litigate history. In Russia, some of the Sovietica is being salvaged and Stalin is being painted positively[36] by Russian President Vladimir Putin.

Budapest, too, is a perfect example of how expediency and opportunism drive politicians and parties to leverage symbols of the past to score popular points today. While a national consensus continues to revile its Soviet past, there is also a movement to use symbolism and a redacted past to rewrite a new national narrative. Freedom Square is now home to a controversial memorial that seemingly absolves Hungary for its Holocaust role,[37] portraying the entire country as victim. In the history game, it is always easier for countries to blame others for their fate, but harder for a nation to face its own past squarely.

The good news? Freedom Square also hosts a striding, sunny Ronald Reagan statue[38] moving confidently toward the still-standing Soviet obelisk. A nearby Budapest tech park privately put up[39] a statue of computer visionary and Apple founder Steve Jobs. In Hungary, enlightened modern history seems in a race to outweigh and out-monument the past.

The United States may be in a similar race. The Smithsonian Institution is the world's largest museum and research center and the premier place for contextualizing U.S. history and storing fallen statues. The Smithsonian's new leader,[40] Lonnie Bunch, would be the perfect caretaker and curator. Bunch was previously the founding director of the National Museum of African American History and Culture—could he oversee a way out-of-the way "Memento Park DC"?

Coda: Many cities and states continue to wrestle with this issue. Some authorities have put problematic statuary in storage. Others try to offer perspective by relocating offensive artwork to designated historical display areas. One strange twist was a proposed law in Alabama which would prohibit the placement of contextualizing signage to monuments that might alter its intended meaning.

---

36 Thoburn, "For Putin, for Stalin."
37 Kirchick, "Hungary's Ugly State-Sponsored Holocaust Revisionism."
38 Birnbaum, "Statue in Budapest's Liberty Square Credits Reagan for Freedom."
39 Crook, "Steve Jobs Memorial Statue Unveiled in Budapest."
40 "Secretary Lonnie G. Bunch III."

CHAPTER 5

FREEDOM OF MOVEMENT

THE WORST REFUGEE OFFENDER: CHINA

Introduction

Be outraged about kids in cages, but save some ire for China, the most egregious abuser of refugees.

Originally published: January 21, 2018

Caging kids at the U.S. border is reprehensible. But as first ladies, governors, celebrities, and citizens of all political stripes line up and strike out against the inhumane practice of separating children from parents seeking refuge, everyone should save some ire and outrage for one of the world's greatest offenders and dissemblers of refugee rights: China.

Despite having signed onto the 1951 Convention Relating to the Status of Refugees,[1] China has gone to incredible lengths to redefine and reclassify foreigners who seek asylum on Chinese territory, allowing an appearance[2] of having received "foreign" refugees. In fact, China is practicing the same type of refugee policy it pursues when it comes to international trade. It is willing to export its massive population at high numbers, send them abroad for education, work, and to establish cultural beachheads and corporate outposts (as with steel[3]), but is unwilling and vehemently opposed to accepting a modicum of duty-free imports or unwashed masses.

---

1 United Nations High Commissioner for Refugees, "The 1951 Convention Relating to the Status of Refugees and Its 1967 Protocol."

2 United Nations High Commissioner for Refugees, "Vietnamese Refugees Well Settled in China, Await Citizenship."

3 Dalton and Wei, "How China Skirts America's Antidumping Tariffs on Steel."

China, unfortunately, is not alone. Russia[4] and Turkey[5] use refugees as weapons, Italy's new government is stalking them[6] and preparing them for deportation, Hungary makes it clear that they are unwelcome public targets.[7] Increasingly, the rest of the West sees them as an unmanageable burden or parasitic horde who threaten nativist cultures, take jobs, drain welfare, change the national character, overwhelm communities, breed terrorists, and create chaos. Refugees and their children are having a hard time finding a new home.

The Trump policy of separating children from parents is a sin and a stain on American society. It further erodes whatever moral high-ground America continues to hold. Caging kids is a new low, a perverse policy that draws parallels to some of the 20th century's darkest state actions. There is no credible excuse for this child endangerment and it should stop immediately. Children are the most vulnerable class of humans. They need care, not cruelty. Full stop.

But as the world rightly condemns the Trump administration for both its callous policies and mendacious excuses, it cannot turn a blind eye to the egregious and selfish policies of another great global power. China exploits globalization's many advantages and privilege but rejects real global responsibility for many of the world's thorniest problems. The lifeboat may be feeling full[8] in some societies and nationalist leaders are definitely taking political advantage of the moment to capitalize on populist sentiments, but it's been a few years[9] and several regimes ago since China was a lifeboat to the scads of international migrants seeking safe-harbor and survival.

If anything, China is adding to the problem, aiding and abetting the Myanmar government that persecutes, uproots, rapes, pillages, and murders the Rohingya population, forcing them to flee[10] across land-mined borders into neighboring Bangladesh. Plenty of kids die in that forced migration. Girls are often rounded-up and sexually assaulted.[11] Violence visits them early in their

---

4 Deutsche Welle, "NATO Commander: Russia Uses Syrian Refugees as 'weapon' against West."

5 Bar'el, "Erdoğan Wields Powerful Weapon in Battle with European Union."

6 Birnbaum, "A Town That Expels Migrants and Celebrates with Cake Wants to Be a Model for Italy."

7 Walker, "No Entry."

8 Hardin, "Lifeboat Ethics: The Case Against Helping the Poor."

9 Meyers, "China Once Welcomed Refugees, but Its Policies Now Make Trump Look Lenient."

10 Kounalakis, "Rohingya Attacks Are the Murderous Version of Trump's Muslim Ban."

11 *Los Angeles Times*, "'I Didn't Want This Baby': Rohingya Rape Survivors Face a Harrowing Choice."

lives and the reward for their forced sexual victimization is either death or a lonely continued struggle for survival in an often parent-less future.

In China, there is both an official and a popular anti-immigrant and anti-Muslim[12] sentiment that aligns well with both its support and strategic goals in Myanmar. China as the region's dominant power not only helps create the conditions for forced migrations from Myanmar, it is setting the terms for the continued permanent internment of populations in North Korea's gulag-state. President Trump may be feeling warm and fuzzy about Kim Jong-un, but the dictator's people continue to suffer the predations and depravity of Kim's totalitarian state. North Koreans regularly risk their lives to escape the heavily fortified border in order to breathe the air of freedom in their Southern sister nation. Few try to cross over[13] into an inhospitable China.

One of China's evolving arguments for American security guarantees for Kim's regime is that Beijing is both unwilling and unprepared to accept a flood of North Korean refugees. In fact, it already immediately repatriates[14] those few who manage to get across. China prefers a Trump-brokered Korean peace that includes some Western demilitarization. This would allow President Xi Jinping to increase his country's own security by growing his border buffer and increasing China's state security while giving him greater influence and power over the region. Xi would prefer that potential North Korean refugees—resulting from any Pyongyang political opening or border loosening—head towards Seoul instead of China. It is a cynical and self-serving policy that is entirely consistent with China's geopolitical status and strategy.

My parents were refugees to an America that opened its arms and heart. I am eternally grateful. It pains me to equate any Chinese state policy to my own country's political behavior. The Trump administration must find neither solace nor support for its soulless edict to wrench kids from parents. On this, China should be left to stand apart.

Coda: One of President Biden's earliest executive orders was to reunite migrant families by reconnecting children separated from parents at the U.S.–Mexico border during the Trump administration. Biden also ended his predecessor's "stay put" policy, forcing asylum-seekers to remain in Mexico.

---

12 Wang, "Why Do Chinese Reject Middle Eastern Refugees?"

13 Human Rights Watch, "World Report 2018."

14 Cohen, "China's Repatriation of North Korean Refugees."

NBA PLAYER GOES ONE-ON-ONE WITH ERDOĞAN

Introduction

Since Enes Kanter labeled President Erdoğan "Hitler of our century," Turkey's dictator labeled the basketball player a terrorist and requested an Interpol "Red Notice" arrest warrant for Kanter. That wouldn't stop his slam dunks on Erdoğan.

Originally published: January 18, 2019

Shoot a 3-pointer, go to jail.

If Turkey's spoiled-sport president gets his way, he will soon be locking up Enes Kanter, a Turkish-American star center for the New York Knicks.

The reason for a just-requested Interpol "Red Notice" arrest[15] warrant is not Kanter's aggressive defensive style, it is his offensive speech[16] calling President Recep Tayyip Erdoğan, among other things, the "Hitler of our century." Erdoğan returned the favor and labeled Kanter "a terrorist."

Unlike in the United States, where public figures can't be libeled,[17] criticism of the Turkish president is illegal.[18] I can write that President Trump is a boob and feel pretty secure that the black helicopters won't descend on my home. Well, maybe not totally secure as the U.S. Attorney General nominee William Barr recently told the Senate that he "can conceive" of instances[19] where journalists might be arrested.

In Turkey, however, Erdoğan's goons make it a daily practice to intimidate individuals and their families, confiscate their property and, of course, throw them in prison.[20]

Erdoğan's crimes are too big to prosecute while Kanter's should be too absurd to pursue. But they're not.

Kanter is not the only U.S.-residing thorn in Erdoğan's side. The aging dissident cleric, Fetullah Gülen, living remotely on a Pennsylvania farm, sends out regular messages to resist Erdoğan's leadership and tactics. Gülen is a former political ally who eventually figured out Erdoğan's long-term plan to usurp all

---

15 Interpol, "About Red Notices."
16 Graham, "Enes Kanter Calls Turkey's Erdoğan 'Hitler of Our Century' after Airport Detainment."
17 Bugh, "Public Figures and Officials."
18 Kardas, "Insulting the Turkish President: Article 299 and Why Europe Says Its Illegal."
19 AOL Staff, "AG Nominee Barr 'can Conceive' of Jailing Journalists 'as a Last Resort.' "
20 Pierson, " 'El Chapo' Paid Former Mexican President $100 Million Bribe: Trial Witness."

power and destroy all perceived personal foes. Erdoğan is making good on the threat and the practice, putting more journalists in jail than any other country and even frog-walking an American cleric held as a prison pawn in Turkey to (unsuccessfully) exchange for Gülen.

Gen. Michael Flynn, President Trump's short-lived national security adviser, was aiding and abetting this process for a long time, even helping plan a Gülen kidnapping and rendition from the United States. The Flynn-Flan man took Erdoğan's money, slowly moved the Turkish president's agenda forward, but then got caught doing dirty deeds for Russia before turning state's witness. That put a damper on any Gülen extradition. And it strengthened Kanter's voice.

Thin-skinned Erdoğan won't abide a challenge from anyone with a fan base, audience or political power, whether athlete, journalist or president of the United States. Just last week, Erdoğan cancelled[21] his meeting in Turkey with John Bolton to discuss protection for American-allied Kurds abandoned by Trump's Syria withdrawal. While Bolton wants a regional anti-Iran coalition and guarantees Erdoğan won't mow down Kurds, Kanter hopes to take down Erdoğan.

The NBA's soft power and global brand equity is so great that it can awaken fear even in a steely national leader. Imagine if there were a contemporary Yao Ming-level player[22] who captured the imagination of his countrymen, but was critical of China's Communist Party or President Xi Jinping. That it would not be easy for Beijing to ignore. The NBA's global stage is that big.

International players usually stay away from politics, however, their celebrity instead being used as a point of national pride or for philanthropic deeds. NBA star power has helped[23] improve healthcare in Africa (Dikembe Mutombo), inspires[24] Greece (Giannis Atentokoumpo), supports[25] Argentine children (Manu Ginobli) and added[26] to Spain's athletic recognition (Pau Gasol).

My recent Bollywood night courtside visit to a Sacramento Kings v. Golden State Warriors game made obvious the growingly global nature of the game. Players and coaches come from everywhere. The hardcourt featured a kings' crown

---

21 Gall and Landler, "Turkish President Snubs Bolton Over Comments That Turkey Must Protect Kurds."
22 Ming, "The Naismith Memorial Basketball Hall of Fame: Yao Ming."
23 Olkowski, "Former NBA Star Lays Out Philanthropic Goals for Democratic Republic of Congo."
24 Antetokounmpo, "Giannis Shares His Inspiring Story on 60 Minutes."
25 ESPN Staff, "In the Twilight, Manu Ginobili Is Argentina's Shining Example."
26 UNICEF USA, "UNICEF Ambassador Pau Gasol Visits Syrian Refugees in Iraq."

underscored[27] by both Chinese and Hindi character logos. The owner, Vivek Ranadivé, a native of India sat a few seats down. The team's general manager, Vlade Divac, is from Serbia.

A few years back, I visited Divac at his modest Belgrade apartment in a city where he has hero status. Outside, we got stopped every few steps of the walk to his corner bakery. Divac was so popular, visible and accessible that he was regularly rumored as a potential Serbian presidential candidate. Such is the power of celebrity and the reach of the new NBA. That is the type of power that Erdoğan fears. Unfortunately for Turkish minorities, there are no Kurdish basketball stars.

Erdoğan is a relatively tall man, but small enough and mean enough to sic[28] his security staff on a few protesters during his short Washington, D.C., visit in 2017. And he doesn't stop at disturbing his opposition in our nation's capital. He is one of a handful of world leaders who goes toe-to-toe with Trump's administration, infiltrating it and co-opting it where he can, bullying it everywhere else.

Gülen, once an Erdoğan ally, is getting old, and his political movement is hobbled back in Turkey. But someone will be his successor, and Kanter can certainly be his high-profile anti-Erdoğan messenger. It appears that Erdoğan has already made that calculation. Which is why Kanter won't travel for the Wizards game to London, a city where foreign autocrats have proven[29] they can brazenly poison dissidents.

Kanter believes he is targeted[30] for assassination. "I think I can get killed there," he has said. If he survives the threats and the season—and even a Senator Marco Rubio-desired trade[31] to the Miami Heat—Kanter will continue to be outspoken and slam dunk on Erdoğan.

Coda: In November 2020, Kanter was traded to the Portland Trail Blazers and planned to become a U.S. citizen in June 2021. He still receives death threats for criticizing the Turkish dictator.

---

27 "Sacramento Kings Debut New Alternative Court Colorway With International Brand, Matching Global Uniform Design."

28 Fandos and Mele, "Erdogan Security Forces Launch 'Brutal Attack' on Washington Protesters, Officials Say."

29 Witte and Birnbaum, "Putin Implicated in Fatal Poisoning of Former KGB Officer at London Hotel."

30 Kanter, "Turkey's Erdogan Wants Me Back in His Country so He Can Silence Me."

31 "Rubio and Enes Kanter Discuss Free-Speech Erosion in Turkey."

EUROPE'S LAST TROUBLEMAKERS

Introduction

Brexit aside, Poland and Italy have also turned against the European Union, as both dominantly Catholic nations reject migrants coming to the EU.

Originally published: January 31, 2019

Poland is free because of a pope, the Vatican and a European dream. Not that long ago, Soviet-dominated Warsaw created a spiritual alliance and common cause with a church-dominated Rome and its dream of an expansive pan-European political union.

That dream is now a nightmare that aligns the two Catholic-dominated nations of Poland and Italy, bound together in an anti-immigrant stance, an unholy alliance ready to take on Europe and cut it down to size.

This latest assault on the European Union comes on top of an uncertain and undefined Brexit brought on by a banger-eating[32] British populace tired of Polish plumbers[33] unclogging their water closets. Europe seems especially brittle right now with the political chaos surrounding Britain's political schizophrenia and the unanswered Irish border wall[34] question. Despite Brexit's severe disruption, however, Poland and Italy are the European Union's newest challenge for survival.

The pope and the Vatican might be all that stand between a divided West that falters and a revived united Europe. Divine intervention gladly accepted. First, the backstory:

In 1989, while Poland's bankrupted Communist leaders and military dictator occupied Warsaw's political institutions, Pope John Paul II provided moral leadership. He was the political ally of the opposition dissident Solidarity movement and its leader Lech Walesa. The pope inspired peaceful demonstrations and unified the Polish opposition. The pope—with a little help[35] from President Ronald Reagan—inspired the revolution against Soviet domination and guided Poland's early return to Western Europe.

Enter Italy. The spiritual and cultural alliance between Rome—the seat of the Holy See—and Warsaw has always been grounded in the authority of the church and the pope's leadership. I experienced this profound relationship.

---

32 "Ultimate Bangers and Mash Recipe."
33 Frayer, "If Britain Leaves the EU, What Happens to the 'Polish Plumber?'"
34 Campbell, "Brexit."
35 Walsh, "Ronald Reagan and John Paul II."

In 1990, when I stood with 300,000 people, mostly Poles and Slovaks, on Czechoslovakia's Letna Plain,[36] bearing witness to the Vatican's unifying political and spiritual power.

Today, there is a lot of passionate and reactionary anti-Europe noise to cut through, but the Vatican faced similar political challenges at the end of the 20th century to help end the Cold War. Pope Francis has already weighed in on America's border-wall hysteria, suggesting that an irrational fear[37] of migration "makes us crazy." Unfortunately, that "crazy" knows no American or European borders.

Now Italy and Poland, despite Pope Francis' profound moral humanism and deep spirituality, are joining in common cause, saying to new European arrivals that there is "no room at the inn." This new approach suggests compassion is theoretically fine, but migration, refugees, and the "other" are unwelcome. Polish and Italian populist leaders claim that migrants are overwhelming their societies, changing their character, stressing their services, inflaming their politics and threatening their stability.

Poland and Italy's leaders are now aligned and allied. They call their anti-EU collaborative electoral project[38] a "new spring" for Europe and have joined forces to gain political power and push out Brussels' often ineffectual leadership. If in power, they plan to undermine European institutions, not build new ones.

Not everyone has the same orientation. I recently joined former Italian Prime Minister Matteo Renzi at a Stanford University dinner. He is one of the last Europeanists. Renzi[39] talks animatedly about a reinvigorated European continent driven by EU investments in culture and art. To save Europe, he envisions investing heavily and wholeheartedly in a 21st century renaissance. Instead of a "new spring," Renzi believes in a European rebirth. It is a positive vision.

Europe must rebuild its confidence and cultural capital, argues Renzi. He says Europe needs to spend euro-for-euro on culture and military: One euro spent for tanks or planes should be matched by a euro for poetry, painting, or opera. Renzi suggests this is the surest way to a common cultural and military defense. He also guarantees his plan would widely promote the blessings of moral democratic systems, Christian-based humanism and charitable, European high-minded culture. It would counter European nationalist fears and give the EU a proud, unifying and unassailable cultural and artistic identity.

---

36 Battiata, "Pope Begins Visit to Czechoslovakia."
37 Samuels, "Pope."
38 Plucinska, "Italy and Poland Want 'New Spring' in Europe."
39 Kramer, "Matteo Renzi's Agenda for Italy."

However, he is nearly alone in this vision among Europe's new short-sighted and small-minded nationalist leaders. Italy's Deputy Prime Minister Matteo Salvini and Poland's ruling Law and Justice Party (PiS[40]) politicians are populists focused on shallow, nationalist measures. They push for near-term tactical political gains that overshadow the need for sweeping, strategic and humanistic value-based leadership.

Poland's unholy alliance with Italy's similarly anti-Brussels, anti-immigrant, anti-foreigner, anti-everything populism brings a lot of riled-up Europeans to the table as game changers. The Italians and Poles live in large and heavily populated nations, and a victory for their ruling nationalist parties in Europe's May 26 parliamentary elections will allow their politicians swing their wrecking-ball widely at Brussels.

Re-enter Pope Francis: With his global perspective and universal appeal, he embodies the moral authority and personal charisma to articulate, promote and propel a contemporary and compassionate European vision as he ministers to the world.

Whether the pope's message can penetrate the heated Polish and Italian political debates is unclear. But his is a spiritually humanistic voice that needs to be amplified to harmonize the voice of God and man.

Coda: In late 2020, Italy slowly and quietly began dismantling Salvini's anti-immigration policy. By contrast, Polish President Andrzej Duda, continued to express strong and popular views against the imposition of EU migrant quotas.

THAT LITTLE FISHING BOAT MIGHT JUST BE A WEAPON OF WAR

Introduction

The United Nations Convention on the Law of the Sea guarantees freedom of navigation to all states on the high seas. But that rule is watered down when civilian vessels are turned into warships.

Originally pubslished: August 1, 2019

Deep-sea fishing charters are a staple of most American coastal marinas—from Miami to the San Francisco Bay. Boats loaded with fuel and fun rock their way out on gentle waves to open waters and ocean sunsets. Summer freedom at its finest.

---

40 Kalan, "Poland's New Populism."

Now imagine if the million registered floating funhouses in Florida and the million plus in California were suddenly impressed into the U.S. Navy to run offensive operations ramming ships or sent on snooping day-sails. If you can picture this, then you have a sense of other countries' new hybrid navies. Around the world, fishing boats have become the new warships.

Fighting on the high seas and in ports of call is always treacherous, but the dangers just got worse. Battling against navy ships and subs trying to sink fleets, stake out seas or show force now also means that every trawler, research vessel, fishing boat and dinghy is also a potential combatant.

A 21st-century maritime adversary no longer looks like a uniformed sailor or Marine. It's just as likely to be a guy hauling up a fishing net or trawling in offshore waters. Paranavies, maritime militias and pirates are rapidly evolving low forms of high-sea crimes and warfare. From the South China Sea[41] to the far reaches of the Arctic,[42] these developments are giving the West's high-tech militaries a new sinking feeling.

Masters and commanders recognize this in part as a back-to-the-future military moment, a reminder of the days when state-sponsored pirates and independent privateers ruled the seas. Sovereign navies were put in place to pursue and punish them. Naval battles in the past regularly involved pirates and other non-state actors.

In fact, pirates are the reason we even have Marines. The Corps was re-established after the Revolutionary War and in 1805 were sent to defend[43] American merchant ships against Barbary pirate attacks at "the shores of Tripoli." The deposed Libyan ruler presented a Mameluke sword to the successful squad's American leader. A sabre remains part of the USMC formal dress tradition. Oorah.

Two centuries later, in October 2000, non-state actors attacked[44] the USS Cole in Yemen with terrorist irregulars sidling up to the ship in a small speedboat laden with explosives. The USS Cole crew tragically failed to attack the C-4 stocked speedboat because it was not identifiable as either a traditional combatant or threat. It blew a hole in the Navy destroyer, killing 17 American sailors and crippling the ship. That case was pursued and indictments eventually unsealed[45] by then-FBI Director Robert Mueller.

---

41 Tay, "US Reportedly Warns China over Hostile Non-Naval Vessels in South China Sea."

42 Peter, "What Makes Russia's New Spy Ship Yantar Special?"

43 "History of the Marine Corps."

44 CNN Editorial Research, "USS Cole Bombing Fast Facts."

45 "Al Qaeda Associates Charged in Attack on USS Cole, Attempted Attack on Another U.S. Naval Vessel."

Of course, Western adversaries are not limiting their new-old tactics to the water. In this latest manifestation of modern gray-zone warfare, Russia, China and other adversaries creatively deploy hybrid forces.[46] Whether unmarked seafaring vessels or innumerable "little green men,"[47] troops lacking flag insignias on their uniforms, the goal is the same—to hide or deny this stealth military's relationship to a state in efforts to avoid retaliatory consequences or escalations.

We have long recognized that soldiers and armies no longer need to wear identifiable uniforms to be enemy combatants. On the ground, these irregulars are known as guerrilla fighters—"freedom fighters" or "partisans" if they are on your side and fighting for your cause. They were effective against America in Vietnam and continue to kill U.S. troops in Afghanistan. Today, Vladimir Putin's Russia has embedded[48] them in Ukraine's Donbass region and occupied Crimea.

Changing military tactics usually alters responses, and the questionable fishing fleet force is getting an answer. Recognizing that a combatant ship no longer needs to be painted gray or bear hull numbers, America's Indo-Pacific fleet recently adapted[49] its rules of engagement. The U.S. Navy now looks at nearly any vessel with flagged by the People's Republic of China as a potential combatant—from fishing boats to Coast Guard vessels. The message? Harass or threaten the U.S. Navy, and be prepared to suffer the consequences.

America's naval forces are also strategically adapting to the growing threats toward their freedom of navigation operations and deployments by revisiting U.S. fleet strength and size. No, the U.S. Navy is not insisting that civilian pleasure craft give up their booze cruises to patrol and secure America's shores. Instead, naval forces will use more robotics, drones, electronics and smaller ships. Unmanned ships, drone subs and killer robots are already patrolling and pursuing[50] those who challenge American interests, whether with conventional or unconventional means, regular or irregular forces.

Globally, what required sending Marines to distant shores is still an active concern for global trade, fishing and free naval navigation. The right of unimpeded seafaring, however, remains more of a centuries-old aspiration

46 *The Changing Story of Russia's "Little Green Men" Invasion.*

47 Peck, "Britain Is Sending Its Special Forces to Fight Russian 'Little Green Men.' "

48 Bickerton, "World War Three: Putin Russia Has 80,000 Troops in Ukraine Crimea Says Petro Poroshenko."

49 Sevastopulo and Hille, "US Warns China on Aggressive Acts by Fishing Boats and Coast Guard."

50 Larter, "US Navy Moves toward Unleashing Killer Robot Ships on the World's Oceans."

than an easily enforceable international law or defensible reality. Given all these challenges, the last thing the world needs on its 140 million square miles[51] of water is new threats from old boats.

Coda: In 2020, according to the International Maritime Bureau, there was a dramatic increase in maritime kidnappings. Most of those targeted container ships were on the west coast of Africa.[52]

THE GREAT TRUMPIAN ESCAPE

Introduction

Until the administration of Donald J. Trump, Americans thought despotic regimes only existed in other countries. Trump's election disproved the title of the Sinclair Lewis dystopian political novel, *It Can't Happen Here*. What other authoritarian dangers lurk in the aftermath of that experience? And where in the world can a would-be authoritarian go?

Originally published: October 29, 2020

Losing an election can be tough. President Trump has publicly mused that being defeated could be so devastating it could cause him to leave the country.[53]

Anyone who was conscious in 2016, however, will know that election predictions and polling numbers are not the same as Electoral College outcomes. Anything can happen. In short, Trump will not be calling a travel agent anytime soon.

If, however, Joe Biden does become the 46th president of the United States and Trump starts seriously thinking about self-imposed exile, where might he go?

The possibilities are endless. But desirable destinations are few and far between. As he looks at the map and tries to find a place to land, he might want to see where other fallen leaders have trod.

Some of his contemporary foreign colleagues struggle to hold onto power, many have planned an emergency exit strategy and keep an eye on the door—just in case they suddenly need to skedaddle.

---

51 Water Encyclopedia, "Ocean Basins—Sea, Depth, Oceans, Temperature, Important, Largest, System, Marine, Pacific."

52 Pratik, "Pirates Are Kidnapping More Seafarers off West Africa, IMB Reports."

53 Collins, "Trump Jokes He Might Leave Country if He Loses to Joe Biden in Nov. 3 Election."

Unpopular leaders are sometimes forced to leave at a moment's notice, like Ukrainian President Viktor Yanukovych's door dash in 2014. He fled his palace,[54] with only enough time to spirit out a few bags of gold bars onto a waiting chopper flying him to safety in nearby Russia, where he still lives. But not all ex-leaders are pushed and rushed out the door. Some are slowly coaxed to leave.

The White House continues to look for ways to pressure[55] Venezuela's ostensible President Nicolás Maduro to depart, but Washington gets foiled every time. Unfortunately, Trump talked big but delivered *nada* when it came to ousting Maduro.

The United States added pressure by slowing Venezuelan oil exports and sanctioning[56] ships. It recognized opposition leader President Juan Guaidó. Nothing worked. Then a failed coup fiasco gave Maduro a huge propaganda win. Maduro got to perp walk[57] American mercenaries who had attempted an ill-advised overthrow worthy of the Keystone Kops.

Part of the White House's failed attempt at regime change in Caracas included discussions for an orderly and safe exile abroad for Maduro. Washington pushed a deal for him to flee and live the rest of his post-bus driving days[58] on a warm beach with a cold beer.

Cuba's Varadero Beach was made to sound super dreamy, but Maduro already has power, wealth and the loyalty of his armed forces. Leaving all that behind has not looked like a particularly good deal. Unfortunately for Maduro, when it does start to sound more compelling, he may be out of more than just a job. Ask Saddam Hussein.

Maduro, however, is in no hurry to forsake his nation—or his oil revenues.[59] In fact, he's fat and happy at home while, disturbingly, his main opposition just got out of Dodge. Leopoldo López took off[60] after years of hunger strikes, harassment, beatings and imprisonment. While Maduro remains in Miraflores Palace, López is now far, far away in Spain.

---

54 Kounalakis, "Home Sweet Palace."

55 Kounalakis, "Florida Could Punish Trump for Failed Latin America Policy."

56 Spetalnick and Saul, "Exclusive: U.S. Turns Screws on Maritime Industry to Cut Off Venezuela's Oil."

57 Goodman, "U.S. Mercenaries Captured in Venezuela after Failed Coup Attempt Compared to a 'Bad Rambo Movie.'"

58 Carroll, "Former Bus Driver Nicolás Maduro Clings to Wheel in Venezuela."

59 Natarajan and Schoenberg, "Venezuelan Oil Official Flees to U.S. with Intel on Maduro's Inner Circle."

60 Facebook et al., "From Spain, Top Dissident Vows to Fight for a Free Venezuela."

Leaders in trouble or out of favor have long sought an easy escape route, avoiding persecution and jail. Sometimes they use their time abroad to regroup and plan to recoup their influence and power. That's what Ayatollah Khomeini did in Paris before riding a revolutionary wave to return to Tehran.

That's also what corrupted Iraqi politician Ahmed Chalabi did after years of living in London. He successfully lied to and coaxed America to attack Iraq in the hopes of wrangling a prime minister position supported by a U.S. military occupation. Both Khomeini and Chalabi returned from exile to strengthen[61] Iran's aggressively dangerous role in the region.

Not all leaders take a self-imposed hiatus abroad in order to plan a strategically timed return like Bolivia's ex-President Evo Morales. He is currently biding his time in Argentina as his allies slowly regain control of the levers of national power. Morales plans to return[62] to La Paz by Nov. 9.

Some former leaders decide to call it quits entirely, leave their country and spare themselves the indignity of popular derision and, possibly, prosecution. Former King Juan Carlos I of Spain made that choice, abdicating the throne for his son, Felipe VI, to rule. A hero of post-Franco Spain, Juan Carlos got a little sloppy[63] in his personal and financial affairs and left Spain for the United Arab Emirates in August. He explained his exile as the best way to save the monarchy, allowing his son to distance himself from the crown's scandals.

Trump may feel the personal desire to take a little time off from any political fallout should he lose and loudly continue to contest the 2020 election. If so, he may go to a Trump property in a foreign country where he actually pays taxes.

Trump should know, however, that American ex-presidents are safe at home when their tenure is up. He can stick around Florida, New York, or even Washington, DC. In places with less democracy, a perverted rule of law and a potentially angry mob at the presidential gates, ex-leaders' options come down to fight or flight.

Coda: After enduring the indignity of a second impeachment, Trump faced the consequences of his many misdeeds. A long series of state and federal charges, both criminal and civil, await him, with nowhere to run and nowhere to hide.

---

61 Borger, "US Intelligence Fears Iran Duped Hawks into Iraq War."

62 Arce, "Bolivia's Morales Calls for Calm after Protesters Demand Junta."

63 Anderson, "Juan Carlos's Fall from Grace in Spain and the Precarious Future of the World's Monarchies."

CHAPTER 6

FREEDOM FROM CORRUPTION

BEYOND PARIS, QUESTIONABLE EFFORTS TO COMBAT CLIMATE CHANGE

Introduction

While countries want to be more environmentally conscious, they also want to maintain comparative advantages. Some have invested in renewable resources for their energy. We must hold everyone accountable to ensure no one cheats the system for personal/corporate gain.

Originally published: February 18, 2016

Germany has long been a leading advocate for confronting and ameliorating climate change. But actions speak louder than words—or signatures on an international accord. The recent Volkswagen scandal is only the latest case of climate policy hypocrisy.

Meeting in Paris last December, countries around the globe finally recognized the generally accepted scientific evidence that climate change is real. They also accepted some responsibility to do something about it.

To much fanfare, 195 countries, including Germany and the United States, signed the Paris Agreement[1] pledging to hit targets to drop emissions, cut carbon and keep our aging Earth from experiencing too many hot flashes and cold extremities.

Developed democratic countries, pushed by their citizens, led the charge for a comprehensive agreement to atone for past polluting and to prevent developing states from repeating their own sins. Canada, England, France— they all chimed in and tried to convince, coerce and cajole those developing

---

1 Harvey, "Paris Climate Change Agreement."

countries to be energy ascetics. That was a tough sell. The developing world now wants its turn to crank out the carbon and catch up to the already rich, gas-burning and global-warming recidivists.

Looking beyond the narratives of the industrialized world's planned sacrifice, however, some of the stories seem a little less noble or credible.

France, for example, is fine with less fossil fuel because it depends mostly on nuclear power[2] for progress: Up to 78 percent of its electrical needs are met by the near zero-carbon-emitting nuclear plants. Future plans to cut its dependency on nuclear plants while also cutting carbon emissions will certainly be a challenge.

Germany laudably boasts that it is able to reduce the amount of carbon it emits and shut down its nuclear power plants because it has developed enough alternative wind and solar power to provide clean and nearly free energy for all. In fact, German statistics recently peaked when satisfying more than 50 percent of its electricity[3] demand through solar power.

In each case of selective carbon curtailment, it is expected that a nation seeks its self-interest while also acting simultaneously to protect its competitive advantages. But Germany recently went one step further by publicly advocating an anti-polluting stance, while at the same time a dominant corporation powering the German economic juggernaut acted surreptitiously to undermine environmental goals.

Volkswagen, Germany's industrial behemoth, figured it could advocate for tougher rules for others, but cheat its way to success by developing a workaround to America's basic EPA auto-emission requirements. VW crafted an elegant, difficult-to-detect and fraudulent solution to the inconvenient pollution standards. It installed software in 11 million diesel vehicles worldwide that triggered a clean-emissions setting calibrated for a laboratory—not actual road use.

Moreover, there is evidence that in the case of auto emissions the European Union was, if not complicit, suspiciously aware of autos failing emission tests years before the VW scandal, according to European tests[4] done as early as 2007.

Denied military clout to build and project power, modern German governments have forged uniquely strong ties with industry. Business-friendly industrial policies and an export-focused foreign policy[5] support and underwrite the economic powerhouse that is a 21st-century Germany's

2 *The Telegraph*, "France Nuclear Power by Numbers."

3 *The Week*, "Germany Gets 50 Percent of Its Electricity from Solar for the First Time."

4 Hakim, "Beyond Volkswagen, Europe's Diesels Flunked a Pollution Test."

5 Adam and Thomas, "U.S. Criticizes Germany's Export-Led Policies—WSJ."

"Wirtschaftswunder"[6] —economic miracle. Achieving that new modern miracle sometimes seems to take precedence over any other policy, principle, norm, standard or goal.

Economics have trumped global environmental and public health concerns in the past. In the 1980s, when the country was still divided, West Germany tried to export domestically unacceptable radioactively contaminated milk[7] to developing countries, including Egypt. Other European countries were complicit[8] in the practice and caught.

So while the world's leaders are self-congratulating and citizens applaud the historic Paris Agreement, the world must not turn a blind eye to the ways that rules can be broken. When a powerful nation like Germany dominantly projects power and influence by export, consumers and countries need to cry foul when those export goods are not so good for the world.

Coda: In February 2021, a Paris court found the French government guilty of failing to adequately meet its climate change goals.

DON'T CHEER CHINA'S CLIMATE PROGRESS UNTIL IT'S FOR REAL

Introduction

Trump's withdrawal from the Paris accords left the door open for California to assert its power and promise. Then-Gov. Jerry Brown visited China to seek its support for the Paris accords and environmental concerns.

Originally published: June 1, 2017

America's abandonment of global leadership during the Trump administration does not mean that Americans are ready to give up the fight for a safe and peaceful future. In fact, President Trump's retreat from challenges to the global commons brings more attention to Gov. Jerry Brown's efforts to act on climate change.

Brown's upcoming visit to Beijing will focus on keeping up the COP21 Paris accords momentum[9] Trump wants to radically reverse. California's aggressive

---

6 Hodder, "Wirtschaftswunder."

7 Tagliabue, "A Nuclear Taint in Milk Sets Off German Dispute."

8 Bannink, "Contaminated Foodstuffs Dumped on World Market."

9 *The Sacramento Bee*, "Paris Climate Agreement More Popular than Trump or GOP Senators Opposing It."

stance on pollution controls and environmental standards will be highlighted. The governor wants to make a lasting difference in the world.

Some are critical of a state's role in concluding agreements with sovereign nations like China, arguing that only the federal government has the right to enter accords. But Trump's climate change denial[10] and waning global influence[11] creates an international opening for California to assert both its power and promise.

Governors Schwarzenegger and Brown traveled internationally both to drum up trade and seek mutual understanding on environmental issues. In 2013 Brown signed a bilateral agreement with China.

California's interest and right to combat climate change and seek China's support is understandable and has precedent. But what's in it for China?

Three things: One, the Chinese get to further chip away at America's fracturing domestic political structure by making deals at the subnational level. Two, they get to step into the global leadership spotlight on an issue that resonates internationally with a world populace that is both acutely aware of and feels directly threatened by pollution. And, three, it allows China to show its own citizens that it is acting on the issue currently posing the biggest challenge to the Communist Party's political leadership, power, and legitimacy.

Internationally, China prefers to make specific, direct deals with smaller political entities, rather than powerful nations or multilateral institutions. It is easier for China to agree with individual states, whether within the European Union or part of the United States, since such deals are likely narrowly defined and not conditioned on larger strategic issues.

When California made a climate deal with China, for example, the state did not condition that deal on China's pressuring North Korea to stop nuclear weapons testing. Making a direct deal with a subnational state allows China both to leverage its relative power and to highlight any policy schisms within larger political structures. That's one reason why China is making multiple bilateral business deals and political agreements with small individual European states while sidestepping larger EU treaties. A dissolving EU and a politically divided U.S. create the perfect conditions for an opportunistic China to hasten the dissolution and grow the divide.

---

10 *The Sacramento Bee*, "Jerry Brown Says Donald Trump's Position on Climate Change Is Backfiring."

11 "As Trump Fiddles on Climate, the World Goes Californian."

China recognizes Trump's feckless leadership, weakening position, undisciplined messaging, nativist pandering, and globally alienating policies and sees an unprecedented opportunity to play the international good cop. The absurdity of this is beyond the pale.

China, the world's greatest coal burner and polluter, is seeking to position itself as the world's leader and standard bearer in climate change policy. Yes, China needs to act and any successful mitigation actions it takes will have a tremendous effect on global warming. But giving China undue and undeserved political credit for climate leadership is like rewarding recidivist serial arsonists for not lighting matches.

Finally, China needs to symbolically—and actually—do something before her people rise-up against a system that makes mask-wearing necessary while it pursues unbridled economic development at all cost. Political rights, civil liberties, the rule of law and Chinese citizens' rights to breathe clean air, drink untainted water and eat safe food has taken a back seat to accelerated economic growth and maintaining the leadership's monopoly on power.

China will undoubtedly score political points for successfully engaging with Brown. Regardless, he should use the visit to affirm and strengthen the climate deal—especially since California has more economic and political throw-weight than most countries.

Solving the greatest environmental threat to future generations should be a priority. In an ideal world, however, individual states should not have to make up for the nation's shortcomings or its leader's weaknesses, failures, or lack of vision.

Coda: On his first day in office as president, Joe Biden signed an executive order for the United States to rejoin the Paris Agreement. The Biden administration has called on China to do more.

NICARAGUA'S "HOUSE OF CARDS" STARS ANOTHER CORRUPT AND POWERFUL COUPLE

Introduction

The power couple of Daniel Ortega and his wife, Vice President Rosario Murillo, siphoned off billions from their nation's wealth to buy political support—the money kept in personal accounts and businesses.

Originally published: November 29, 2018

Nicaragua is a political stage where a real-life "House of Cards" is now in its second season. President Daniel Ortega and his wife and partner in crime, Vice

President Rosario Murillo, have together run the country as an increasingly violent family business for the last couple of years. Ortega has been continuously in power for the past decade and, all in all, for four long terms with no term limits. The next elections are scheduled for 2021.

Ortega and Murillo make the Netflix series' Frank and Claire Underwood seem like law-abiding, Constitution-respecting, selfless public servants. The Ortega family runs everything, owns the ruling Sandinista Party, dominates media, monopolizes power, skims profits and loots the nation. They are living proof of Lord Acton's axiom[12] that, "Absolute power corrupts absolutely."

The United States has now decided to shut down parts of the Ortega-Murillo gang's operation by freezing funds and flummoxing any financial transactions using American banks or brokers.

Is this the right thing to do? Absolutely!

This week, the White House delivered an executive order to coordinate punishment for the Nicaraguan regime with legislative passage of the Nicaraguan Investment Conditionality Act (NICA[13]). American financial pressure on Nicaragua's ruling couple along with domestic unrest at home are intended to deliver a political death blow to Managua's imperious masters. Whether the United States is also coordinating international action or supporting Nicaraguan resistance is unknown—if likely—but an outcome that brought a more democratically responsive government to this Central American nation would be welcomed both at home and abroad.

U.S. meddling comes at a cost, of course, and the 20th-century history of American involvement has included CIA covert action, support for the graft-ridden and brutal Anastasio Somoza dictatorship and President Ronald Reagan's greenlighting a dirty little Contra war that ignored the will of Congress, traded arms for hostages and ran dark money through Beirut, Tel Aviv, and Tehran. Reagan's Iran-Contra scheme[14] was opposed by my Hoover Institution colleague,[15] then-Secretary of State George Schultz, but its sordid story and public revelation only added to a lasting legacy of distrust toward Washington throughout Latin America.

All stories evolve and plots twist, however, and the contemporary drama headquartered in Managua is as sordid as they come. The revolutionary Sandinistas, who overthrew Somoza in a country reeling from devastating

12 Acton Institute, "Lord Acton Quote Archive."

13 Ros-Lehtinen, "H.R.1918—115th Congress (2017–2018)."

14 PBS, "The Iran-Contra Affair."

15 Brown University, "Understanding the Iran-Contra Affairs—The Legal Aftermath."

geological and political earthquakes, have now become as vile and corrupt as the regime they deposed. Ortega and Murillo were baptized in Central American revolutionary fire and Robin Hood ideals to deliver justice and power to the nation's impoverished. A loosely interpreted[16] "liberation theology" provided a clear Christian conscience and justification for violent government overthrow.

In 1987, Ortega and his Sandinista leadership spoke in the critical and compassionate language of liberation to me and my fellow students at Columbia University's Graduate School of Journalism, the alma mater of then-Nicaraguan Foreign Minister Miguel D'Escoto.[17] Earlier that October day at the United Nations, the American delegation had walked out on Ortega's fiery General Assembly speech as he blasted Reagan, derided America's role in the region and claimed superior moral standing. The Nicaraguan firebrands were energetic and committed revolutionaries, both espousing an uplifting program for Nicaragua's poor and unsheathing critical rhetorical daggers aimed at America's heart.

That revolution has now eaten its children and delivered a matrimonial couple who dispense corporal—and lethal—punishment to critics and competitors. How did Ortega's Sandinista government devolve this badly?

For years, Ortega and Murillo were the personal beneficiaries of the oil-diplomacy policies of Venezuela's then-dictator President Hugo Chavez. Venezuela continued this policy under its current President Nicolas Maduro, allowing the Ortegas to siphon off billions both to buy political support and to sock away in personal accounts and businesses.

Once global oil prices tumbled, Venezuela faced a serious financial and political crisis at home, so last year it stopped the oil subsidies[18] that kept the Ortegas flush and Nicaragua afloat. With no more funny money flowing into Nicaragua, the dynamic duo decided to cut pensions, raise gas prices, end utility subsidies and punish the poor, resulting in nationwide rioting. The Ortegas' power was challenged by this growing unrest, so they set out to silence the opposition, imprison protesters and use militias and military to murder party challengers to the ruling Sandinistas.

Nicaragua is now in a full-blown crisis. Its power duo's corruption and monopoly on power have forced otherwise law-abiding and mostly impoverished citizens to flee the country. The majority of them seek refuge in neighboring

---

16 Sigmund, "Christianity and Violence: The Case of Liberation Theology: Terrorism and Political Violence."

17 Navrozov, "The Saxon Soul."

18 Waddell, "Venezuelan Oil Fueled the Rise and Fall of Nicaragua's Ortega Regime."

Costa Rica, while a smaller number skip from Nicaragua to join the migrant caravans arriving at the U.S. border. The Nicaraguan house of cards is poised to fall, especially with fresh pressure from America's NICA and U.S. Treasury actions.[19]

Fictional Claire Underwood, who is in her sixth and final season, ascended to the presidency upon her husband's death, after serving as first lady, then vice president. Nicaraguan Vice President Murillo's run may face early cancellation well before she achieves her ultimate presidential ambition.[20]

Drama lovers need not despair—Azerbaijan's President Ilham Aliyev last year appointed his multi-talented[21] wife, Mehriban Aliyeva, as the country's new first vice president. The political actors may be different, but the Azeri House of Cards spin-off already feels like a rerun.

Coda: Joe Biden began his presidency by proposing legislation to tackle corruption, violence and poverty in Latin America.

FACEBOOK AND ITS GLOBAL VILLAGE NEEDS A MAYOR TO REPRESENT US

Introduction

As online communities keep growing into the billions and across borders, the scale of social media networks' problems also has grown. As businesses, they operate to make money, and their "dark sides" are not addressed as they are not democratic.

Originally published: April 5, 2018

Facebook is the largest community in the world. It is also one of the least democratic institutions on earth. That's why Facebook needs a mayor.

In non-virtual communities—meaning "IRL" (In Real Life) physical cities and states —where people interact face-to-face daily, societies have developed self-governing structures and policing institutions to serve and protect them. Private companies like Facebook, however, were not organized around democratic ideas or social justice principles. Despite the often-lofty mission

---

19 Treasury Department, "Treasury Targets Nicaraguan Vice President and Key Advisor over Violent Response to Protests."

20 Debusmann, "Nicaraguans See First Lady as Power behind Throne."

21 "Mehriban Aliyeva—Biography Site—The First Lady of Azerbaijan."

statements[22] of social media companies, they are businesses put together for one reason: To make money. Oodles of it.

Thanks to the "network effect,"[23] unplanned, but highly profitable, communities have grown on these internet platforms to number in the billions. Greater in size than any nation-state. More politically powerful than any party or person. They cross borders and span the globe.

As they have grown, so have the scale of their problems and the onus of their responsibilities. The network effect cuts both ways. What has not grown apace has been the capacity to deal with the downside of a digital community's size and scale. Systems are inadequate to manage communities' dark side. The bigger these diverse social networks get, the less responsive they are to their complexity and breadth. Worse, they are undemocratic.

Many people reside, interact, and organize within these social networks more than they do in their physical, local community. How do they participate in Facebook's governance? Who reviews and settles their grievances? And when did they give up their rights to safety and representation? By clicking "I agree" to a Terms of Service Agreement they never read?

By sad-face emoji-ing, individuals might feel at times as if they are lodging a meaningful political protest, but an anonymous algorithm can willy-nilly silence a voice or mute dissent.

Whom do you call when you want to fill the propaganda potholes or arrest violence-inciting cyberbullies? Who monitors and manages the daily self-donations of personal, private data? Which social media platforms get to decide 21st century campaign finance laws?

To function healthily, these platforms need representational roles for their global communities. Mayors, sheriffs, judges, educational boards, regulatory bodies. These platforms must democratically open up to typical community representatives and roles to manage cross-border political speech, for example, or develop bodies to hear and settle accusations of libel. It's time to recognize that Facebook has become a real global commons that needs a real public governing structure.

Today, however, Facebook denizens are not Facebook citizens.

Sure, people can drop out of the community and live a Walden-like life in the analog outback with other digitally disconnected and disaffected humans. But everyone knows that even if they now choose to leave digitized society, it

---

22 Moscaritolo, "Facebook Has a New Mission."
23 Hagiu and Rothman, "Network Effects Aren't Enough."

is impossible to erase their past and purge the digital breadcrumbs of their previous searches and interactions.

Surviving in a 21st century society means a dependency on digital life, whether banking, finding a job, or staying connected with friends and family. We are neither willing nor able to make the trade-off between being a digital subject or an analog citizen.

Regardless, the choice should not be binary. Why should we be subservient to a big data behemoth and "voluntarily" relinquish the rights we have accrued since 1776? Since when is "I Agree" enough to strip us of a participatory role and make us subject to psychographically advanced targeting of our preferences and person? Who's looking out for us?

Tech leaders like Facebook's CEO Mark Zuckerberg have argued they should be entrusted with this role. Zuckerberg has made a personal commitment[24] to defend democracy. Despite his good intentions, anyone who understands democracy's evolutionary history, should feel slightly uncomfortable when someone powerful says "trust me" or that he alone can fix[25] a problem.

Further, while digital "platforms" are entrusted to secure the data and dreams of billions, they need to recognize they are not immune to the vagaries of a market that values them on projected revenue and future growth. The last few weeks have reminded us that tech stocks can be volatile and markets fickle. A market's normal functioning can lead to failure.

What happens if a social media company collapses under the weight of debt, the failure of leadership, or the loss of potential growth. Who owns the data of the dispossessed? How does that community re-form itself and find new expression and connection? This is not a theoretical question.

The virtual world is made up of tentative topographies and ephemeral communities. In 1994, Apple Computer (disclosure: I used to consult Apple) once hosted a social site called "eWorld,"[26] where I established an identity and built a community. I lost both when eWorld went bell-"e"-up after two years. If only I could have called eWorld's mayor to complain or offer help.

In a future social media democracy, I would own my data, ask my representatives to shut out political advertising paid for by Russian rubles, and

---

24 CNN Business, *Zuckerberg*.

25 Appelbaum, "Trump's Claim."

26 Edwards, "Remembering EWorld, Apple's Forgotten Online Service."

vote for my teenage boys to learn less about condom snorting[27] and more about civics. I bet I'm not alone.

Coda: Facebook CEO Mark Zuckerberg has called for more government regulation of social media. In 2021, the Australian government tried to force the social media giant to pay publishers for using their content. Zuckerberg responded by threatening to block users there from posting news content. The fight for social responsibility by social networks continues.

A PANDEMIC OF PIGS

Introduction

Before the COVID-19 crisis, China was already experiencing a porcine version of a pandemic. A devastating blow to animals, traditions, markets and, perhaps, politics.

Originally published: March 12, 2020

One little piggy went to market, one little piggy got sick, one little piggy got culled—and joined 40 percent of China's little piggies that went wee-wee-wee all the way to burial pits.

During the past 19 months, the world's largest pork market lost almost half of its pigs to an illness that went unreported and unchecked, and is now crossing borders threatening livestock elsewhere in Asia and the world.

Global worries about the coronavirus as a global pandemic are just the latest public-health scare that took flight in China. The African Swine Fever has run rampant in the People's Republic since 2018 and has devastated the country's pork production and markets.

The collapse of oil prices and demand, the wildly volatile stock market, and the social disruption across America due to the Coronavirus pandemic are all serious. So is any global threat to food stocks.

Pork is a staple meat for the Chinese and a primary source of protein in the People's Republic of China. The bad news? The hog stock has collapsed, and the pig population is decimated. There is little to do about this immediately in a country where pork production is done in conditions dominated by small farms[28] and backyard pigsties. Industrialized production is not widespread.

---

27 "Why Are Teens Snorting Condoms?"
28 Bradsher and Tang, "China Responds Slowly, and a Pig Disease Becomes a Lethal Epidemic."

China lacks an effective USDA-type system to manage the domestic quality and conditions for pork production. It was only a matter of time before China got hit with the type of widespread animal disease that is now running rampant—and often unreported—in the country.

The good news is that there is little time between a moment of pig infection and death. That means very little time for farmers to take infected, contagious, and dangerous pork to market for human consumption—though there are plenty of cases of tainted pork making into foodstuffs.[29] So many of China's pigs are infected nationwide that all pork is suspect. Only half of the current pig populations—which have tripled in price—survive to make it to the dinner table.

A quarantine is the best chance for containing the menace, but the swine sickness is slipping across regional borders and slowly making nearby pork production vulnerable. Add to the problem a general unwillingness to share information about the infected stocks, and you have a wider global catastrophe in the making. Australia has already detected and interdicted tainted pork products and just invested[30] $43 million for biosecurity personnel, equipment and preventive measures.

Countries are not always happy to air their dirty laundry or share news of their latest health scares or viral epidemics with the rest of the world. There is the danger that it will cause panic, force businesses and travelers to avoid the country and highlight the difference in public health and medical standards between developed and developing nations.

In China's case, it can also challenge the Core leader's political standing and party power. Chairman Xi Jinping is likely feeling the smoldering social backlash from the virulent and initially unmanaged novel coronavirus. Xi is also sweating bullets in his quietly contested position, where the long knives are not visibly out, but whispered criticism and raised eyebrows suggest questions about whether his stewardship in times of crisis has been competent and coherent.

Xi recently moved quickly to express symbolic leadership and responsiveness to the coronavirus in Wuhan, showing up[31] in a face mask to walk around city markets. China, too, has used its autocratic power and upped its state surveillance tools to force quarantines and social behavior to slow the COVID-19's outbreak spread among citizens.

---

29 Staff, "Chinese Frozen Food Firm Recalls Products Suspected of African Swine Fever Contamination."

30 Locke, "$66m African Swine Fever Detection Boost at Sydney and Melbourne Airports, Mail Centres."

31 Yuan, "'Political Show.'"

China's proactive measures are not limited to humans, with a top-down directive[32] that pigs be increasingly produced and slaughtered in controlled, scalable and standardized pig farms. Thirteen-story high-rise[33] "hog hotels" are being built in parts of the country.

For local and regional Chinese rulers, it is often more important to hide from Beijing a problem like infected pigs and sick people than to have to deal with bad news and expensive solutions. In all parts of the world where government authorities are seen as part of the problem, political leaders and bureaucrats give this narrative credence by behaving badly and avoiding accountability. It becomes a vicious cycle.

Developing countries often cut corners. Petit corruption and payoffs are everywhere. Every official form signed or checked permit becomes an opportunity for shady transactions and payoffs. The smaller the stakes, the more desperate the conditions, the more prevalent the "baksheesh" bribery system of profiteering from poverty.

If Xi successfully turns around the narrative of China's early structural failures regarding the coronavirus pandemic, he could come out as a stronger leader with more pervasive and threatening tools[34] to control society. If, however, the pork crisis continues into a third year, the big, bad urbanly dense Chinese population might just huff and puff and blow Xi's house down.

Coda: In early 2021, Chinese scientists found a natural mutation in the African swine fever virus which, they said, could be less deadly than the strain that decimated that nation's largest pig herd in 2018 and 2019.[35] Early reports pointed to illicit vaccines as the likely cause.

AMERICA NEEDS A KING

Introduction

U.S. presidents have too much power. Maybe it would be better to have modern, toothless monarchs who cut ribbons and not much else.

Originally published: May 21, 2020

---

32 Huaxia, "China Promotes Large Pig Farms to Ensure Stable Pork Supply."
33 Ying and Li, "China Focus: Smart Tech Helps Whole-Hog Reshaping of China's Pig-Raising Industry."
34 Kuo, "'The New Normal.'"
35 The Pig Site, "China's ASF Woes Could Linger in 2021."

Three co-equal branches of government was a fine idea when America was in its post-revolutionary fervor, having just rejected the vilified royal sovereign[36] King George III of mighty England.

If the Broadway musical[37] "Hamilton" did not make you laugh at the diminished and divorced-from-reality kingly figure, then any number of modern-day royals will remind you of the insulated[38] nature of a dying and dated institution hanging by a fragile golden thread. In most countries where a monarchy endures, however, the royals' level of engagement, authority and power are threadbare.

That's why in the age of Donald Trump, the United States needs to welcome back a king. An updated, modern-day American monarchy with all the royal trappings and none of the real juice. Someone like militarily-bedecked King Philippe of Belgium, for example.[39] This respectable modern royal is a powerless pussycat compared to 19th century despotic King Leopold II of the Belgians.[40]

Kings in other countries today can open parliaments and dub knights; be the patrons of regattas and oversee philanthropic causes; endorse products selected by the royal court and pimp out their titles for a share of commercial profits.[41] In almost none of the modern constitutional monarchies are kings, queens, princes, princesses, dukes and duchesses anything more than ceremonial celebrities and a contemporary throwback to cultural traditions or non-democratic tyrannical pasts.

America could use a bit of the celebrated role but skip past the tyranny part while cutting back some of the runaway executive power.

New York's Gov. Andrew Cuomo recently reacted to President Trump's assertion that the federal government could decide by fiat on the fate and laws of an individual state. Trump said, "When somebody is the president of the United States, the authority is total." Cuomo's comeback was crisp: "We don't have a king … the president doesn't have total authority."[42]

In fact, the Constitution prevents that total level of executive overreach and power. That didn't stop the president from his declaration or temper his attitude. It took a governmental reality check, states' pushback and a whole lot of eaten

36 Editors, "George III."
37 Magical Magnus, *Hamilton—King George—All Three Songs.*
38 All about History, "The Dangers of Royal Inbreeding."
39 Moens and Gijs, "Of Race and Royalty."
40 Cox, "Author Hochschild Recounts Lost History of Horror in the Belgian Congo."
41 Gellene, "Fergie Takes On a Heavy Load as Spokeswoman"
42 Pengelly, "'We Don't Have a King.'"

crow for him to back down and recognize that, in fact, thanks to federalism the states are really in charge of decision-making.

If America, however, had a modern toothless monarchy in the reign of King Trump—even continuing on through an endless Trump family dynasty—the so-called "sovereign" could say anything he or she wanted. Outbursts, tweets and proclamations wouldn't ultimately matter except to the degree that the king or queen had true moral authority, credibility, governing alliances, trust and a common touch. Bluster and balderdash would lead to nothing but irrelevance and be seen as folly. Not so our modern presidency.

America's president is today imbued with too much power. When this country parted with King George III, the limits on the executive were substantial. Running the country was not so complex. 18th century presidents did not sit on a nuclear football, sign bills to print $3 trillion dollars instantly or tell states much of anything, let alone how to manage stay-at-home orders during global pandemics.

The world has gotten a lot smaller, the government a lot bigger and the authority and power of the presidency has become near limitless. That power is awesome, in fact. It is also too much power for one person—especially one who discounts expertise, ignores institutions, degrades government departments and claims supremacy over the judiciary and legislature. Over the years, the executive branch has moved from respecting checks and balances to operating on cash-and-carry.

Other countries have figured out how to maintain titular heads of state while also formally limiting the authority and power of those leaders. In constitutional monarchies, royalty is always a vote away from being discarded. Greece ran a referendum against its monarchy.[43] Britain, too, regularly threatens to dump its royal family by plebiscite[44]—and that was before Meghan and Harry moved to Malibu.

Maintaining modern monarchs makes sense for some nations because royals represent continuity, bring in a few tourist dollars and sell some tabloids. They get trotted out to host state dinners and greet visiting heads of state. They then go back to their palaces and properties to live their quiet lives while the day-to-day business of governing is left to elected officials who grind away at balancing budgets, building bridges and banging out laws.

---

43 "Constantine II of Greece."
44 Walker, "Clive Lewis Says Labour Should Consider Referendum on the Royal Family."

Many countries without monarchies also have figurehead leadership represented by weak and relatively powerless presidents who do much the same as weak modern monarchs. They even have palaces.[45] America can figure out a happy medium—a "president king" who would be far different from an executive who seeks and claims total authority while shunning real responsibility.

Coda: Modern day monarchies are not what they used to be. Royals have lost much of their power as well as their shine. And now they are losing their numbers. The heir apparent to the British throne, Prince Charles, plans to reduce the size of the monarchy after his ascension. Democracies with a strong executive branch might learn a thing or two from contemporary kingdoms.

CAPITAL PUNISHMENT IS A DOUBLE-EDGED SWORD

Introduction

The United States has yet to come to terms with its abhorrent practice of executions for capital crimes. In addition to the tragic cases of killing mistakenly convicted defendants, the American justice system is saddled with inherent inequities toward people of color and the economically disadvantaged, as well as those represented by inept counsel. Ironically, America's inconsistent death penalty policies allow the most egregiously guilty to escape punishment while overseas. All this contorts the very definition of "justice" while undercutting national security.

Originally published: September 12, 2020

Bill Barr is killing Americans but sparing terrorists.

In July the U.S. attorney general directed his Department of Justice to resume[46] the death penalty. Since his directive this summer, he's used lethal injection to kill five federal Death Row inmates.

Barr executed[47] five murderers, rapists and torturers of children and the elderly. Men who inflicted unimaginable pain and suffering on their victims and surviving families. Barr unapologetically resumed capital punishment after a two-decade hiatus, "bringing justice to the most horrific crimes." Barr's tough on crime.

Unless, of course, he's not.

---

45 Segretariato generale della Presidenza della Repubblica, "The Quirinale Palace."

46 "Federal Government to Resume Capital Punishment after Nearly Two Decade Lapse."

47 Death Penalty Information Center, "Execution List 2020."

Barr also decided this summer to skip the death penalty for a pair of foreign ISIS terrorists who clearly qualified for the ultimate punishment. Shockingly, Barr wrote[48] a three-page letter dated Aug. 18 to British Home Secretary Priti Patel to say he won't seek the death penalty for two terrorists in U.S. military custody in Iraq. The despicable duo, nicknamed "The Beatles" because of their British accents, are accused of kidnapping and beheading several hostages in Syria in 2014, including James Foley, an American journalist.

And Barr's assurances to Patel went further,[49] saying that even if a death penalty were imposed, "It would not be carried out." That's right, he's both killing Americans and guaranteeing not to kill terrorists. This disparity is offensive and needs to change.

Society is currently debating[50] whether there are two systems of American justice as the 2020 presidential election forces the question: Is there one harshly punitive system for Black America and another less-severe system for the rest of America? That answer may come as early as Nov. 3.

What's clear now is that there is a two-tier system of American justice.[51] One says the death penalty is OK for criminals inside U.S. territory. The other essentially gives criminals residing outside the United States a get-out-of-jail-free card.

The reason? Countries can't—and won't—extradite to America criminals eligible for the death penalty. Sen. Dianne Feinstein recognized this crazy reality in 2003 when she said,[52] "If you steal a car in the U.S., Mexico will return you to face prosecution and punishment. If you kill the driver, Mexico will protect you." That's right. The more heinous the crime, the less likely the chance of being extradited to the United States.

As a result, America can't get its man. In the case of the "Beatles," the United Kingdom won't even give evidence unless Barr cries "Uncle."

Bill Barr currently is in charge of this longstanding and absurd two-tiered system of capital injustice. He freely applies the death penalty to guilty parties at home while, at the same time, guaranteeing that those committing monstrous acts abroad either escape justice or receive greater leniency than criminals at home. It's perverse.

---

48 Strohm, "Barr Tells U.K. Islamic State Suspects Won't Face Death Penalty."

49 "ISIS 'Beatles' Will Not Face Death Penalty in US."

50 Politico, "Harris."

51 Kounalakis, "Death Penalty in the U.S. Protects Edward Snowden."

52 Vote Smart, "The Voter's Self Defense System."

Civilized countries around the world have stopped[53] capital punishment. Those nations refuse to extradite or provide evidence to places that execute criminals: Saudi Arabia, Iran, Iraq, Egypt, China and the United States.

Our country has to make an important choice. Will it maintain its death penalty, recognizing that the trade-off means some of the world's most wanted criminals will get away with murder? Or, will the United States give up capital punishment entirely and join the community of nations that condemn the practice and fully collaborate on cross-border justice? America can't have it both ways.

James Foley's family has been incredibly understanding of the flawed U.S. legal policy requiring official "assurances" to mete justice. A merciful and spiritually strong Diane Foley told the BBC, "I feel that the death penalty is too easy. It allows them to be martyrs… They really need to face life imprisonment, so they have a chance for redemption themselves."[54]

America gave Russia assurances[55] that there would be no death penalty if they sent NSA leaker Edward Snowden back home. The United States promised the Mexican government that drug kingpin "El Chapo" Guzman would not be subject to capital punishment.[56] After the 9/11 terrorist attacks, the Brits said if they caught Saudi mass-murdering terrorist Osama bin Laden, he would not have been extradited to the United States.[57] The list of criminals escaping swift—or any—justice continues to grow because of America's backward approach to capital punishment.

While America may kill its own and spare those on foreign soil, Saudi Arabia just practiced the exact opposite. A Saudi court overturned five death sentences for the gruesome murder of Jamal Khashoggi, the Washington Post journalist suffocated and dismembered in Istanbul.[58] In a country that otherwise wholeheartedly embraces the death penalty, Khashoggi's killers instead received between seven and 20 years in jail. Is it ever possible to apply the death penalty equitably here or anywhere?

America must sync up with most of the world around capital punishment or accept that while some get executed, others will get away with murder.

---

53 Amnesty International, "Death Penalty in 2019."

54 "ISIS 'Beatles' Will Not Face Death Penalty in US."

55 "DOJ: No Death Penalty for Snowden—POLITICOBack ButtonSearch IconFilter Icon."

56 NPR.org., "Notorious Drug Lord 'El Chapo' Pleads Not Guilty To Federal Charges."

57 Kounalakis, "Death Penalty in the U.S. Protects Edward Snowden."

58 Agence France-Presse, "Jamal Khashoggi Murder."

Equal justice requires us to end capital punishment.

Coda: Barr used his authority to order, for the first time in U.S. history, the execution of more federal death row inmates than in any of the 50 states. In 2020, Americans elected anti-death penalty advocates Joe Biden and Kamala Harris.

CHAPTER 7

FREEDOM FROM FEAR

A SOLUTION TO ELIMINATE CHEMICAL WEAPONS

Introduction

After seeing images of the use of chemical weapons on Syrian civilians, Donald Trump said he was particularly moved. He failed, however, to work with allies to eradicate the world of chemical weapons or strengthen international organizations fighting use of chemical weapons.

Originally published: April 18, 2017

Gassing children is abhorrent. Killing children in any way is abhorrent, but President Donald Trump said he was particularly moved by the images[1] of the recent Syrian chemical weapons attack. That is understandable because the use of chemical weapons in warfare is arguably worse than other types of wartime battlefield killing.

The reason: Modern killing by chemicals is a cruel and calculated way to destroy humans but preserve physical structures, roads and machines. A warmonger who wants to preserve infrastructure but destroy the lives of opposing armies, collaborating civilians and innocent bystanders has decided that life is cheap but buildings are not.

In Syria, the civilian population is terrorized not only by rockets, bullets and bombs, but they are also subjected to murder by starvation and poison gas. Only the last two approaches kill people without destroying their homes, schools or places of worship.

---

1 "U.S. Launches Missles into Syria in Response to Chemical Attack, NBC Reports."

A look at the rubble that was once the Syrian city of Aleppo[2] is a reminder to all that a violent, explosive war with conventional weapons can destroy nearly everything. Aleppo was under siege for four years, with President Bashar Assad's government fighting opposition rebel forces dug-in and fighting amidst civilians.

The Syrian government took Aleppo late last year, claimed a victory and won back a decimated city where once stood a vibrant town.

Chemical weapons like the sarin and chlorine gas used by Assad, however, change the fighting calculus. Killing with chemistry prevents a town's destruction. Infrastructure survives; buildings are preserved. Chemical weapons allow for a war victory with the spoils remaining intact.

In the late 20th century, an enhanced radiation weapon[3] was developed that did the same thing. The neutron bomb, also known as the "capitalist bomb"[4] or "landlords' weapon,"[5] was developed and nearly deployed by the United States and France. It was a bomb with less explosive and heat-generating power but with radically more radioactivity and the ability to kill life but keep structures and machines in good working order.

Politics, fear and strategic considerations[6] kept this weapon out of production. International outrage forced countries to abandon work on the neutron bomb, seen popularly as an immoral and indiscriminate weapon. Chemical weapons share the neutron bomb's negative values.

Trump expressed his emotional reaction[7] to the horrendous imagery of beautiful children gasping for air, their lungs burning, their bodies paralyzed. His military response was meant to be punitive and a warning against Assad's further use of chemical weaponry.

The final part of his presidential action should now be preventive. Stop chemical weapons entirely, not only in Syria but around the world.

Use of chemical weaponry must never be normalized, and the president should use this moment to take a strong, moral and consistent stand to promote extreme verification internationally. The previous vetting process for Assad's secretly stockpiled or recently manufactured sarin and chlorine gas was

---

2 Loveluck, "The Battle for Aleppo, Explained."

3 Kaplan, "Enhanced-Radiation Weapons."

4 Strauss, "Though It Seems Crazy Now, the Neutron Bomb Was Intended to Be Humane."

5 Vinocur and Times, "France to Produce Neutron Bomb with U.S. Help, Allied Aide Says."

6 Cato Institute, "Precision-Guided Munitions and the Neutron Bomb."

7 Parker, Nakamura, and Lamothe, "'Horrible' Pictures of Suffering Moved Trump to Action on Syria."

inadequate. Only extreme verification with global partners can move the world toward total eradication of this scourge.

This may sound aspirational, but it is imaginable and achievable. Trump should use his deal making business prowess to build a coalition of military powers prepared to enforce the current Organization for the Prohibition of Chemical Weapons[8] work.

OPCW is a 2013 Nobel Peace Prize-winning international organization[9] with a 98 percent world membership. But OPCW needs to be given stronger tools and expanded international legal authority if it is to more aggressively enforce[10] standing treaties. One way might be to empower a United Nations that Trump already wants to rationalize and reform.[11]

Stopping chemical weapons could be Trump's signature foreign policy initiative, one more immediately achievable than previous presidents' attempts to eradicate nuclear weapons.[12] The United States, too, still has stocks of chemical weaponry it plans to eliminate by 2023.[13]

Negotiating a means to accelerate the destruction of foreign and remaining American chemical weapons[14] could also open a door to dealing with other future problems that threaten the global commons. Now is the time.

Coda: Izumi Nakamitsu, UN High Representative for Disarmament Affairs, told the Security Council in a February 2021 virtual briefing that the COVID-19 pandemic was limiting the ability of the world body to work toward elimination of Syria's chemical weapons program.

STEVE BANNON'S NIGHTMARE

Introduction

Muslim migrants fleeing their troubles at home arrive in Lesbos, Greece, looking for a brighter, safer future. To political strategist Steve Bannon, this is where the terrorist march across Europe started.

Originally published: July 27, 2017

---

8 OPCW, "Organisation for the Prohibition of Chemical Weapons."

9 NobelPrize.org., "The Nobel Peace Prize 2013."

10 Sucato, "Enforcing the Ban on Chemical Weapons."

11 Popovski, "Can the U.N. Adapt to Donald Trump?"

12 EURACTIV, *Obama's Prague Speech on Disarmament.*

13 Nuclear Threat Initiative, "United States | Countries | NTI."

14 Centers for Disease Control, "CDC—Chemical Weapons Elimination."

Docked alongside Greek fish taverns and cafes, multi-flagged naval vessels unload their human cargo, and their crews' depleted spirits, onto this postcard-perfect island. Muslim migrants and refugees flow onto Greece's shores, fleeing troubles at home and looking for a better, European future.

It is the stuff of Steve Bannon's nightmares.

Humanitarian images on Lesbos' sunny beaches and camps likely look to President Donald Trump's chief strategist like the geopolitical frontline in his perceived war on Western civilization. Bannon sees here the starting point for a great Muslim march across Europe—a condition he identifies as "civilizational jihad personified by this migrant crisis."[15] His boss has picked up on the theme.

Trump went to Poland earlier this month and, in a speech heavily influenced by Bannon's worldview, challenged the West to muster "the will to survive."[16] Trump, who actively conflates immigration with terrorism,[17] refugees with sleeper cells,[18] called on Europe and America to determine whether they have the will to defend themselves. "Do we have enough respect for our citizens to protect our borders? Do we have the desire and the courage to preserve our civilization in the face of those who would subvert and destroy it?"

It is this worldview—Bannon's and Trump's and Russian President Vladimir Putin's—that paints the refugee crisis and mass migrant flows to Europe as an existential threat. These new, self-proclaimed defenders of Western cultural heritage and democracy look at modern Greece as the place where their values are being slaughtered at the hands of approaching Muslim hordes. On these shores.

It is an argument that should seemingly go far here in the birthplace of the very Western civilization that this *Trumputinon* triumvirate says it wants to buttress.

It was not, historically speaking, so long ago that Greece and this island were under Islamic Ottoman rule. Lesbos' main town of Mytilene is crowned by a Castle fortress[19] that was overtaken by the Turkish Ottomans in 1462 and then housed madrasas and mosques. Their now-ruined structures are a prominent and stark reminder of a recent past where Greek culture and Orthodox Christianity were subordinated to Turkish rule until the early 20th century. And today, a freshly belligerent and all-powerful Turkish President Recep Erdoğan is rhetorically reasserting his military might[20] and self-understood historic right to parts of Greece.

---

15 Green, "Inside the Secret, Strange Origins of Steve Bannon's Nationalist Fantasia."

16 "Trump Says Western Civilisation at Stake in Warsaw Speech."

17 Fullerton, "Trump, Turmoil, and Terrorism."

18 Schow, "Donald Trump."

19 AFAR, "Castle of Mytilene."

20 Smith, "Tensions Flare as Greece Tells Turkey It Is Ready to Answer Any Provocation."

Overpaid human smugglers charge around 2000 euros each from desperate Syrians, Afghans, Iraqis, Pakistanis and Bangladeshis and then launch them on dangerously overloaded rubber rafts toward the nearest EU entry point. They wish their passengers luck and point the barely floating deathboats toward Lesbos' lights.

And yet, instead of feeling resentful or threatened, Lesbos' islanders receive these people with open arms and few complaints, despite their own economic hardships and dropping tourism revenues. In this moment of global political cynicism and financial misfortune, it is a rare and reaffirming phenomenon to observe Greeks' selfless acts toward helpless souls.

Since 2015, over a million people[21] have been processed through this island, primarily inside the Moria camp, a dusty holding center surrounded by barbed wire and chain link fence. Moria is currently at twice capacity, full of too many single men hoping for a shot at permanent residency somewhere in Northern Europe. Greek residency was never their goal and this island was never their final destination. Frustrated by the slow pace of extreme vetting and the growing certainty that those from non-asylum qualified African nations are stuck, camp residents often clash with security forces. Last week, the camp was evacuated due to riots and fires.

Bannon may be right to suggest migration is a threat. It is a threat to Western establishment politics, if not civilization. Fresh waves of foreigners washing ashore put enormous pressure on European governments and ruling parties. Immigration contributed to the Brexit[22] "Leave" vote, with the referendum interpreted as the British heartland's repudiation of an open, welcoming and cosmopolitan London.

Is the migration wave a Trojan Horse ruse? Is political Islam wheedling its way into Western institutions, waiting for the opportune moment to undermine the entire system? It is certainly a justification used by the paranoid and the newly powerful to justify a potential grand bargain between Washington and Moscow. It seems the rationale for Trump and Putin to work together to defend Western civilization.

Despite the political fearmongering and Lesbos' own history, there is little obvious concern on the island. Instead, there is widespread belief here that tourists, military, and modern EU institutions protect Greece from modern day Islam's demographic dominance.

---

21 UNHCR, "More than One Million Refugees Travel to Greece since 2015."
22 Travis, "Fear of Immigration Drove the Leave Victory—Not Immigration Itself."

People like Bannon, however, see a growing strategic threat. For them, this is a clear and present danger that probably keeps them awake at night.

Coda: As of January 2021, there were about 17,000 migrants and refugees on Greek islands in the eastern Aegean Sea, according to Greek asylum authorities. Greece petitioned the European Union to help ensure the return of 1,450 asylum-seekers to Turkey. This issue is part of the larger ongoing conflict between the two NATO members.

PUNISHING PUTIN FOR POISONING SKRIPAL

Introduction

The West should hold Russia accountable for spy murders or prepare to face bolder attacks.

Originally published: March 15, 2018

Global spy games just got a little more dangerous with the byzantine poisoning of Sergei and Yulia Skripal in the medieval-era UK city of Salisbury.

Extraterritorial assassination attempts are usually precisely targeted with the victim attacked in an unmistakable, but quiet, surgical strike. Among developed nations, there is not supposed to be any collateral damage and the attacking nation tries to maintain plausible deniability.

But the Skripal case using the Russian Novichok[23] nerve agent just changed things.

The message to double-crossing double agents? There is no place to hide. The message to host countries harboring these defectors? Drop dead. More and more countries are witnessing targeted foreign assaults and assassinations on their soil in a wanton and reckless disregard for diplomatic norms, innocent bystanders and respect for national sovereignty.

Prime Minister Theresa May is showing both warranted outrage and unprecedented backbone regarding this poisoning. She has rightly noted the attack on the Skripals has harmed British citizens on British soil and exposed a larger citizenry to dangerous toxins. Further, she railed that England's security forces were contaminated, and, most importantly, that this was a direct attack against her island nation. A NATO consultation may be in the works. Twenty-three Russian diplomats have been expelled. Even deeper retaliation is on the lips of an offended and angered political class.

23　"Russian Spy."

While President Trump has been characteristically restrained regarding all things Russian, U.S. Sen. John McCain, R-Ariz., stated[24] that "we must recognize Putin will not hesitate to engage in state-sponsored assassination. He must not be allowed to treat the UK or any other nation as a venue for political murder."

Secretary of State Rex Tillerson, too, responded quickly and unequivocally to the attack, saying[25] the poison used "clearly came from Russia" and that the "really egregious act" will "trigger a response." The response came quickly. He and Under Secretary for Public Diplomacy, Steven Goldstein,[26] were fired.

Russian Foreign Minister Sergei Lavrov said "we have nothing to do with this."[27] Tillerson's gone while Lavrov's star continues to rise. Where will a post-Rex America stand on Britain's findings and any of its calls for further action against Russia?

How a post-Brexit-vote Britain and her dwindling Western allies react and respond to this new crisis is going to redefine the unwritten rules of how nations deal with growing, stealthy and murderous incursions on their territory. UK actions will help redefine the way national intelligence services behave abroad,—both in what is acceptable and how they will unilaterally act in cases where they aggressively seek to protect national security and deeply held secrets. Are defectors off-limits? Does the killing of traitors have a statute of limitations? Are there any applicable standards and norms in a covert world where rules don't easily apply? Should countries get away with anything as long as they are not caught red-handed?

These are difficult questions. The conditional ethics of covert behavior and intelligence activities are complex and alterable. That's why John le Carré[28] novels, like "The Spy Who Came in from the Cold," are so deeply engaging. They force the reader to explore the personal conflicts of patriotic demands and the moral ambiguities of duty-bound action.

Britain's most notorious double-agent, Kim Philby, was a part of the Cambridge Five spy ring before defecting to the USSR. Whether the Brits tried to kill Philby in Moscow is unknown, but he lived to an alcohol-pickled 76, honored for his Soviet service with the Order of Lenin and the issuing of a five-kopek postage stamp.

---

24 Applebaum, "How the Use of a Nerve Agent on British Soil Exposes the UK's Isolation."

25 PBS NewsHour, "Tillerson Says Poisoning of Ex-Spy in Britain 'Clearly Came from Russia' and 'Will Trigger a Response.'"

26 Atwood, "Trump Fires Steve Goldstein, a Top Tillerson Deputy, in State Department Shake-Up."

27 Herszenhorn, "Sergey Lavrov on Spy Attack in UK."

28 Kroft, "Ex-British Spy on Leading a 'Double Life' as a Famous Author."

Edward Snowden, the former NSA contractor, is a contemporary intelligence asset living in Russian exile. Snowden does not yet have a postage stamp, but he does, so far, get to live securely in an undisclosed location in Moscow. The Skripal assassination attempt must be upping his already high paranoia and fear that "they will put a bullet in my head or poison me when I come out of the supermarket."[29] Even former Texas congressman Ron Paul believed[30] that "somebody in our government might kill him with a cruise missile or a drone missile."

True, American government officials do want Snowden dead, but they want Snowden's death to take place in the good old USA, not under cover of darkness in another country. CIA Director and Secretary of State-designee Mike Pompeo has called or Snowden's execution[31]—not in Russia, but by bringing him home, giving him a trial, and handing him a death sentence.

The American and British approach to defectors, spies, and other wanted criminals or convicted enemies of the state is to actively try to get them back. In the meantime, they get to live out their miserable lives abroad.

Russia thinks differently and is double-daring Western nations to do something about it. Theresa May's Britain just might.

Coda: The Kremlin boss didn't stop with poisoning spies. In August 2020, Putin reportedly ordered a similar attack on his main political opponent, Alexei Navalny. He survived a dose of Novichok while campaigning in Siberia. Navalny was airlifted to Berlin for treatment. Russian authorities promptly arrested him upon his return to Moscow. The charge: Violating the terms of his parole by not checking in while undergoing treatment in Germany.

THE AMERICAN KKK BRAND OF HATE TRAVELS WELL

Introduction

European extremists "admire" the American Klan as it is growing throughout Europe. Grand Wizard David Duke and "Alt-Right" spokesperson Richard Spencer are just two people banned from European countries for their extremist ideologies.

Originally published: August 30, 2018

---

29 Stewart, "Edward Snowden Says U.S. Secret Service Are Trying to Kill Him."

30 Madison, "Ron Paul Fears NSA Leaker Assassination."

31 "Meet Mike Pompeo, Trump's Likely next Secretary of State Who Wants Snowden Executed."

Film director Spike Lee's most recent film about a black cop joining the Ku Klux Klan is a caustic reminder of America's "original sin"[32] of slavery and our raw, homegrown racism. The KKK is truly an American original, but it has not remained within U.S borders. No wall of ideas has corralled this toxic concept from jumping the Atlantic and infecting Europe, where the KKK has found a new home.

KKK promoters do not regularly crow about their network or membership numbers. The European Klan plays a coy game, often masking its illegal affiliations and private intentions while publicly sugar-coating its rancid message. But their goals are clear. As German investigative journalist Frederick Obermaier told Deutsche Welle, "The German groups admire the American Klan, and they hope to be as big as the KKK in the U.S."[33] Blood and soil is their refrain.

European public officials and national laws regularly stop the organization and assembly of KKK adherents. A high-profile case concerned former Grand Wizard David Duke, who started the neo-fascist, paleo-racist European-American Unity and Rights Organization[34] (EURO). Duke, whose character starred in Lee's "BlacKkKlansman,"[35] was expelled from Italy a few years back,[36] with a Venice court finding him guilty of trying to establish "an organization aiming to exterminate the black and Jewish races in Europe."

Duke is not the only American banned from rallying European white supremacists. "Alt-right" spokesman Richard Spencer is prohibited entry in 26 European Union countries.[37] KKK branches rise and fall in countries such as England[38] and Germany,[39] but the racist ideology, spirit, and practices endure— a German parliamentary inquiry found four active Ku Klux Klan groups.

While Duke and Spencer may provide red meat for racist fire and fury, others are feeding Europe an anti-immigrant-rooted "anti-globalist" ideology. Steve Bannon calls it the Movement.[40] Bannon may have become *persona non grata* in the Oval Office, but his ideas are welcomed in Europe's far-right populist circles.

---

32 Wallis, "America's Original Sin | Racism, White Privilege, and the Bridge to a New America."

33 King, "'The KKK Is Active Here in Germany'."

34 Southern Poverty Law Center, "EURO."

35 Lee, *BlacKkKlansman.*

36 Beirich, "David Duke Tossed Out of Another European Country."

37 Oppenheim, "Neo-Nazi Richard Spencer 'Banned from 26 European Countries.'"

38 Parry, "We Expose Vile Racist Biker as British Leader of the Ku Klux Klan."

39 "Four Ku Klux Klan Groups Active in Germany, Says Govt."

40 Beauchamp, "Steve Bannon in Europe: A Dubious Plan for the 2019 EU Parliament Vote."

His arguments for the defense of Christianity and preservation of European culture has found fertile ground. Earlier this year he spoke at a French National Front party congress, telling the crowd "Let them call you racists. Let them call you xenophobes. Wear it as a badge of honor."[41]

Racism itself is no stranger to European shores, of course. Fear and hatred of recent immigrants drives today's politics in Germany, Sweden, Hungary, Austria, Italy and all around the continent. Reactionary far-right parties are rising to stoke the sentiments of a fearful populace in countries that are seeing a rapid rise in newcomers from Africa and the Middle East. This week's mass anti-immigrant demonstrations in the streets of Germany's Chemnitz are the most recent manifestation of organized popular ire.[42]

A steady and barely controllable stream of asylum seekers from nearby war-torn regions and economically devastated nations are a daily reminder of imperfect immigration and unmanageable refugee policies. With no easy solutions, Europe's political populists are callously using the immigrants' arrival, race and religion to craft a credible narrative of invading hordes who are diluting European cultures, languages and tradition.

Two of those populists, Italy's Interior Minister Matteo Salvini and Hungary's Prime Minister Viktor Orban, met in Milan[43] earlier this week to plot a course for shutting down borders, deporting immigrants and drumming up wide anti-EU political sentiment.

Not all European countries are standing idly by when a coalescing rightist leadership faction plots an electoral overthrow of European laws and border norms to impose new nationalist identity politics. Both French President Emmanuel Macron[44] and the Swedish foreign minister, Margot Wallström, are aiming to defeat the Hungarian-Italian duo, with Wallström threat-tweeting, "Bring it on."[45]

Wallström's tough talk may also be masking the real fear in Sweden that its Sept. 9 election will reward far-right Sweden Democrats party with a first-place finish.[46] Sweden Democrats have disavowed their white-supremacist roots but continue to ride high on the anti-immigrant populist wave.

---

41 Ganley, "Bannon to French Far-Right Party: 'Let Them Call You Racist ... Wear It as a Badge of Honor.'"

42 Benoit, "German City Becomes Rallying Point for Anti-Immigration Protests."

43 Foster, "Populist Duo Viktor Orban and Matteo Salvini Call for Deportation of Migrants from Europe."

44 France 24, "Macron Accepts Orban, Salvini Challenge."

45 Wallström, "Margot Wallström on Twitter."

46 Brown, "Sweden Freaks Out."

I personally experienced some of Sweden's early anti-immigrant attitudes in the 1980s, when I was a University of Stockholm graduate student. Initially, I was naïve to the societal prejudice aimed at Southern Europeans, primarily Greeks, Turks, and Yugoslavs who made up a large cohort of workers in Sweden. In Sweden, our skin tone and hair color became our identifying characteristic; we were called *Svartskalle*—black-skulled people—and not in a good way.

I eventually made a black t-shirt with *Svartskalle*[47] emblazoned on its front and, despite my confrontational approach, was able to have healthy conversations about race and ethnicity with most Swedes. I never feared violence. But in today's heated political climate, it is not clear that those same rational conversations can exist. Can they take place in the United States in the run-up to our November elections?

In a week when America honors Senator John McCain's life, he reminds us in his final statement[48] that America is "a nation of ideals, not blood and soil." America's obligation must be to remind other nations that these ideals—not hate, exclusion and racism—are universal. Unfortunately, the KKK happens to be one of our more violent and virulent exports.

Coda: Several members of Congress, along with the NAACP, invoked the 1871 Ku Klux Klan Act to sue former president Trump and his former attorney, Rudy Giuliani, for allegedly conspiring with hate groups to storm the U.S. Capitol on January 6, 2021.

FOREIGN TYRANTS RELISH TRUMP'S "SOVEREIGNTY DOCTRINE"

Introduction

The unpunished murders of Khashoggi and Mikhail Lesin, the Russian poisoning of British spies and an assassination plot in Denmark showed how little the United States—or any nation—can do to pursue justice for crimes committed by determined countries.

Originally published: November 1, 2018

Jamal Khashoggi's horrific murder was a message to journalists, dissidents and regime critics everywhere. You are never safe. Anywhere, anytime.

---

47 "Svartskalle—Wiktionary."
48 Phillips, "'Do Not Despair of Our Present Difficulties.'"

Khashoggi was guilty of practicing journalism. He mistakenly bet he would be safe traveling to a NATO member nation to take care of personal business. Why? Because nations generally follow both international law and formal diplomatic practices that respect foreign laws and sovereignty.

Increasingly, however, more nations are exporting fear and practicing lethal intimidation with a new form of global vigilantism. They go abroad to get outlaw revenge.

The Khashoggi case is the latest example of exceptional and perverse murderous state-related behavior that targets and takes out perceived opponents living in exile. It's not just journalists abroad practicing their profession that are singled-out for murder. Turncoats living in other countries are targets, and killing them, too, is a clear warning to future defectors and detractors.

In 2015, Russia's media honcho Mikhail Lesin was murdered[49] in a Dupont Circle hotel the night before meeting with the Department of Justice in Washington, D.C. The spying Skripals barely survived a Russian poisoning attempt in the United Kingdom. In Denmark, an assassination plot aimed at an Iranian dissident recently was foiled.[50]

Vigilante state justice abroad is a disturbing trend. It challenges a nation's sovereignty by committing crimes on foreign soil. It is also a direct and bald-faced challenge to President Trump's clearly articulated—perhaps only—core foreign policy principle: his "sovereignty doctrine."[51]

President Trump's doctrine is an extension of his "America First" platform. He articulated this forcefully at his U.N. General Assembly speech this year when he said every nation has the right "to pursue its own customs, beliefs and traditions" as long as they "honor [American] sovereignty in return." The problem, of course, is that those customs and traditions can range from foreign countries' authoritarian[52] structures to public beheadings[53] to female genital mutilation.[54]

---

49 Leopold, "High-Profile Russian Death in Washington Was No Accident—It Was Murder, Officials Say."

50 Noack, "A Foiled Assassination Plot in Denmark May Have Just Cost Iran a Partner against Trump."

51 *Washington Examiner*, "The Sovereignty Doctrine."

52 Sanger and Haberman, "Trump Praises Duterte for Philippine Drug Crackdown in Call Transcript."

53 "Saudi Arabia Criticised for 48 Beheadings in Four Months of 2018."

54 UNEPA, "Girls Are Saying No to FGM—and They Need Political Champions."

"You do you" is the sovereignty doctrine in a nutshell. Here's the rub: In the past—in rational, real life—U.S. leaders could respect other nations' sovereignty, while decrying their attacks inside other countries. Not so with Trump, however, for whom "sovereignty" extends to ignoring or downplaying a nation's despicable acts far beyond its borders.

The uptick in foreign assassination attempts means a weakly-enforced Trump doctrine is creating both a safe space for despicable regimes at home while also turning a nearly blind eye to their butchery abroad.

Unfortunately, America's split policy personality is not new. A conflicted America has long professed a preference for democracy abroad but looked the other way when friends and allies transgressed their citizens' rights. During the Cold War, anti-democratic military coups were often catalyzed and countenanced by America.

Despite this checkered history, pre-Trump America also insisted that human rights were both universal and paramount. The United States signed on to a U.N. "responsibility to protect" doctrine[55] that sometimes overruled national sovereignty and allowed direct intervention in foreign lands to protect their populations, as in the Kosovo war.[56] Kosovars will tell you that America got it right, the jury is still out on Iraq and Libya.

During the late 20th century America focused its diplomatic and military power on maintaining and expanding rights around the world. The United States was highly critical of the Soviet Union's imprisonment of dissidents, and summit meetings between President Reagan and Mikhail Gorbachev always kept "refuseniks"[57] on the agenda.

A conflict-averse and sovereignty-first Trump, however, avoids bringing up uncomfortable human-rights issues with foreign leaders in the belief that he can get a better deal by leaving thorny subjects and the internal affairs of other nations off the table instead of using them as leverage. Foreign leaders preempt tensions and appease the president by forcefully denying any complicity in election interference, foreign assassinations or military aggression.

In the past, even where the negotiation stakes were high and where decoupling human rights from other policies could have assured a faster and smoother outcome, the rights agenda remained on the table, and American adversaries always knew to expect it.

---

55 "United Nations Office on Genocide Prevention and the Responsibility to Protect."
56 Bellamy, "Kosovo and the Advent of Sovereignty as Responsibility."
57 Jewish Virtual Library, "Refusniks."

That has all gone by the wayside.

Kim Jong Un is now seen not only as a legitimate dictator by President Trump, but also as someone with whom an epistolary relationship[58] can lead to a love affair. Begone thoughts of torture, murder, enslavement for the people residing within North Korea's borders. They are seen as birth lottery[59] losers, and their lot is treated with indifference by POTUS.

American presidents have always given hope to oppressed peoples and inspired fear in desperado leaders. Now that the presidency no longer occupies any moral high ground, the hopes of foreign individuals for equality, democracy, independence and the promise[60] of FDR's "four freedoms" no longer look to the American president for hope. They now look directly to the American people.

Their hopes reside with an enlightened and activated American society to help alleviate their oppression by voting for wise and empathetic leaders who will pursue not only America's national interests but also universal human rights and dignity.

In fact, the global hope of the tyrannized and downtrodden is that America's leaders will again equate the international pursuit of human rights with America's national interests. That U.S. leaders will again recognize that our intertwined values and interests are essentially one and the same.

Vote.

Coda: And we did. Trump lost by more than seven million votes.

NEW ZEALAND GETS THE JOB DONE

Introduction

It was not only its response to the novel coronavirus that made New Zealand a global outlier. Having a tough female leader was a major factor.

Originally published: July 20, 2020

Florida is a red-hot COVID-19 zone, Texas is on a one-way ride up the infection escalator and California is reversing course after early lockdown success.

---

58 Bacon, "President Donald Trump on Kim Jong Un."

59 Save the Children, "The Lottery of Birth: New Report Reveals World's Most Disadvantaged Children Are Being Left Behind in Global Efforts to Improve Child Survival."

60 "FDR and the Four Freedoms Speech."

Together, these three states make up 20 percent of all new global coronavirus cases.[61] The United States is a pandemic-policy mess, and the whole world is watching the meltdown.

Not every nation, however, is experiencing Washington's infighting, chaotic approach and inability to implement a nationally coordinated pandemic response. New Zealand is an odd exception in a coronavirus world in turmoil.

How did such a small place take on such a big role on the world stage to lead the fight against infection's spread throughout its country?

Basically, there are two reasons: First, it had an almost airtight month-long lockdown[62] during which only supermarkets and pharmacies remained open. Second, the population trusted its public leadership and complied with strict safety protocols. Pretty basic. As a result, on June 7, Prime Minister Jacinda Ardern announced that New Zealand had "eliminated transmission of the virus."[63]

New Zealand's government and public-health officials were not alone in clearly articulating the problem and getting their people to accept and implement tough behavior. Greece and Iceland,[64] both heavily reliant on tourism, swallowed the bitter pill of shutting out visitors and closing down commercial activity. While Iceland has the population of a small American city, Greece has more than twice the number of people of New Zealand.[65]

Greece deserves international accolades for its COVID-19 response, especially since the country is surrounded by threats and still recovering from economic depression. Greek Prime Minister Kyriakos Mitsotakis, for example, simultaneously is controlling the virus' spread and managing refugees weaponized by Turkey to enter into his country.[66] Unlike Greece, island nations can more easily manage who gets in and out of the country. New Zealand has totally shut down.

New Zealand may also seem exceptional because its distantly remote location has kept it safe during this global crisis. That geographic isolation has given Silicon Valley entrepreneurs an earthbound survival destination. In fact, it's where hardcore 2016 Trump supporter Peter Thiel, who founded PayPal and

---

61 "Florida, Texas and California Account for about One-Fifth of the World's New Coronavirus Cases."

62 Lederman, "The Pandemic Roadmap."

63 Menon, "Ardern Dances for Joy after New Zealand Eliminates Coronavirus."

64 Sturluson, "How Iceland Flattened the Curve."

65 Smith, "How Greece Is Beating Coronavirus despite a Decade of Debt."

66 Tolliver, "Turkey Weaponizes Refugees against Europe."

Palantir,[67] plans to escape the global apocalypse. It's unclear what his plan will be to escape the effects of climate change or nuclear fallout, but at least New Zealand will be a kinder, gentler place than the venture capital centers of the world.

Marianne Williamson, who ran in the Democratic presidential primary, recognized New Zealand as a special haven. At the Miami debate, Williamson challenged Ardern's goal to make New Zealand "the best place in the world to be a child."[68] Author-candidate Williamson boldly asserted the next U.S. president should earn this title for America. A tough sell but a noble goal for the USA, especially when it comes to issues like kids and guns. Just ask the grieving family of Jace Young, a 6-year old Black child randomly shot dead in his San Francisco neighborhood on Independence Day.[69]

New Zealand is not immune to gun violence. In March 2019, it experienced a horrific, racist shooting at two mosques that left 51 people dead.[70] The response? The country made assault weapons illegal. Parliament voted 119–1 in favor of the weapons ban similar to one once in force in the United States.[71] Even after that terror attack, most New Zealand police still don't carry guns.[72]

Policies in nations such as New Zealand may seem distant and irrelevant to big industrial nations, but its size and remote location have not divorced it from geopolitics. Far from it. It is a critical partner to a consortium known as The Five Eyes—five English-speaking nations that have coalesced around common security concerns and intelligence sharing.[73]

The United States, Canada, the United Kingdom, Australia and New Zealand are part of the same-secrets club, recognizing that it is not only a common language that binds them, but also a shared commitment to democratic values, universal human rights and free markets. The language commonality means that they operate relatively seamlessly across national boundaries. They may not all spell "color" the same way, but they do see "colours" similarly,

---

67 Shead, "Peter Thiel's New Zealand Estate Lies Neglected as Coronavirus Drives Preppers into Hiding."

68 Arciga, "Marianne Williamson's First Act in Office."

69 Cassidy, "Family, SF Leaders Plead with Community for Help in Solving Slaying of 6-Year-Old Boy."

70 Graham-McLay and Roy, "Christchurch Gunman Pleads Guilty to New Zealand Mosque Attacks That Killed 51."

71 Faidell and Wright, "New Zealand's Parliament Votes 119-1 to Change Gun Laws after Christchurch Massacre."

72 Warner and Antolini, "As New Zealand Police Pledge To Stay Unarmed, Maori Activists Credit U.S. Protests."

73 Nicholson, "Suspicion Creeps into the Five Eyes."

although Wellington clearly saw COVID-19's red warning signs to which other anglophones were blind.

New Zealand's overall pandemic response and vigilance has kept the virus at bay for two-and-a-half months.[74] It's easy to credit its distant isolation and adherent society, but some focus on a special leadership characteristic: Women get the job done.

A popular meme credits multiple nations led by women as being more effective in managing a nation in crisis. Prime Minister Ardern makes the list along with Germany, Taiwan, Iceland, Finland, Norway and Denmark.

Not a bad line-up of successful women leaders, especially when they are juxtaposed against more than a few presidents and prime ministers who have failed miserably in the age of the coronavirus.[75]

Coda: On February 14, 2021, after three members of a family in Auckland tested positive for COVID-19, New Zealand put the entire country on lockdown.

THE PURSUIT OF HAPPINESS

Introduction

In addition to life and liberty, the Declaration of Independence calls "the pursuit of happiness" an inalienable right—not a mere nicety or privilege, but something essential to our future security—a self-evident truth.

Originally published: September 18, 2020

When Rep. John Lewis (D-Ga.) was recently laid to rest and as his coffin was being walked out of Atlanta's Ebenezer Baptist Church, everyone in the pews was asked to dance to Lewis's favorite Pharrell Williams song, "Happy." Solemnity mixed with sheer joy that day to span the spectrum of Lewis's life—from struggle to song.

Congressman Lewis loved this song and it showed. A video of him dancing to the tune went globally viral a few years ago.[76] Around the same time that Lewis's video was circulating, Iranian citizens were being arrested and jailed for doing the same thing: Dancing freely and joyously to that positively infectious hit song.[77]

---

74 Graham-McLay, "Ardern Warns New Zealanders against Covid-19 Complacency."
75 Wittenberg-Cox, "What Do Countries with the Best Coronavirus Responses Have in Common?"
76 O'Neil, *Congressman John Lewis Dancing to Pharrell Williams' "Happy."*
77 Schilling, Schilling, and Schilling, "How Pharrell and a Cast of Hundreds Got Happy for a 24-Hour Interactive Video."

Iran, and recently Egypt, has cracked down on the expression of creative personal freedom. These thinly legitimated dictatorships have made it a point to be big-time party poopers.

To see the absurdity of the Iranian and Egyptian officials' concerns, go to YouTube[78] or Oracle's TikTok[79] and view joyful innocence before it is punished. A group of young people is exuberant as they prance about an apartment rooftop or sweetly lip sync while driving along Cairo streets. The young Iranians' crime was their video showing the co-eds gathering, women without head coverings dancing with men, bouncing and singing "Happy," goofing and expressing themselves with wanton abandon. Their crime is they were happy.

In Egypt, Mawada Eladhm went out and did what millions of other people do around the world—dance, sing, pose for selfies. Doing this in Egypt, however, got Eladhm and other women arrested, sentenced and fined.[80] Egypt has become less and less tolerant of Western cultural norms.

Prior to the Arab Spring, Egypt was slowly opening up. After the revolution, there were radically different and competing demands. One set of citizens called for quick reforms, freedoms, and jobs while another larger one voted in a stricter Shrariah law-oriented Muslim Brotherhood. President Abdel Fattah el-Sissi—formerly General el-Sissi—led a coup against the Muslim Brotherhood and has since had the enormously difficult task of trying to provide economic opportunity while actively suppressing political freedom.

The Egyptian president is trying to appease political Islamists and democratic activists in a fraught environment and challenging neighborhood. Just next door in Libya, a civil war and proxy battles rage, threatening to draw in Egyptian forces. Oh, and the pandemic.

Still, why would a once cautiously reforming Egypt punish innocent singing and dancing? Why does Iran rapidly rebuke young people and make them publicly recant and repent their joyful acts?

Individual expression threatens totalitarian regimes and dictatorships. Free, uninhibited, publicly expressed joy is a powerful repudiation of these regimes' most effective governing tool: Fear.

Smiling, singing, and dancing are expressions of an unbreakable spirit. If a mind is liberated from fear, it no longer is bound by regime-imposed social

---

78 CBC News: The National, *Iranians Arrested for Pharrell Williams' "Happy" Tribute Video.*

79 Pham, "How Oracle Ended up with TikTok."

80 Kappler, "Women on TikTok in Egypt Are Being Arrested for 'Indecent' Videos."

constraints. How do you fight humor? How do you keep people from humming or foot tapping?

Joy is subversive. Ask some of the former Communist leaders who tried ruling with an iron fist and a closed mind. Fear works. Until it doesn't.

When the Soviet empire finally collapsed, it was both financially broke and morally bankrupt. What accelerated the downfall was that citizens finally lost their fear. They wanted a better, more representative, responsive, and rejuvenating form of republican government. They wanted markets that functioned, freedom of expression and movement. They wanted the freedom to pursue happiness.

Egypt and Iran continue to rob their people of widespread freedom, hope, and joy. Ultimately, that approach harms these nations socially, economically, and politically. Keeping people down is an expensive proposition. The costs are huge.

Here's the reason why: Freedom from fear and repression leads to popular demands for less societal corruption, better functioning government, and more efficient markets. While dictators don't like giving up power, research shows that the more people get to share freely in decision-making over society, business, and their own lives, the better the outcomes over time.[81] Freedom can lead to success.

America is one of the freest societies ever to exist. This freedom also has some downsides. Collective action is difficult. It's tough to evenly distribute common goods—things like healthcare, housing, or jobs.

What this system excels at, however, is unhindered, incentivized and rewarded creativity and innovation. In this, America remains unrivaled. It is the air that Silicon Valley entrepreneurs and Nashville musicians breathe. It's what Pharrell meant when he sang "clap along if you feel like a room without a roof." Limitless creativity, boundless joy.

Pharrell's lyrics inspire us to "clap along if you feel like happiness is the truth." John Lewis clapped along his whole life because he believed in freedom's truth and America's fundamental goodness. He was a joyful and fearless warrior who fought for fairness, equality, and justice. His true song continues to ring loudly from Atlanta and Washington to Cairo and Tehran.

Coda: On July 30, 2020, *The New York Times* posthumously published an inspirational op-ed piece written by Lewis shortly before his death titled, "Together, You Can Redeem the Soul of Our Nation."[82]

---

81 Ober and Manville, "Beyond Empowerment: Building a Company of Citizens."
82 Lewis, "Opinion | John Lewis."

CHAPTER 8

FREEDOM FROM OPPRESSION

MYANMAR, THE MURDEROUS VERSION OF TRUMP'S MUSLIM BAN

Introduction

The Myanmar military massacred Rohingya Muslims and ran them out of the country. The UN declared that what happened in Myanmar constituted "ethnic cleansing."

Originally published: September 21, 2017

Kill the Muslims. That's how the latest version of the Muslim ban is shaping up. Started shortly after Donald Trump made it clear to the world that Muslims were not welcome in the United States, other countries started their own, more brutal and deadly effective ban.

The Myanmar military maims and massacres Muslims as they run them out of their country. In Myanmar, it's not enough to ban Muslims; they are being permanently banished. Army regulars are chasing Muslim Rohingya toward and over a recently beefed-up border wall that is a low-tech, high-risk strip of land made of land mines and barbed wire. There is no big, beautiful door in this border wall.

Without mincing words, the United Nations has now declared what is happening in Myanmar "ethnic cleansing."[1] Yale researchers and Nigeria's President Muhammadu Buhari agree that it looks like genocide.[2]

---

1 "The 'Ethnic Cleansing' of the Rohingya."
2 Staff, "Nigerian President Likens Myanmar Crisis to Bosnia, Rwanda Genocides."

Enter an expressly "America First" administration as ethnic cleansing returns to the world stage and hits the headlines. Not our problem, apparently. In this new world, Rohingya are as likely to see the American cavalry coming as Midwesterners are to experience Martians landing in Chippewa Falls.

As in most attacks on minority groups and their human rights, the issues are complex, justifications sometimes seem rational, and a few bad and violent actors amidst a larger innocent civilian population suck up all the attention and force decisively violent reactions. The Rohingya are no different. The Arakan Rohingya Salvation Army (ARSA) is accused of attacking police stations and killing officers. Myanmar's military calls ARSA a terrorist organization, claiming the organization has ties to foreign groups.

ARSA's terrorist label gives foreign nations cover for their official support of Myanmar's measures. China and India show sympathy for the Myanmar leadership.[3] Pakistan and Bangladesh, on the other hand, focus on Rohingya civilian suffering and the very real humanitarian crisis. These two Muslim-majority nations lead the criticism of the Myanmar military and the nation's leader, Nobel laureate Aung Sun Suu Kyi.

Terrorism charges aren't the only thing complicating international intervention for the hounded Muslim minority. Rich oil, gas, and deep port Chinese naval basing opportunities in the Rohingya's Myanmar state of Rakhine add significant geopolitical concerns to the mix.[4] China is hoping to complete an oil pipeline through the Rohingya territory and loosen its dependence on today's easily cut off foreign oil deliveries. The Chinese recognize that if they further befriend and side with the Myanmar leadership, they win the spoils.

Neighboring Bangladeshis are not holding their breath waiting for the Americans to intervene (or even notice), and Bangladesh Prime Minister Sheikh Hasina recognizes refugees fleeing Myanmar are her problem alone. Hasina won't waste her breath requesting American help, telling Reuters that "[Trump] already declared his mind…so why should I ask?"[5]

It hasn't always been this way. The last big ethnic cleansing action that got the world's attention also got the world to intervene. In 2014, thousands of Yazidis chased to an Iraqi mountaintop got choppers and water and a whole lot of help during the Obama administration. It may have been late and it may not have been enough, but the Islamic State's attack on this Iraqi minority was

---

3 Gao, "On Rohingya Issue, Both China and India Back Myanmar Government."

4 Meyer, "With Oil and Gas Pipelines, China Takes a Shortcut through Myanmar."

5 Nichols, "Exclusive: Bangladesh PM Says Expects No Help from Trump on Refugees Fleeing Myanmar."

stopped. It helped that American troops and materiel were nearby and ready to act.

What can be done? Praying for the salvation of innocent souls is a start, but not very effective. An imperfect United Nations—still reeling from President Trump's pointedly critical General Assembly speech—could supply a moral voice, political pressure, international condemnation, refugee relief, and perhaps even a few peacekeeping troops carrying peashooters. For the most part, however, collective intervention by the international community is shut out.

Myanmar's civilian leader, Aung Sun Suu Kyi, is nominally in charge of her government and finally made some late, if welcome, conciliatory remarks regarding the 500,000 Rohingya Muslims that have crossed over as refugees from Myanmar to Bangladesh.[6] U.S. Secretary of State Rex Tillerson gave Suu Kyi a call to tell her he was aware of the abuses—214 Rohingya villages have been destroyed—and to ask that Myanmar curb the violence. Suu Kyi, however, is careful not to criticize Myanmar's military, conscious that she is always only a few speeches away from a potential return to prison or house arrest.

America First downplays universal human rights, privileges national sovereignty, rejects refugees, and actively seeks to ban Muslims at home. That combo is the Rohingya's worst nightmare. Donald Trump's U.N. speech[7] has given further license to other nations to be as bad as they want to be at home, so long as their behavior does not directly threaten American territory or disadvantage the American economy. Everything else gets a pass.

Banning whole categories of people, singling out and deriding individuals for their appearance or affiliations, or saying it's OK for patriots and police to rough-up others keeps viewer ratings up and Twitter followers coming, but is unworthy of a great nation's leader. President Trump needs to knock it off.

Border walls and willy-nilly condemnation of diverse groups and people is interpreted abroad as open season on minorities and greenlighting state violence. What's happening in Myanmar is an extreme and murderous version of Trump's Muslim ban.

Coda: On February 1, 2021, Myanmar's military overthrew the civilian government and declared a state of emergency. Since then, soldiers have used lethal force to stop anti-coup protesters.

---

6 Slodkowski and Brunnstrom, "Suu Kyi Silence on Myanmar Ethnic Cleansing Charge Draws Cool Response."

7 Borger, "A Blunt, Fearful Rant."

VENEZUELANS WERE ON THEIR OWN IN FIGHT FOR DEMOCRACY

Introduction

From one dictatorship to another, Venezuelan elections have been ballot-stuffed and bought. Despite the Trump Administration's bluster, the United States could not—and would not—fight for Venezuelan democracy.

Originally published: May 2, 2019

American presidents—and all political leaders—inevitably face trade-offs between conflicting priorities. In Venezuela, President Trump is stuck between a policy rock and a preference hard place, caught between a democratic and humanitarian demand to side with the Venezuelan people and the tough reality that there is very little he can—or really wants—to do.

Trump's declared "sovereignty doctrine" is now in direct conflict with his desired petro-policy and the reinvigoration of the Monroe Doctrine[8]—and it is all playing out in the streets of Caracas.

The losers? Invariably the good people of Venezuela. They are victims of "President" Nicholás Maduro and his regime's continual and cynically systemic use of food and energy resources to keep political friends and allies happy while shunting and starving his opponents. Millions have chosen to leave and live in exile as refugees, while others head to the Venezuelan streets to topple Maduro. They bear the brunt of simmering tensions and escalating violence.

Interim President Juan Guaidó earlier this week called men and women into the streets for "Operación Libertad." Images of protesters run over and injured by troops and gangs loyal to Maduro create an immediate sense of a national crisis. The numbers of new martyrs for the cause of Venezuelan freedom and democracy are growing, increasing global outrage and fueling loose administration talk about American military options.

This week's premature and now seemingly fizzled[9] "final phase" of the Venezuelan opposition to oust Maduro was fed and nourished by Trump's own assertive National Security Adviser John Bolton and Secretary of State Mike Pompeo. Florida Sens. Rick Scott and Marco Rubio added to the sense

---

8 Kounalakis, "Secretary of State Rex Tillerson Handled Venezuela Deftly—Until He Fumbled."

9 DeYoung, Dawsey, and Sonne, "Venezuela's Opposition Put Together a Serious Plan. For Now, It Appears to Have Failed."

of urgency, while Trump's political instincts led him to understand a stiffening anti-Cuban and anti-Maduro position could help to build a stronger and more loyal Florida voter base.

American rhetoric about democracy and freedom continued to escalate at the same time that the expected Maduro regime defections failed to materialize on May Day. Bolton ominously says that, "All options remain on the table;"[10] Pompeo says that "military action is possible."[11]

Here's the reality: Even though Trump wants Venezuelan regime change and his subordinates keep pushing for "all options," the president is keenly aware that U.S. military intervention is not a credible option. It's not even a good bluff. Even if greater control over Venezuelan oil and American regional hegemony is a likely outcome of regime change in Caracas, it is nearly impossible for Trump to commit U.S. troops to making that happen.

This is Trump's conundrum.

POTUS is unlikely to send troops for two reasons: First, he is stuck with the "Trump Doctrine" that recognizes the sanctity of sovereignty. According to this policy, what happens domestically in any nation is that country's business. He has articulated this at every turn, defended it in multiple settings and circumstances, and has paid the political price for enshrining its primacy in cases ranging from the Jamal Khashoggi killing to Kim Jong Un's unchallengeable leadership and unrequited love. The Trump Doctrine justifies both Russian President Vladimir Putin's and China's President Xi Jinping's weak-sauce electoral legitimacy.[12]

Second, Trump wants to end foreign entanglements and not start new "stupid" military conflicts.[13] He clearly articulated this during the campaign and in office.

These two factors—an aversion to American military engagement and a privileging of nation-state sovereignty—combine to give authoritarian leaders and regimes confidence that they can do what they want without consequences as long as they keep it within their borders.

American voters soon will figure out that the tough talk on Venezuela does not match up with the weak response of the administration's policies. Bolton is not the president. He cannot force Trump's hand. Rubio and Scott,[14] while

---

10 "Bolton on Venezuela."

11 Shesgreen and Jackson, " 'Military Action Is Possible' in Venezuela, Secretary of State Mike Pompeo Says."

12 Westcott and Carvajal, "US President Trump Says He Called Xi Jinping the 'King' of China."

13 Trump, "Twitter/Tweet Deleted."

14 Daugherty and Copp, "Florida Lawmaker Wants U.S. Military to Help Juan Guaido."

sincerely articulating the human-rights case for involvement, might also try to appeal to the president's transactional political sensibilities and argue that Venezuelan oil reserves and Florida voter reserves are there for the taking. Trump is unlikely to be moved, and America's military will also advise that it keep its powder dry.

Trump has not personally overreached on Venezuelan regime change. He has let Bolton and Pompeo go down that path while he simply articulates his support for Venezuelans' democratic aspirations. As a result, if Guaidó crashes and burns, Trump keeps his political distance and options, weakens an otherwise powerful and blustering Bolton[15] and maintains the latitude to quietly make dirty deals with an ever-meddling Russia to resolve the situation peacefully.

Images of protesting Venezuelans run down by armed personnel carriers in the streets is a sickening sight. They drive any compassionate person toward a call to action and a need for resolve against Maduro's repressive and reprehensible regime.

Unfortunately, recent history tells us there is not much America can do to effect easy regime change. The bottom line: The Venezuelans are on their own.

Coda: The Biden presidency ushered in new hope for U.S. involvement in Latin American democracy. In contrast to the previous administration, Biden's State Department announced it would work with allies to target "regime officials and their cronies involved in corruption and human rights abuses."[16]

POTUS IS NOT A KING

Introduction

Donald Trump was definitely imperious, but absolutely not infallible. The President of the United States is not a monarch.

Originally published: November 21, 2019

Distinguishing a monarchy from a republic is a civics lesson once taught in school. Our education system dumped civic literacy a while back, so it might be time for a national refresher course. We all need it, especially he of self-proclaimed "great and unmatched wisdom"—Trump the Infallible.[17]

---

15 Filkins, "John Bolton on the Warpath."

16 "Department Press Briefing—February 3, 2021."

17 Jackson, "On Syria, Donald Trump Cites 'My Great and Unmatched Wisdom'—Others Say No Way."

But if ever there were a fallible man—true of me and all men—the current White House occupant certainly qualifies.

Unlike President Trump, I'm usually willing to admit my mistakes, apologize when I've wronged someone and try to make up for my screw-ups. Being ready, willing and able to deal with my imperfections is a result of my Sunday school moral training and the ethical lessons I was taught at home.

Trump? Whether it's deliberately part of his shtick or simply his obtuse nature, Trump has never confronted a problem or a failed policy that wasn't someone else's fault and, therefore, undeserving of an apology. He is all offense and no defense. Infallibility means never having to say you're sorry.

Trump's unbound and haughty arrogance, while noxious, could be tolerable if the only people affected were those in his small personal and professional coterie. Here's the problem though: He's the most powerful person in the universe and sits atop the greatest nation in this planet's history. A little humility on his part would go a long way.

Unfortunately, Trump's attitude and governing style have led to a constitutional confrontation where the president and his defenders insist that, as a matter of his role and authority, he is essentially infallible and his power absolute.[18] Of course, even those of us who have forgotten the basics of our three-branch system of government and the primacy of Congress—the "First Branch" under Article I[19]—recall "checks and balances."

Checks and balances ensure a president can't just do whatever he feels like doing. Trump demurs. He says he has a constitutional "right to do whatever I want as president."[20] So, we're at an impasse.

Trump says he can do anything. Congress, the press and, traditionally, the courts have said he can do a lot, but not anything he pleases. Can he try to shakedown a vulnerable, newly elected foreign leader in Ukraine to do his domestic political bidding?

This is a pivotal moment. House Speaker Nancy Pelosi paraphrased Thomas Paine, saying, "We think the times have found us now."[21] Impeachment is the tool Congress has to test the limits of presidential power and try potential high crimes and misdemeanors. It is a tool that is now being used to determine if, in fact, the president has committed acts worthy of punishment up to and

---

18 Illing, "Are We in a Constitutional Crisis Yet?"

19 LII, "Article I."

20 Brice-Saddler, "While Bemoaning Mueller Probe, Trump Falsely Says the Constitution Gives Him 'the Right to Do Whatever I Want.'"

21 Brownstein, "Nancy Pelosi's Predictions for Impeachment."

including removal from office. It is a process that distinguishes a republic from a monarchy, a president from a king.

Crown heads can decide policy by proclamation, as Trump tried in the past when he "hereby ordered"[22] American companies to stop doing business in China. Their majesties can determine that criticism of the sovereign is illegal, as with the *lèse-majesté* laws in Thailand. When Trump acts to marginalize and methodically vaporize the press corps critical of him, he is effectively trying to exert *lèse-majesté*.[23] Finally, royalty is not subject to any higher law. They are recognized not only in the plural form, but as the absolute power with no higher earthly authority. This is how Trump perceives himself.

Kings and queens are not subject to removal. They can be dethroned by deposition, abdication or decapitation. Usually, a popular revolt or an act of God takes monarchs from power. But civics reminds us that longevity is no guarantee of permanence in U.S. office.

Benjamin Franklin famously said, this is a republic—not a monarchy—if we can keep it.[24] We fought a revolution against King George III to establish that there is a higher authority than a monarch's on this God-given Earth: the power of the people, a sovereignty of citizens.

Americans' power has not been granted by anyone, it has been fought for and earned and codified in our elegant, if imperfectly executed, Constitution. Here's what's being tested: Do we live in a nation of laws or a nation of men?[25]

We may not need to go back to our history books to learn the lessons we rightly expect our naturalizing citizens to master. All we have to do is pay close attention to what is happening in Congress and decide for ourselves the kind of country in which we wish to live.

Will our representatives defer to one man's grip on power, inflated ego, and sense of absolute infallibility? We pray they be just and choose wisely.

Coda: Although Trump is not a monarch and was voted out of office after being twice impeached, in early 2021 he continued to lead with near-imperial popularity polls and fundraising ability among Republican voters.

---

22 Trump, "President Trump Says 'I Hereby Order' US Companies to Stop Doing Business with China."

23 "Lese-Majeste Explained."

24 Beeman, "Perspectives on the Constitution."

25 Samuelson, "A Government of Laws, Not of Men."

TRUMP WAS THE HITMAN IN CHIEF

Introduction

A former president put the bad guys on notice. Candidate Donald Trump infamously said in 2016 that he could "shoot somebody and I wouldn't lose voters."[26] In retrospect, that might have been literally true.

Originally published: January 1, 2020

"Hitman: Agent 47" was a fictional movie about a trained assassin who killed the Nigerian warlord Bwana Ovie before his mission to take out the Russian president. It was popularly panned, but did fantastic at the box office.

Hitman: POTUS 45 is a real-time, televised and Twittered political program where the American commander-in-chief whacks Iranian terrorist Qassem Soleimani before setting his sights on the next target. The reviews are still coming in, but 45 is already doing well at the fundraising box office.[27]

Agent 47[28] navigated foreign cities, used stealth to deceive well-trained security forces and put himself in vulnerable positions before he could pull off the kill.

POTUS 45 had it relatively easy. He just gave an order to pull a metaphorical trigger.

Agent 47 had plausible deniability and no identity or nationality to make any single country accountable for his murderous actions.

POTUS 45 made it clear to the whole world that he alone was responsible for the American high-tech hit. As a result, his actions have made it clear to distasteful foreign leaders and adversaries sitting in an office or on a tarmac anywhere that they are fair game. If U.S. advanced military technologies can get a bead on them, they might be next.

Kim Jong Un cannot be comforted knowing that a targeted attack can snuff him wherever he sleeps. It may be one of the reasons his predecessors rarely traveled outside North Korea. Step off your sovereign territory and anything that happens to you—"accidentally" or otherwise—is no longer a direct attack against your country and might not be an act of war.

Miscalculation or a heated reaction by an aggrieved and suddenly leaderless nation could ignite a war, of course. That's still a risk with Iran. So far, the

---

26 Dwyer, "Donald Trump."
27 Uberti, "Trump Is Congratulating Himself in Facebook Ads for Killing Soleimani."
28 "Hitman: Agent 47 (2015)—IMDb."

Iranian reaction has been rhetorically hot, but practically restrained. The word from the White House? Iran "appears to be standing down."[29] We'll see.

For years, the Israelis avoided taking out the PLO's Yasser Arafat, though they likely knew his movements better than he did. The costs of eliminating him were too great. Creating a martyr and actively rallying the Middle East against Tel Aviv were highly likely and too risky. Better to have the non-telegenic, corrupt and ineffectual Arafat[30] leading, hyperventilating and hiding than a potentially new, more radicalized, legitimated, and regionally supported one at the Palestinian helm. Better the devil you know than the devil you don't. The Israelis kept him alive.

The Soleimani hit took place in a third country: Iraq. That means he was not mowed down on his home turf, just in his regional neighborhood and de facto domain. That makes no difference to the dead, but from a strategic and legal[31] calculus, that means the United States did not attack Iran's sovereign territory. Just its leadership.

Similarly, Iran uses both proxies and paramilitary abroad to attack military, governments and soft targets—a euphemism for innocent men, women and children. It does so with plausible deniability, whether launching attacks from Yemen, Syria, Lebanon or Iraq. It's all part of what the Islamic Republic sees as a cat-and-mouse game allowing it to conduct low-grade lethal warfare without holding the theocratic leadership accountable or demanding strong retribution from targeted nations.

Riding the edge of outrage and testing the limits of adversaries became sport for Tehran. Destroy Saudi oil fields.[32] Knock down American spy drones.[33] That kind of stuff. Other countries practice this form of passive aggression. Iran has become expert. Whether on the battlefield, in urban cafes or in the deep darkness of cyberspace, Iran has freely conducted gray-zone warfare.

Early optimistic views hold that America's Soleimani action will lead to a lull. Maybe even open a path to negotiating a nuclear freeze. But it's just as likely a step up the escalation ladder.

---

29 Voytko, "Trump."

30 Rees, "Where's Arafat's Money?"

31 Callamard, "The Targeted Killing of General Soleimani."

32 Lister, "Attack on Saudi Oil Field a Game-Changer in Gulf Confrontation."

33 Karimi and Gambrell, "Iran Shoots Down US Surveillance Drone, Heightening Tensions."

Regardless, the United States has put all its unsavory and previously secure-feeling enemies on notice that it could easily unleash new lethal targeting capacities. Every foreign adversary now knows they are always in America's sights. Make a wrong move, get a super-smart bomb dropped on your head with little to no collateral damage (another euphemism for dead innocents).

Are political leaders, representatives, military attaches, diplomats and other state assets now fair game anytime, anyplace? Or is there going to be a truce preserving the more-or-less gentlemen's agreement that countries don't take out other countries' leaders? Who makes such an agreement and how does it get enforced?

Up to now, what's kept countries from killing other countries' leaders was deterrence and diplomacy. Tit-for-tat deterrence works, after all. Diplomacy keeps a dialogue open and its rules provide the protection needed for bad guy leaders to travel safely to Geneva or the United Nations in New York.

POTUS 45 is now America's hitman-in-chief. Come 2020 or 2024, POTUS 46 will either double down on this policy or constrain the executive's right to global targeted killing in the sequel.

Coda: In an ABC News interview on March 16, 2021, Joe Biden agreed that Russian President Vladimir Putin was a "killer" and would pay a price for interfering in U.S. elections. In his first 100 days as president, there were no public reports of Biden ordering any assassinations.[34]

AUTOCRATS ABANDONED TRUMP AND EMBRACED CHINA

Introduction

The enemy of my enemy is not always my friend. The 45th president tried unsuccessfully to persuade autocratic adversaries through flattery.

Originally published: February 13, 2020

Venezuela is a bipolar nation in the eyes of the world. More than 50 countries recognize[35] the government of interim President Juan Guaidó. The rest of the world—most significantly Russia and China—continue to support and strengthen the grip of President Nicolás Maduro.

---

34 Gittleson, "Biden Talks Cuomo, Putin, Migrants, Vaccine in ABC News Exclusive Interview."
35 ShareAmerica, "More than 50 Countries Support Venezuela's Juan Guaidó," 50.

It's bad enough that the Trump administration has been all bark and no bite, trying to flip the failed Latin American state's leadership with tough rhetoric and State of the Union ovations. What's worse is that America under its current leadership has shown that there are neither significant consequences nor consequential actions that can be taken when a foreign country snubs Washington in favor of Moscow or Beijing.

The latest nation to reject President Trump's foreign policy puffery? The former American colony and current conflict-ridden country of the Philippines.[36]

Flattery is not foreign policy, and Trump's fan-boy attitude towards Rodrigo Duterte has not convinced the populist Filipino leader that Manila's future and his personal power are assured by remaining allied with the United States.[37] Instead, he has chosen to throw in his lot with Xi Jinping and the promise posed by China as a regionally rising economic superpower.

This is not only bad news for America's strategic rebalancing in the Pacific and for regional security. It is really bad news for those other Southeast Asian nations looking around their neighborhood and trying to figure out how to balance their economic and security interests against their long-standing American trading and security alliance partners.

Any way you look at this, Duterte's move is big. On Tuesday, Duterte let the United States know that he was dumping the 69-year-old treaty alliance that allowed American forces to remain and train in the Philippines.

It's not just the carrot of Chinese capital that has attracted Duterte to Beijing. The Philippine president feels insulted and justifies turning away from the United States by saying "America is very rude" to Filipino friends accused of human-rights violations.[38]

Human rights, however, have never been a priority for the Trump administration. POTUS arrived in the White House ready and willing to toss democratic principles, values, norms and rules in the dumpster.[39]

Duterte has it all wrong.

Trump is a true ally who embraces Duterte's autocratic rhetoric. Trump envies Duterte's dictatorial style and tough-guy approach to law enforcement and politics. Trump entered office encouraging American law enforcement to use extrajudicial measures—whether slamming perps heads into cop-car roofs

36 Hincks, "A Brief History of U.S.-Philippine Relations."

37 McLaughlin, "A U.S. Ally Is Turning to China to 'Build, Build, Build.'"

38 Yilek, "'America Is Very Rude.'"

39 Finnegan, "Hours after Being Fired, Emotional Tillerson Tells His Side of the Story."

or encouraging the illegal actions of Arizona Sheriff Joe Arpaio.[40] The latest outrage is Trump's admiration for summary death penalties for drug dealers.[41]

Duterte has encouraged vigilantism by everyone from civilians to police to government forces.[42] His approach has been to give a pass to anyone who kills a suspected drug user or dealer.[43] He flaunts his own tough-guy credentials by bragging about personally killing criminals.[44] He waves around guns to prove his seriousness and reinforce his power.

Trump has tried to court Duterte's loyalty to—and love for—America. POTUS practices a populism aligning his personal leadership style with Duterte's. Despite the anti-charm offensive, and regardless of the two countries' clearly shared interests, the Philippine leader just bet his country's future on the People's Republic of China.

In effect, long-standing military relations have just been reversed, and America has been told to go home.

The U.S.-Philippine relationship has never really been smooth. Duterte still harbors resentment for a 1906 Moro massacre so fierce and unjust that it drew the attention of Samuel Clemens—Mark Twain. Volcanoes and tightening American budgets in the 1990s shut down Clark Air Base.[45] Entire Filipino communities that relied on employment and business from U.S. bases suddenly were out of luck.

The two countries' relationship survived the Marcos regime and the destructive Mt. Pinatubo volcano. In fact, the Yellow Revolution that overthrew full-fledged dictator Ferdinand Marcos brought to power an Aquino family boasting deep American training and credentials. Corazon Aquino felt both grateful and indebted to the United States for supporting the overthrow of the Marcos regime and the successful transition to a civilian-led and functional electoral democracy.

The bad news? Philippine's successor democracy gave voters the conditions to sweep into office the tough-talking populist politician Duterte in 2016.

---

40 Wong and Gambino, "Donald Trump Pardons Joe Arpaio, Former Sheriff Convicted in Racial Profiling Case."

41 Sanger and Haberman, "Trump Praises Duterte for Philippine Drug Crackdown in Call Transcript."

42 Human Rights Watch, "The Philippines' Duterte Incites Vigilante Violence."

43 Coronel, Padilla, and Mora, "The Uncounted Dead of Duterte's Drug War."

44 Holmes, "Philippines President Rodrigo Duterte Says He Personally Killed Criminals."

45 Broder et al., "U.S. Reaches Accord with Manila, Will Leave Clark Air Base."

Philippine democracy is now threatened, in part, because China is happy to support reliable autocratic leaders and because Trump's feckless and personality-driven foreign policy toward Asia has alienated and pushed away Manila. The Trump administration's foreign policy lacks strategic coherence. Instead, it favors super-summitry and presidential high-fives.[46]

From Manila to Caracas, rightist and leftist leaders calculate which allies will serve them best and where to place their bets. Throwing off perceived post-colonial American shackles for neo-colonial Chinese chains is a bad choice. Unfortunately for the West and democracy, both Venezuela and the Philippines have wagered against Trump's America.

EXTREME MEASURES TO ESCAPE INJUSTICE

Introduction

Despite international extradition treaties, Interpol red notices and even extraordinary measures such as the CIA rendition program, some wanted suspects still manage to evade prosecution.

Originally published: February 20, 2020

Argo was a Ben Affleck film based on the true story of how a little CIA ingenuity and stealth freed a group of hiding humans.

A CIA team planned a low-tech, high-risk fake Hollywood movie production to sneak Americans out of Tehran. If caught, the Americans would have faced assured injustice and quickly turned from fugitives to hostages of the new Iranian regime. From Iran to China, Afghanistan to Bolivia, the story is a familiar one: Desperate individuals sometimes need to escape a foreign country's authorities and get beyond a nation's jurisdiction.

All countries—whether revolutionary regimes or democratic governments— pursue sovereign justice. National judicial systems reign supreme in the international system. Nations get to decide what to do inside their borders and who is guilty or innocent within their countries. President Donald Trump's foreign-policy doctrine[47] defending the primacy of national sovereignty further cements this custom into practice.

---

46 Doubek, "Trump Meets North Korea's Kim Jong Un And Says Nuclear Negotiations Will Resume."

47 Kounalakis, "Under Trump's 'Sovereignty Doctrine,' Foreign Tyrants Have Nothing to Worry About."

In 1980s Iran, the newly formed interim government sought flimsy justice for what Iranian student revolutionaries believed were historic U.S. human-rights transgressions. The new and freshly violent Iran wanted retribution, remuneration and just plain revenge against America.

When governments persecute foreigners, the individuals targeted are often subjected to unjust accusations, detention, judging, sentencing, and incarceration—or worse. Iran is an extreme example of foreign sovereign justice run amok.

To this day, policy victims in foreign countries abound, while ways to avoid foreign injustice are limited. Here are some options:

- Escape: The *Argo* solution was rare and extreme. Diplomacy is a much more common approach to freeing those in foreign detention. But what happens when the CIA is unavailable or diplomacy is unsuccessful at getting a foreign national's release?

There is always escape. Ask Carlos Ghosn.

The Brazilian-born Lebanese auto executive showed that even Japan's modern technology and surveillance tactics can be outwitted.[48] Facing charges of financial wrongdoing in Japan, his recent Houdini-like, perfectly planned and executed disappearing act used former military special forces teams and human-sized anvil cases to leave Japanese authorities slack-jawed. Lebanon, which has no extradition treaty with Japan, is now heralding and housing the ex-con.

- Exchange: A Taliban trade for two Westerners held for three years led to a ceasefire and a potential peace agreement with America. The deal that Trump officials cut will allow U.S. troops to come home and the administration to save face. Yes, it's partly a hostage negotiation—something the United States says it does not do—but three Afghan insurgents were returned to the Taliban.[49]

Hostage trades are highly controversial, as when President Barack Obama swapped five Guantanamo prisoners for Taliban-held Army Sgt. Bowe Bergdahl,

---

48 Maremont and Kostov, "Behind Ghosn's Escape, an Ex-Green Beret With a Beef About His Own Time in Jail—WSJ."

49 Nelson and Amiri, "Taliban Release Two Western Hostages in Exchange for Militants."

an accused deserter. Despite the Bergdahl controversy, hostage exchanges take place regularly. Two Americans who spent years at Club Jihad are now free.

As wars end, the practice of trading prisoners is a regular, more-acceptable practice. The remains of POWs often are part of a package for trade-deal concessions or improved relations. North Korea returned the remains of American GIs from the Korean Conflict,[50] which were used as a trading chit by Kim Jong Un to entice Trump to the Singapore summit.

China is hoping to work a similar deal with Canada for the Huawei executive arrested for breaking international sanctions on Iran.[51] But first, the Chinese government needs a few pawns and a little more leverage before they can force a trade. For that reason, China has been applying economic pressure on Canada while also finding thin excuses to arrest Canadian citizens. Imprisoned hostages and trade could force Ottawa's hand in this high-stakes game of prisoner poker.

- Exile: Bolivia is trying to get back at both Mexico and Spain for harboring and transporting criminals and political prisoners out of the country and into exile.[52] One man's criminal, however, can be another country's former president. Evo Morales found his way to a safe haven in Mexico, and the new Bolivian government wants him back. In the meantime, La Paz is using its few diplomatic levers to force a return, starting with the expulsion of Mexican and Spanish diplomats from Bolivia.
- Rendition: The practice of rendition is where one country decides another country has an asset or a wanted criminal within its borders, but disregards that country's sovereign rights. Powerful countries just go and get their perp out of a foreign nation giving harbor. Kidnapping, basically. Though illegal, international courts lack the authority or enforcement tools to stop it.

In the case of the Nissan auto executive, high-flying CEOs are known for their chutzpah and survival skills. Japan should have been aware that creative corporate cowboys are hard to wrangle, with or without another nation's intervention.

Convicted criminals abroad certainly cannot count on U.S. presidential pardons or commutations to have an effect. Internationally, might is what often makes right. When diplomatic, intelligence and military tools fail, however, a little stealth can be pretty effective.

---

50 Sisk, "Trump, Kim Commit to 'Immediate Repatriation' of Korean War Missing | Military.Com."

51 McNish, "Huawei Executive's Extradition Hearing in Canada Begins."

52 Harrup, "Bolivia Expels Mexican and Spanish Diplomats."

Coda: In early 2021, Carlos Ghosn remained a wanted man. He said that French investigators were planning to question him in Lebanon concerning alleged financial violations. Ghosn continued to deny all charges against him. Meanwhile, the U.S. Supreme Court refused to halt the extradition to Japan of two men charged with helping Ghosn to escape.

HUNGARY'S AUTOCRAT PLUNDERS HIS NATION'S RICHES

Introduction

Viktor Orbán is a threat to democracy in Europe. The COVID-19 crisis gave him perfect cover.

Originally published: April 4, 2020

In the 1949 film, *The Third Man*, set in post-war Vienna, the Austrian capital is a bombed-out city where Orson Welles' character, Harry Lime, makes a killing on the black market for medical supplies. Lime steals military stocks of penicillin, dilutes the antibiotic and sells it to unsuspecting patients who die from the watered-down drug.

Profiting in desperate times is immoral and unjustifiable.

It is also common.

While most people are conscientious, showing strangers compassion, love and selflessness, craven examples abound of certain individuals profiting from the COVID-19 crisis, and others, by hoarding, price gouging or simply leveraging market forces. The $138 bottle of hand sanitizer is the poster child product of this lockdown moment.[53]

Money motivates the unscrupulous and greedy. Power is the other potent aphrodisiac.[54] In its pursuit, power hungry leaders fan the flames of popular fears and exploit nativist anger.

Money and power are a killer combo.

Across the world, from Ankara to Beijing, Caracas to Moscow, powerful (and newly rich) leaders see the current crisis as a way to build themselves an unassailable permanent political role. Case in point? Hungary's Prime Minister Viktor Orbán now rules by decree.[55]

---

53 Tiffany, "The Hand-Sanitizer Hawkers Aren't Sorry."
54 Sherwell, "The World According to Henry Kissinger."
55 Tharoor, "Hungary's Viktor Orban's New Coronavirus Law Is a Blow to the Country's Democracy."

He just shut down opposition and locked down his power. This week, the charismatic Orbán wrangled his party's parliamentary majority to vote him all-powerful. They handed down a legal edict to declare a limitless state of emergency, suspend Parliament, cancel elections, allow for draconian eight-year prison sentences when forced quarantines are broken and permit shutting down inconvenient press. It's unclear how much European Union crisis funding Orbán might be able to direct toward his cronies and family in this power consolidation. But what is clear is that he has accumulated more power than even the Hungarian Communist regime and overlord Soviet Union he once valiantly and honorably fought.[56]

Here comes the big disclaimer: I know Viktor Orbán. As a journalist, I covered some of the most dramatic moments of modern Hungarian history, starting with my on-the-ground reporting of the March 15, 1989 nonviolent street demonstration. President Obama appointed my wife to be U.S. ambassador to Hungary from 2010-2013 when she actively sparred with Orban and fought to strengthen civil society and democratic institutions. She wrote the book *Madam Ambassador* about this time.[57] During those three years, our entire family lived in Budapest, and I earned my political science doctorate at Hungary's Central European University. CEU was founded by financier-philanthropist George Soros, a man Orbán has publicly demonized and ostracized.[58] Orbán recently succeeded in kicking CEU out of Hungary,[59] forcing the university to relocate to neighboring Vienna, the rebuilt capital where *The Third Man* was filmed.

Orbán is the Harry Lime of democratic politics. He has leveraged liberal electoral practices to destroy his opposition, muzzle critical voices, threaten political dissent, systematically rig elections and, in the process, dilute democracy.

In *The Third Man*, Harry Lime nearly got away with his profitable but deadly medicine-dilution scheme, using the chaos of post-war Austria to hide in Vienna's underground sewers. Budapest was once Vienna's sister-capital of an empire now vanished, but it is there that Orbán sits in his ornate Parliament building, scheming with his comrades and sycophants about how to steal as much money, power and authority as possible at this critical moment. He moved quickly to consolidate power now because the public health crisis provides the

---

56 Kingsley, "How a Liberal Dissident Became a Far-Right Hero, in Hungary and Beyond."

57 Kounalakis, "Madam Ambassador."

58 Beauchamp, "Hungary Just Passed a 'Stop Soros' Law That Makes It Illegal to Help Undocumented Migrants."

59 Kelly, "American University CEU Kicked Out of Hungary, Says It Will Move to Vienna."

perfect opportunity to take advantage of Hungarians' sense of vulnerability, fear and anger.

The tyrant looks upon crisis and sees nothing but selfish opportunity. The democrat inspires people to act selflessly, rise above fear, believe in society's common humanity. The democrat engenders compassion, and understands sacrifice for a greater good.[60]

Orbán is peddling his autocratic prescription to his society.[61] His diagnosis is that the current public health crisis needs an injection of strongman tactics, subordinated institutions and centrally controlled messaging. In this worldview, the people cannot be trusted to act selflessly, but rather must be managed, directed and threatened to follow the leader's social, political and legal dictates. To make matters worse, the European Union appears toothless while American diplomacy is enabling, if not outright supportive of, Orbán.[62]

Like Harry Lime, Orbán is a ruthless charmer. He's smart, quick witted and smooth. His illiberal behavior is facilely rationalized.[63] Orbán-dependent national media propagate and justify his political acts, easily selling the autocrat's narrative to an accepting popular political base for whom xenophobia and intolerance has historic precedence and contemporary resonance.

Orbán plays to people's basest instincts. Like Harry Lime, whose smile betrayed his dark acts and murderous behavior and who was guilty of poisoning people, Orbán is guilty of poisoning the body politic. For democracy-loving Hungarians, this is a dark movie they've seen before.

Coda: In June 2020, the Hungarian parliament ended the state of emergency. It also gave the government the power to declare future "medical" emergencies by decree without parliamentary approval.

THE MURDER OF GEORGE FLOYD

Introduction

The murder of George Floyd united the Americans against injustice at home and ignited demonstrations against racism globally.

---

60 Kolodny, "California Health Corps Site Scored 25,000 Sign-Ups in Its First Day, Governor Newsom Says."

61 Diamond, "Saving American Democracy."

62 Stevis-Gridness and Novak, "E.U. Tries Gentle Diplomacy to Counter Hungary's Crackdown on Democracy."

63 Dettmer, "Orban Presses On With Illiberal Democracy."

Originally published: June 5, 2020

In 2001, New York and Washington, D.C., were attacked, and the world responded[64] by saying, "We are all Americans." The greatest ever military coalition formed to come to America's defense. Nations—including Cuba, Iran, Libya, and North Korea—condemned[65] the terrorist attacks. Countries rallied to express sympathy and send material support.

That was then.

In 2020, the United States is facing an attack by the invisible COVID-19 virus and has a shaky economy in a self-induced coma. And, now, nationwide protests are highlighting racial injustice, with peaceful gatherings to rightly mourn George Floyd's murder in Minneapolis.

But during this time of crisis, all of a sudden, the rest of the world no longer identifies with America. In fact, populations across the globe are looking at the United States as a pariah state. George Floyd protests are breaking out in foreign capitals worldwide, emotionally flavored with strong anti-Trump sentiments. Adversarial nations and leaders are gleefully enjoying the momentary comeuppance and trying to rub salt in this nation's open wounds.

This is now.

In the eyes of the world, America has changed. We are no longer seen as a nation leading on human rights, press freedom, civil rights, democracy, justice. Foreign TV screens either show an executive indifferent to the world's suffering or selfishly seeking advantage for an "America First" policy agenda—even during a pandemic that requires international collaboration and multilateral solutions.

They are wrong, of course. America still promotes justice and democracy abroad; still provides security and humanitarian aid in far-off lands. But America's reputation has suffered. The perception abroad is that America has dangerously backslid. The current president—with his penchant for sharp divisive talk and harsh reactive policies—has sucked up all the oxygen in the global media. He is America's loudest and most visible representative. He and his peccadilloes now embody America in the world, and the world does not like what it sees. The majority of America does not like it, either.[66]

---

64 Blocker, "'Le Monde' Editor Says Anti-Americanism Has Ceased to Be Relevant."

65 Editors, "Reaction to 9/11."

66 Silver, "How Popular Is Donald Trump?"

Floyd's brutal asphyxiation under the knee of a cruel and callous cop is the catalyst for current domestic unrest. It has also reinforced a global citizenry's increasingly critical attitude toward the United States.

Poll numbers in allied nations—where we once freely traveled pre-COVID-19—have sunk lower than a diked Dutch lowland. While those favorability numbers have dropped significantly for America as a nation, they have nearly bottomed out for the U.S. president. The two are, of course, inextricably tied. The Pew Research Center recently found that globally there are "more negative ratings for President Trump than for other world leaders."[67] That's right, Xi Jinping and Vladimir Putin rank higher globally. Take a moment to grok that reality.

America's downgrade in the global public's estimation has a lot to do with Trump, as Pew has shown. The popularized international caricature of a grotesquely evil Trump—whether the Trump Baby balloon[68] or daily editorial cartoons[69]—is a big part of the perception problem. Trump, of course, does his best to fit the two-dimensional villain role, wantonly demeaning both people and places while also tweeting divisive inanities.

But it is not just Trump. America presents a confusing face to the world with our relative openness toward our societal problems. We publicly air our dirty laundry. That's both a curse and a blessing.

When reprehensible actions against innocents are caught on camera, like mass shootings or racist killings, we don't hide these acts from the world. Everybody gets to see all sides of America. They see how we painfully work through problems and seek solutions. The process sometimes brings our society to a breaking point. As difficult as it is, everyone gets a gander at systemic racism, police brutality, economic inequality, impeachments, demonstrations, riots. The world gets to watch as we struggle through reforms, fight for freedoms, wrangle for rights.

By contrast, we rarely see the brutality that occurs in closed societies—and what's out of sight is often out of mind. China's concentration camps have imprisoned[70] and "re-educated" a million Uighurs. Emotionally charged images

---

67 Wike, et al., "Trump Ratings Remain Low around the World, While Views of U.S. Stay Mostly Favorable."
68 Mackintosh, "'Trump Baby' Balloon Takes Flight in London Protests—CNN."
69 US News & World Report, "Editorial Cartoons on Donald Trump."
70 BBC News, "Data Leak Reveals How China 'brainwashes' Uighurs in Prison Camps."

of Uighurs, if they exist, do not play every hour on cable news. Russia's war[71] in Ukraine is not distilled into an eight-minute and 46 second video.[72] The foreign broadcast networks of Moscow's RT or Beijing's CGTV do not show images of those nations' victims of injustice.

This hidden hideousness may keep Russia and China from taking a reputational hit, but it also shields their systems from domestic and international pressure to reform.

Ours is a messy system. It's also a preferable system. We tend to correct our mistakes and make progress over time. That won't bring back George Floyd, but it may bring back America's reputation and role in the world.

Coda: On April 20, 2021, former police officer Derek Chauvin was found on all charges of murder and manslaughter for killing George Floyd. He and three other former Minneapolis policemen subsequently faced prosecution in Floyd's death.[73]

---

71 Zerkal, "Russo-Ukrainian War: Putin Must Be Held Accountable."

72 Hill et al., "How George Floyd Was Killed in Police Custody."

73 Williams and Li, "Derek Chauvin, Three Other Ex-Minneapolis Police Officers Indicted by Federal Grand Jury."

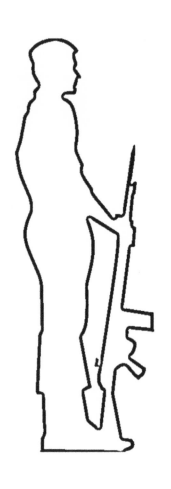

CHAPTER 9

FREEDOM THROUGH SECURITY

NUKE DEALS ARE FOR SUCKERS

Introduction

Donald Trump did not seriously negotiate over weapons of mass destruction while president. Instead, he dumped American partnerships and agreements made across the globe.

Originally published: October 5, 2017

Nuke deals are all the rage these days. The United Nations sees nuclear accords as a path to world peace. President Barack Obama worked toward a "global zero" nuclear-free future.

President Trump, on the other hand, is highly skeptical of deals with Iran and North Korea because he understands what Tehran and Pyongyang leaders already know: Nuclear disarmament deals are for suckers.

Countries generally balk at giving up their hard-won and expensive nuclear capabilities because nuclear weapons are a time-tested and reliable deterrent.[1] Giving up these weapons requires faith that any agreement inked is rock solid and that the countries agreeing to unilateral nuclear disarmament are assured they will not wind up like Ukraine or Libya—invaded or overthrown.

Trump does not inspire this faith. Neither does he have faith that the other side will do as it's told.

That's why the Iran deal may soon get scrapped and why Trump tweeted at Secretary of State Rex Tillerson to stop "wasting his time"[2] working to negotiate

---

1 Waltz, "'The Spread of Nuclear Weapons: More May Better,' Adelphi Papers, Number 171."
2 Baker and Sanger, "Trump Says Tillerson Is 'Wasting His Time' on North Korea."

one with Kim Jong-Un. Depending on unpredictable policy pronouncement or stated goals, treaty breakdowns could lead to a Middle East arms race or a reignited North Korean conflict.

If the Iran deal is broken by the United States, there will certainly not be a North Korean deal, or any future deals with rising nuclear states, because foreign leaders will instantly have evidence of what they have always suspected: These agreements are a trap. A deal must be worth more than the paper on which it is written. And history shows, it is not.

Trump already has dumped the Trans-Pacific Partnership, withdrawn from the Paris climate accords, and decided (but not announced) whether to recertify the Iran deal. Every agreement, treaty, commitment, and pinky-promise made by America is now in question. A few months back, even NATO wondered if collective defense[3]—the main premise of the treaty organization—was on the table.

"Global statecraft relies on trust, reputation and credibility, which can be all too easily squandered," wrote my Hoover Institution colleague, former Secretary of State George P. Shultz, in making the business case for sticking with the Paris climate deal.[4] "If America fails to honor a global agreement that it helped forge, the repercussions will undercut our diplomatic priorities across the globe." North Korean nuclear disarmament is one of those priorities.

Putin, like Trump, does not concern himself with previously done deals, convention or expectation. In 1994, the Budapest Memorandum was signed by the U.S., UK, Russia and Ukraine.[5] When the Soviet Union dissolved, Ukraine had the world's third largest nuclear arsenal and the Memorandum called for all 1,900 nuclear weapons to be moved to and disassembled in Russia. In exchange for the nukes, the parties all agreed to "respect the independence and sovereignty and existing borders of Ukraine," including Crimea, of course, and to "refrain from the threat or use of force" in the post-Soviet country.

What is the likelihood that Putin would have invaded, occupied, and annexed all of Crimea or started a hybrid war in Ukraine's Donbass region if Kiev still controlled its arsenal?

Zilch.

The lesson learned by other aspiring nuclear powers?

It pays to have nukes.

---

3 "NATO—Topic: Collective Defence—Article 5."

4 Shultz and Halstead, "The Business Case for the Paris Climate Accord."

5 Pifer, "The Budapest Memorandum and U.S. Obligations."

Putin is not the only double-crosser. NATO's duplicity in Libya provides a lesson for potential disarmament partners. It is impossible to defend Gaddafi's murderous rule or to be critical of the sense of urgency and humanitarian impulse for regime change felt by the world and led by France and Britain.[6] But here, too, dictators and despots grew to understand that even a disarmament deal with the West is not a guarantee of survival. Gaddafi gave up his WMD and nuclear weapons program in 2003 and, in return, saw painful sanctions removed and received an invitation to join the international community. Then he was killed. Long story short, it was a bad deal for him personally. The country has not fared that well, either.

That all happened way back when Obama was president, but dictators have pretty good memories. As a result, Kim Jong-Un is looking closely both at bad precedents and Trump's potentially reneging on the relatively fresh Iran nuclear deal.

Iran is key. If Trump grudgingly recertifies the despised Iran deal for a third time, then maybe North Korea might be open to negotiating away its own nukes. Unlikely, but possible. Especially with a little stiff prodding from Beijing.

All indications are that Iran, despite its reprehensible regime and human rights violations both at home and abroad, is following the deal's conditions. Under those circumstances, Trump's team favors recertification. Secretary of Defense James Mattis (Disclosure: Mattis is also a Hoover colleague) just told Congress that the U.S. needs to stick with the Iran deal. A still-serving Secretary Tillerson concedes, "Iran is in technical compliance with the agreement," even though he holds his nose and believes Tehran is violating the accord's "spirit."[7]

Trump may be trying to imitate Mohammed Ali and aggressively "rope-a-dope" Kim Jong-Un into a nuclear deal. The president's global reputation, however, as a sometimes (to some people) charming but blunt prevaricator[8] is not likely to trick Kim Jong-Un into an act of self-toppling political suicide.

Which means that Trump might just do as he tweets by ordering a preemptive strike on Kim to try to land a sucker punch.

Coda: Trump's self-proclaimed deal-making skills led to no improvements in U.S. relations with its adversaries. In February 2019, Trump announced that the United States would withdraw from the hard-won Intermediate-Range

---

6 BBC News, "Libya: US, UK and France Attack Gaddafi Forces."

7 Lee, "After Meet on Iran Nuke Deal, Tillerson Says Iran Complying but Violating Spirit."

8 *The Charlotte Observer,* "Donald Trump's Lies Have Consequences. We're Seeing Them Now."

Nuclear Forces Treaty with Russia. The Biden administration announced its intention to renew arms control talks and extended the New START Treaty.[9]

STAR WARS AND DRONE SPIES

Introduction

As fears of a high-altitude electromagnetic pulse (HEMP) strike that would cripple American satellites and communication grow, the Pentagon and latest US defense budgets prepare for such doomsday scenarios.

Originally published: December 14, 2017

Star Wars' newest episode "The Last Jedi" is hitting screens nationwide this week, but less entertaining is this season's latest space weaponry and commercial drone deployments that increasingly threaten America's national security.

Kim Jong Un may be planning to use his nuclear and missile technology not to land an explosion on U.S. soil, but to blast it in space.[10] Such an explosion would trigger a high-altitude electromagnetic pulse (HEMP) that could cripple satellites and blind any nation that relies on orbiting communications for everything from airline navigation to financial transactions.

A HEMP strike would bring about a "doomsday scenario" and an act of war that kills no one directly but plunges everyone into the first stages of a technological dark age.[11] An October 2017 congressional hearing on this threat brought testimony that a North Korean HEMP attack could "shut down the U.S. electric power grid for an indefinite period, leading to the death within a year of 90 percent of all Americans."[12]

Former House Speaker Newt Gingrich has been ringing this alarm bell for years, but despite HEMP hawks' fears and warnings,[13] the current Republican-led Congress decided to shutter the 16-year-old Commission to Assess the Threat to the United States from Electromagnetic Pulse.[14]

---

9 Blinken, "On the Extension of the New START Treaty with the Russian Federation."

10 *The Economist*, "HEMP-Induced Anxiety—America's Utilities Prepare for a Nuclear Threat to the Grid | Business."

11 Bedard, "Congress Warned North Korean EMP Attack Would Kill '90% of All Americans.'"

12 US Government Publishing Office, "Empty Threat or Serious Danger."

13 Weldon, "Washington Absolutely Must Save the EMP Commission."

14 Kester, "The Trump Administration Has No Plan for Dealing with a North Korean EMP Attack."

If the HEMP threat sounds like a worst-case and extreme act, the Pentagon thinks and prepares for such acts. It's why the military has a Cyber Command and does scenario planning that lays out battle plans and retaliatory strikes for a state-launched HEMP attack. The just signed record $700 billion military budget is also meant to build defenses against any North Korean plans to launch and land a nuke both above or on America.

Militaries need to plan for the unthinkable, but some experts believe a commonly feared HEMP attack would likely be a dud, more science fiction than serious threat. Jeffrey Lewis, a nuclear weapons expert at the Middlebury Institute of International Studies, told NPR that while an ICBM nuclear attack on the American homeland is a real threat, a HEMP attack would unlikely do more than flicker a few street lights.[15]

New battle strategies, missiles, and drone technologies are in place to fry everything from America's electrical grid to spy on critical infrastructure. North Korea's nuclear-tipped ICBMs can now be pointed at American allies and territory, while China's best-selling consumer drones are flying off the shelf and swooping around the country, suspected to be stealthily sending their flight patterns and photos of critical infrastructure to a foreign adversary.[16]

As the holidays approach, some of these drones will be bought, assembled, and deployed by American hobbyists innocently flying their new toys, potentially capturing sensitive data for foreign nations. Darth Vader's light saber is child's play compared to today's spy and fry tech.

Elsewhere in the world, low-tech snapshots are still illegal. Foreign travel lands American tourists at airports, train stations, near military bases and power plants where photography remains strictly forbidden. Arrests are still made in some countries where taking photos near sensitive areas can land sightseers in jail. In an irony-free UAE, an elderly American was arrested for taking a picture of a "No Photography" sign.[17]

Cyberspace, however, has no borders or police, so foreign-manufactured drones flying freely in American airspace, constantly gather and upload images stamped with both time and space data. Foreign-coded computer software and foreign-made hardware supplement the information gathering by collecting America's personal and private digitized insights.

---

15 Brumfiel, "The North Korean Electromagnetic Pulse Threat, or Lack Thereof."
16 Mozur, "Drone Maker D.J.I. May Be Sending Data to China, U.S. Officials Say."
17 Yaqoob and Fisher, "American Grandfather Faces Five Years Jail in Arab Emirates for Taking Picture of 'no Photography' Sign |."

Together, they are processed into big data crunching, artificial intelligence machines spitting out real-time physical and psychological mapping of the world, from street level views of cities to what's coursing underground through the veins of America's fiber optic cables. Topography, geography, habitual behavior, predictable movement, traffic patterns, financial transactions, commuter density. It's all there. A skilled marketer and internet behemoth can use the information to manage and manipulate consumer behavior. A determined adversary can easily target and weaponize that same data.

Preventing the collection and exploitation of that valuable info should be a national priority, even if foreign hacks and popular indifference have already allowed foreign countries to tap into a rich trove of Americans' private data and state secrets. U.S. government agencies have taken some action, banning the use of Russia's Kaspersky Lab[18] anti-virus software and grounding Chinese-made DJI drones for some official use, even though Kaspersky and DJI deny they engage in spying.

At a time when President Trump tweets that America's own law enforcement and intelligence agencies are "in Tatters—worst in History!"[19] America's adversaries are stocking their information gathering equipment on American Christmas store shelves and seeking intelligence advantages in a data giveaway underwritten and executed by holiday shoppers, municipalities, and the federal government.

"The Last Jedi" is an expansively dramatic battle between good and evil. In the real world, however, the stage and theater of war being prepared is not the local cinema or a galaxy far, far away. It is the land, sea, sky and cyberspace that envelop America. May the force be with her.

Coda: In the autumn of 2020, Azerbaijan used drones supplied by China, Turkey and Israel to overwhelm Armenian forces in Nagorno-Karabagh. It was, in effect, a test of NATO's high-tech military resources against Russian defense capabilities.

CHINESE AGENTS POSING AS JOURNALISTS

Introduction

The US Department of Justice announced that the China Global Television Network and the Chinese Xinhua news service must report under the foreign

---

18 Volz, "Trump Signs into Law U.S. Government Ban on Kaspersky Lab Software | Reuters."
19 Lewis, "President Trump Claims the FBI Is Tainted and Its Reputation in Tatters. This Graph Shows He's Wrong."

agents' registration act. Western journalists are usually neither spies nor diplomats, although the same cannot be said of China's and Russia's global news networks.

Originally published: September 21, 2018

China's television network and news wire service have long worked as intelligence gathering operations around the world and in the United States. The American government just did something about it.

On Tuesday, the Department of Justice announced that the China Global Television Network (CGTN) and the Chinese Xinhua news service must now report to the U.S. government under the Foreign Agents Registration Act (FARA).[20] This is a big move. A move that was a long time coming.

My book, "Spin Wars & Spy Games: Global Media and Intelligence Gathering," is a primer on how news organizations operate in the world and how non-Western journalistic organizations take advantage of open societies like the United States.[21] While Western journalists are usually neither spies nor diplomats, the same cannot be said about both Russian and Chinese global news networks.

China just got its notice to register under FARA while Russia's broadcaster RT (formerly Russia Today) and Sputnik were forced to register as foreign agents earlier this year. I began noting Russian and Chinese media organizations' growth, activities, and direct challenge to American media's global primacy a few years back.[22] The challenges have since grown.

In my book, I explain how Chinese state-owned news networks use their presence and power to perform both diplomatic and intelligence operations.[23]

On the diplomatic side, Xinhua and its foreign bureaus have been de facto embassies, performing multiple tasks usually reserved for trade missions, cultural representatives, or ambassadors in places like Hong Kong before the handover, for example, as well as parts of Latin America.

On the intelligence gathering front, the Chinese news organizations use Western practices of investigative reporting, access, brand equity, and

---

20 O'Keeffe and Viswanatha, "Chinese State Media Giant CGTN Registers as Foreign Agent in U.S."

21 Kounalakis, *Spin Wars and Spy Games.*

22 Kounalakis, "The Conversation: America's International Broadcasters Are Losing the Air Wars."

23 "Meet the Author: Markos Kounalakis | USC Center on Public Diplomacy."

credibility—often granted by their unwitting employees, reporting subjects, and regular commentators and guests who are host country nationals. A number of my Hoover Institution colleagues and I have consistently refused to appear or provide analysis on either the Russian or Chinese television network programs.

The Trump administration's general antipathy towards China's trade practices and state behavior is culminating in a full-spectrum economic and political confrontation with the People's Republic. The FARA move is another White House reaction to China's unfair media and industrial practices that include trade "dumping" to achieve advantage and primacy in certain industries, such as solar panels.[24] Equally irksome is the long-accepted Chinese practice of restricting Western journalists' visas, open access, distribution, and audience in the PRC.

China uses its global news networks to extend and project its power with great success around the world, in particular on the African continent.[25] With a headquarters in Nairobi, Kenya, and with a clear mission to ally with African leaders, develop African infrastructure, and dominate African media, China and its government-underwritten journalistic operations pursue state-driven political agendas. CGTN's Nairobi Center headquarters (the only other foreign CGTN broadcast center is located in Washington, DC) is a launching pad of pro-Chinese, pro-China business, and pro-regime reporting and messaging that is reinforced with all-expense paid trips and media training for African journalists in Beijing.

Chinese journalism training does not teach the public advocacy tools to check government that I learned at Columbia University's Graduate School of Journalism. Rather, it is a combination of propaganda training, China-state indoctrination, and outright editorial directive learning that places China's party-state and China-Africa state relations in a privileged position and their promotion as sacrosanct. The media becomes the message.

The bad news? Not only are China and Russia using their growing state-owned and operated news organizations as diplomatic and intelligence gathering institutions but, concurrently, the West's media capacities are dramatically diminishing.[26] The old news business model is collapsing, which means that Western news organizations no longer expend as many resources to send foreign correspondents abroad or to open foreign news bureaus.

---

24 World Trade Organization, "WTO | Anti-Dumping—Gateway."

25 Essa, "China Is Buying African Media's Silence."

26 World Affairs Council, "The Decline of Western News."

Western journalists do not operate as either formal intelligence agents (with a few exceptions) and do not engage in formal state diplomacy on behalf of the United States or European nations (except in some extraordinary circumstances, such as CBS's John Scali during the Cuban missile crisis).[27] Western journalists and global news networks do their reporting, condense and analyze their findings, and produce their news product for mass consumption. It is available to everyone. Americans, Europeans, Chinese and Russians alike. In the intelligence business, this publicly available, but officially useful information is called "Open Source" intelligence (OSINT).

With fewer and fewer Western journalists overseas, the amount of Western-oriented OSINT diminishes while Chinese and Russian globally available news, information, and perspectives are both ascendant and increasingly dominant.

The really bad news? American policymakers, analysts, and citizens are relying more and more on amplified and official, if often masked, Russian and Chinese-generated news, analyses, and social media to make decisions about politics and foreign policy.

Making Russian and Chinese global news networks register under FARA is just one step in the right direction. Saving and enhancing Western news organizations and journalistic practices is also necessary to combat this troubling trend.

Coda: In 2020, Britain's MI5 intelligence agency uncovered three Chinese spies posing as journalists in the UK. The trio were expelled without publicly revealing their identities.

GEORGE H. W. BUSH, PEARL HARBOR AND AMERICA'S OTHER FALLEN

Introduction

While some soldiers are remembered more than others for remarkable contributions, we must remember and recognize every soldier and their contributions. As the country mourned the death of President H. W. Bush, we mourned and honored all fallen service members, both identified and unknown.

Originally published: December 7, 2018

George H.W. Bush survived an airplane crash in Japan's Pacific Ocean in September of 1944. Seventy-four years later, on Wednesday of this week, two

---

27 Gelder, "John A. Scali, 77, ABC Reporter Who Helped Ease Missile Crisis."

Marines were recovered in the same Bush-ditched cold waters when a couple of planes went down in a mid-air collision.[28]

In both incidents, the majority of the crew went missing. Time teaches us that some soldiers are remembered more than others, but that everyone's military sacrifice must be recognized and revered.

Men who go on to greatness and achieve power are remembered in remarkable ways, with eloquent words, in lasting tributes.

For others, as with a military burial I once happened on for a Vietnam-era veteran, the ceremonies are only attended by a few good men, brothers-in-arms of the recently deceased.

My unplanned witness came on a cold dewy morning in Sacramento's Old City Cemetery.[29] Long stretches of stone monuments filled my view, the hard earth below my feet. In the background, a mausoleum-crowned mound dominated the view at the freshly dug and barely marked soldier's grave before me.

That nearby prominent rise hosted the remains of famous men and Robber Barons who rose to prominence in the late 19th century.[30] Piercing the solemn morning silence was a cassette tape recording of a bugle playing "Taps" sounding distant and forlorn. Station in life is irrelevant in death.

Soldiers who die in the field, in the air, or on the seas, whether in combat or training, are always prepared for the finality and anonymity of death in service to their country. There is no promise of glory. What is assured is the quiet and enduring honor that is paid a fallen soldier by his family, his military branch, and the national inheritors of that sacrifice.

On this Pearl Harbor Day, it is fitting that Americans are reminded of the spirit of the enlisted soldier who survived and went on to become the 41st President of the United States. But it is as important to honor the long-lost crew members who died when Navy airman Bush's plane went down after a bombing run near the Japanese island of Chi Chi Jima. The names of those two men—John Delaney and Ted White—are harder to find than Bush, but their collective legacy was a defeated Imperial Japan and a stronger, safer America.[31]

---

28 Stripes, "One Marine Dead, Five Missing after Jet and Tanker Collide off Japanese Coast."

29 "Sacramento Historic City Cemetery."

30 Kelley and Wile, "America's Robber Barons."

31 Smith, "72 Years Ago, Former President George H.W. Bush Almost Died In World War II."

Airman Bush recognized their sacrifice and America's blessings. Upon reflection immediately after his rescue, Bush wrote a letter to his parents about that fateful day in the Pacific. He recounted for them the events and his actions to get Delaney and White out of his burning, smoke-filled plane, realizing his crew was likely dead. He recalled that prior to the arrival of the rescue submarine that fished him out of the water, "I sat in my raft and sobbed for a while."[32]

The nation now mourns its fallen president. As importantly—perhaps more importantly—it is a time both to mourn and honor the fallen service members, both ID'd and unknown, famous men and forgotten heroes. The three American soldiers who last week were killed by roadside bombs in Afghanistan and the ones who likely died in this week's refueling air crash off Japan.[33]

This week's incident, taking down a Marine Corps aircraft, a F/A-18 Hornet fighter jet and a KC-130 Hercules aerial tanker, is only the latest reminder that preparedness and training come at a cost. Sometimes the ultimate cost.

Ceremonies will not be held at the National Cathedral for these dead. Their funerals will not be televised, nor will there be large processions and presidents. They are known by some and forgotten by many—especially in an era where the military–civilian divide, recognized by Defense Secretary James Mattis, is growing ever wider and the generations that knew conscription are aging towards oblivion.[34]

Pearl Harbor, Dec. 7, 1941. President Franklin D. Roosevelt said it was "a date which will live in infamy"[35] and marks when FDR asked Congress to declare war. Many of the soldiers stationed in Hawaii that fateful day went to their watery grave. While we may not know their names, we remember them for their sacrifice. Pearl Harbor events are what animated the then-17-year-old George H.W. Bush—and so many other young Americans—to volunteer for military service.

FDR's Pearl Harbor speech said that "always will our whole nation remember the character of the onslaught against us." Many would perish from the extreme brutality of the Pacific battles and captures, depicted so vividly in Ken Burns's 2007 documentary, "The War."

Bush was an energetic flyboy in that Pacific theater. An aviator through and through, I am reminded of his youthful service whenever I fly through George

---

32 Harrington, "Shock of Combat Changed George H.W. Bush's Life."

33 Nordland and Azadzoi, "3 U.S. Soldiers Died in Afghanistan: Why This Fight Drags On."

34 Keller, "The Key to Bridging the Civil–Military Divide, According to Mattis."

35 Roosevelt, "'A Date Which Will Live in Infamy': FDR Asks for a Declaration of War."

Bush Intercontinental Airport in Houston, where a bronze statue depicts him flinging his flight jacket over a shoulder as he gazes optimistically ahead towards a determined future of American greatness.

To honor this service, his funeral services in Texas include the largest-ever 21-aircraft missing man formation.[36] The honorary formation flies for not only for Bush 41 but for those who fell beside him at war in '44.

They fly for all American soldiers. May they all rest in peace.

Coda: According to the U.S. Department of Veterans Affairs, of the 16 million Americans who served in World War II, approximately 300,000 were still alive at the beginning of 2021.

WE KNEW COVID-19 WAS COMING

Introduction

In 2016, the Obama administration established the Directorate for Global Health Security and Biodefense to monitor worldwide health risks. America knew a pandemic was on the horizon.

Originally published: March 19, 2020

Two years ago, the stock market was on a one-way trajectory: Up.

In 2018, we watched how bioengineering advances and a technology[37] called CRISPR held the promise of personalized medicine and cures. People lived longer, healthier lives.

That year also was the 100-year anniversary of the globally devastating[38] Spanish Flu pandemic. That silent viral scourge killed more people than World War I. The Spanish Flu took between 50 million and 100 million lives worldwide.

World War II's occupations, trench warfare, shooting and bombing, and the starvation that followed, killed 20 million. The war's casualties split nearly evenly between military and civilian deaths; Americans and Europeans.[39]

Since then, lethal pandemics have lurked as a danger to our globalizing societies. The real threat and risk were always understood by public-health policy analysts and scenario-planning government agencies.

---

36 Eckstein, "Navy Will Perform Unprecedented 21-Fighter Flyover for Bush Funeral."
37 Plumer, "A Simple Guide to CRISPR, One of the Biggest Science Stories of the Decade."
38 All about History, "Spanish Flu."
39 "World War I Casualties."

Publicly, we had our own recent reminders: SARS, MERS, H1N1, Ebola. Citizens and leaders judged this threat to be off in the far distance. That illusion was a more comfortable way to go about our daily lives. It was easier for us to focus on our routines, invest in future markets and defer, or completely ignore, historic precedent. In the best case, we thought we could confront threatening outbreaks when the time arrived, before they became epidemics. In the worst case, we told ourselves we could head off those epidemics before they developed into pandemics.

That seemingly distant dystopian future has arrived, and we all feel as if we were somehow caught off guard, unprepared.

Here's the thing: We should not be surprised. We should have been ready.

This is not an "I told you so" moment. For years, people such as Dr. Peter Piot have been telling us this was going to happen.

The warnings have not been subtle, either. Piot wrote the 2012 book "No Time to Lose" declaring that the world was not planning for the next big, hard-to-contain pandemic. His experience told him that next time—this time?—perhaps millions of people worldwide could die.

Piot is not a fearmonger. He is the microbiologist credited with discovering Ebola. He's been a senior official at the World Health Organization, the United Nations and the Gates Foundation. He currently is the director of the London School of Hygiene & Tropical Medicine. I had a long talk with him in 2018 and walked away shell-shocked, fearful that a public health pandemic was looming.

Piot said a pandemic like COVID-19 was inevitable. For years now he's been telling us what to do as a society, and how to do it.

First, society needs to recognize that an outbreak's containment begins locally. Local action failed in this case, China's repressive political system prevented[40] the honest dissemination of information on the initial outbreak. By the time the real news got out and the rest of China and the world became aware of the coronavirus' contagious spread, it was too late. Early containment was the key to stopping this thing in its tracks, buying time to develop a vaccine and gaining public confidence that the disease could be controlled.

Instead, we have witnessed failure all around.

Piot says that containing a potential pandemic requires political leadership and will. We have seen an absence of both. What was a preventable public health problem has now mutated into a global economic crisis.

---

40 Lawler, "China's Coronavirus Cover-up Was among Worst in History, Congressman Says."

Piot was not the only one to warn us. He used his amplified voice and platform, but so did others, such as Laurie Garrett in her award-winning 1994 book, "The Coming Plague."[41] Movies, too, presented us an extreme and graphic version of a pandemic's consequences, as in Steven Soderbergh's 2011 "Contagion."[42]

Despite the warnings, the fears and the expectation that this was coming, the COVID-19 virus is all around us now. Global preparation was weak, and the initial American response was anemic.[43]

Seemingly normal, safe, everyday life is upended by a simple, invisible, potentially invincible virus. We shelter in place. We worry about society's most vulnerable: the elderly, those with weak immune systems, the ones who slip through the cracks of our healthcare systems or struggle to keep a roof over their heads.

Our executive leadership ignored the warning signs and the experts. Our federal government had the tools and the resources to do something, but failed to target them and failed to plan. As we continue to suffer the consequences and wake up daily to a new challenge—more deaths—and early finger-pointing, how can we be certain that the next big global threat will be met?

Heed the warning signs.

Nuclear-weapon agreements are lapsing.[44] Sophisticated cyber weapons can take down a nation's strategic infrastructure.[45] Biological hazards abound. There are plenty of experts and authors sounding the alarm. If this pandemic achieves anything positive, it should be to prepare us for future threats to our survival and way of life.

Coda: On his first day as president, Joe Biden signed an executive order restoring the White House office to address global health security. That directorate was established by the Obama administration and disbanded under ex-President Trump.

---

41 Garrett, "The Coming Plague."

42 Soderbergh, *Contagion.*

43 Pilkington, "Unprepared America Wakes Up to Coronavirus, Gradually Then All at Once."

44 Borger and Sabbagh, "Lapse of US-Russia Arms Treaty Will Heighten Missile Threat, Says UN."

45 Koppel, *Lights Out.*

ENVIRONMENTAL INVASIONS

Introduction

If it's not one thing, then it's a swarm of murder hornets.

Originally published: May 7, 2020

Just when you thought it was safe to go outdoors again—with face coverings, of course—news of a lethal, stinging insect could scare people back inside. The Asian giant hornet has just shown up in our beehives and on our doorsteps.[46]

Airlines are going bust, vacations getting canceled and study-abroad programs marooning college kids in other countries, but that doesn't mean all overseas travel has stopped. Microscopic viruses and big, bad invasive species are still roaming the world, finding new homes on distant shores.

When it comes to nature, there is no justice, only reckoning.

Today's novel coronavirus arrived at the end of 2019, an unwelcome guest that snuck in—undetected—from China with infected transcontinental travelers.[47] Now, as we hunker down to stave off COVID-19, the so-called "Murder Hornet" is the latest invasive species to make it to America, delivering psychic shock waves and deadly stings. Big, visible foreign invaders like the hornet are easier to detect and a lot less worrisome than the invisible coronavirus microbes rapidly jumping from person-to-person.

The story of the traveling deadly virus is not a new one. Any modern history of the Americas recognizes the devastation brought from Europe to the New World. Attacks did not arrive only in the form of weapons or troops, but were conducted primarily by new diseases; especially smallpox, a hidden virus with a 12-day incubation period. Jared Diamond, author of the Pulitzer Prize-winning book "Guns, Germs and Steel,"[48] points out that Europeans introduced the new diseases of smallpox, measles and flu that killed an estimated 90 percent of Native Americans—around 20 million people.[49]

Darwinism kicked in, allowing the strongest to survive and for immunity to set in. Antibodies developed, generations evolved, and we—the successors of those survivors—still stand.[50] Globalization has exposed more people to the

---

46 Main, "'Murder Hornets' Have Arrived in the U.S.—Here's What You Should Know."
47 Kelly and Thomas, "Disaster in Motion: Where Flights from Coronavirus-Ravaged Countries Landed in US."
48 Conan and Diamond, "Understanding History with 'Guns, Germs, And Steel.'"
49 Diamond, "Guns Germs & Steel: Variables. Smallpox."
50 Hoodbhoy, "The New Coronavirus Has Reminded Us of Our Debt to Darwin."

varied diseases and pestilence that exist around the world and, in the process, helped strengthen our systems and fostered our own survival.

Microbes may make it through our Customs and immigration walls, but there are other critters and cuttings that sneak in to sully our native ecological balance. In Florida alone,[51] imported invasive creatures include feral hogs,[52] Burmese pythons,[53] lionfish, and fire ants while habitat is overtaken by aquatic hydrilla weeds and climbing lygodium ferns.

Globalization and urbanization may have accelerated the reach and velocity of both viral infection and the spread of invasive species, but, again, this is not a new story.

Anyone familiar with Western movies has seen shootout scenes in dusty town squares marked by the sound of desolate winds blowing iconic tumbleweed through the streets. What can be more Western than tumbleweed? Russia and China gifted the first invasive species[54] of tumbleweed to the Americas around 1877, only to be crowded out by a new tumbleweed coming from Australia and South Africa that has since hybridized.[55] The U.S. Department of Agriculture has been fighting a losing war against this invader for over a century.[56]

In some parts of the world, native species of flora and fauna face extinction because of hunting or environmental degradation. Wild tigers, for instance, are sought for their supposed aphrodisiac qualities[57] and resplendent hides. Enter, ironically, Joe Exotic and his nemesis, Carole Baskin.[58] Together they and their ilk have more tigers alive in captivity than exist in the wild.[59]

While we are now freaking out about the latest Asian import, the Murder Hornet, we can at least spend a few lockdown hours on Netflix watching "Tiger King," that uniquely American story of hubris and hucksterism. The show is now a major globalized export and a leading example of how viral American entertainment can infect the minds of the world.

---

51 The Nature Conservancy, "Invasive Species in Florida."

52 US Department of Agriculture, "USDA APHIS | Feral Swine-Managing an Invasive Species."

53 Cohen, "Agency Wants More Python Hunters in the Florida Everglades."

54 *Smithsonian Magazine*, "Monster Invasive Tumbleweed Is Outgrowing Its Parent Species."

55 University of California, Riverside, *The Good, the Bad and the Tumbleweed*.

56 CGP Grey, *The Trouble with Tumbleweed*.

57 "Tiger Penis Soup."

58 *Miami Herald*, "President Trump Weighs Pardoning 'Tiger King' Joe Exotic."

59 Leigh, "5 Things Tiger King Doesn't Explain about Captive Tigers."

Well before the Tiger King, 15th century globalization gave the Americas an opportunity to spread native joys and stimulants to the Old World. Explorers brought back to Europe the most remarkable of agricultural products: tobacco and chocolate.[60]

Smoking kills, of course. Tobacco became an export that has since taken many lives and, despite its addictive qualities, was easier to avoid than the killer smallpox brought to America.

While new smokers and vapers are cropping up globally, smallpox no longer exists thanks to a worldwide vaccination program. Smallpox, in fact, was the world's first eradicated disease.[61] Let's hope the imported COVID-19 virus is soon No. 2 on that short list so we can all get outside—where the Murder Hornets thrive.

Coda: A film called *Attack of the Murder Hornets* by director Michael Paul Stephenson was released in February 2021, and showed how the Washington State Department of Agriculture worked with local beekeepers to stop the species.[62] Researchers predicted that if the giant hornet were not stopped in the Northwest, it could spread across the entire continent and beyond.

MAYBE AMERICA NEEDS TO GO VEGAN

Introduction

Let's get to the meat of the matter: After COVID-19, we have to change the way we eat. The coronavirus has beef producers around the world back on their heels and hooves.

Originally published: May 14, 2020

COVID-19 has changed everything, highlighting one of the meatier issues during this crisis: the politics of beef production and export. From ranches to feedlots, slaughterhouses to global markets, beef is now one of the most important products under threat in a high-stakes international food-supply game.

Meat supplies are so important, in fact, that President Trump intervened to keep meatpacking plants in operation.[63]

---

60 Norton, "Sacred Gifts, Profane Pleasures."

61 Bradford, "Smallpox."

62 Ouellette, "Attack of the Murder Hornets Is a Nature Doc Shot through Horror/Sci-Fi Lens."

63 Polansek and Mason, "Trump Orders U.S. Meat-Processing Plants to Stay Open despite Coronavirus Fears."

Meat consumption makes up a big part of Americans' protein intake—with milk and dairy being the most important.[64] Anything that threatens its availability on the market or dramatically raises its price is of national concern. Recent shortages and store limits on meat purchases have further raised the alarm. Supply and demand are strained.

Cattle ranchers are certainly feeling the squeeze: Demand for beef has dramatically dropped as restaurants close. However, those fast-food chains and markets with customers seeking burgers and steaks are finding a stark supply reality—cattle can't get from feedlots to fork because of supply constraints. Coronavirus outbreaks in factory slaughterhouses are hampering the ability to process, package and deliver the product.[65]

With more than 4,900 meatpackers infected and 20 reported deaths, fewer animals are being butchered and processed. Less processing capacity means fewer heads of fattened cattle get churned through the system. Less processing capacity means lower demand for animals at the plants, dropping the price per head and significantly raising costs as stay-at-home cattle are expensive for ranchers and feedlots to keep.

Fewer cattle entering processing plants also means fewer packaged meat products coming out. In the marketplace, that translates into shortages and higher prices in supermarkets. Not enough meat explains why 1,000 Wendy's burger joints were suddenly short on patties.[66]

The problem is not just at home. The human preference for beef is stressing a system that also depends on global markets. Australia's producers, for example, rely heavily on beef and barley exports to China.[67] This week, China cut off Australian exports because the island continent wants to investigate the Chinese origins of the coronavirus. Beijing is punishing Aussies for their alleged COVID-crisis finger-pointing, attacking food exporters through economic coercion.[68]

China is blatantly doing what other powerful countries often get away with—marrying trade policies to political goals. This linkage happens all the time. The Trump administration, for example, has vigorously reintroduced this into its

---

64 *Current Trends in Consumption of Animal Products.*

65 Vettese and Blanchette, "Covid-19 Shows Factory Food Production Is Dangerous for Animals and Humans Alike | Troy Vettese and Alex Blanchette."

66 Burginger, "Wendy's Removes Burgers from 1,000 Locations Due to Meat Shortage."

67 Lim and Ferguson, "In Beef over Barley, Chinese Economic Coercion Cuts against the Grain."

68 Needham, "Australia Rejects Chinese 'economic Coercion' Threat amid Planned Coronavirus Probe."

own policy toolkit, making import tariffs a staple of creating economic leverage to achieve policy outcomes.[69] From Europe to China, steel to cars, tariffs are this administration's preferred means to extract trade concessions and political favor.

China's move is intended to change Australia's political posture and help put the Canberra government out to pasture. Beijing visibly winks, denying the politics of the beef ban, arguing instead that Australia violated food inspection standards. Both could, of course, be true. Food inspection can be spotty in the best of nations.

America's meat industry has a long and sordid history, highlighted early in the 20th century in Upton Sinclair's "The Jungle," an eye-opening novel exposing the meatpacking industry's unsanitary processes and unsavory labor practices.[70] The novel generated a public uproar, and new safety and sanitation laws were passed, but the meat industry continues to have problems exacerbated by globalization.

Mad Cow disease,[71] the controversial use of hormones, targeted trade barriers and adversarial nations' policies that undermine foreign agricultural sectors are just some of the attacks and inherent weaknesses of today's fragile and globally interlinked food-supply chain.[72]

Vulnerabilities ranging from pandemic to political whim should motivate both consumers and policymakers to rethink the system of food production and delivery— independent of the many ethical considerations surrounding meat consumption.[73]

Unreliable and bottle-necked supply chains alone have led to today's beef shortages. Some countries have awakened to this challenge. China has a heightened sensitivity to food shortages, for example, as the nation suffers from a decimated pork supply, down 40 percent because of African swine fever.[74]

From a consumer perspective, we must reconsider eating habits that require enormous energy and resources to bring beef from hoof to hamburger. Thankfully, there are more and, increasingly, better options, including plant- and-lab based substitutes.[75]

---

69 Brown and Kolb, "Trump's Trade War Timeline."

70 *New York Times*, "Upton Sinclair, Whose Muckraking Changed the Meat Industry."

71 Centers for Disease Control, "Bovine Spongiform Encephalopathy (BSE) | Prions Diseases."

72 foodnavigator-usa.com, "US Beef Industry Sets out Japan Trade Goals."

73 Mark, "Toward a Moral Case for Meat Eating | Sierra Club."

74 *Miami Herald*, "Chinese Pork Production Beset by African Swine Fever."

75 Piper, "The Rise of Meatless Meat, Explained."

Governments, too, need to reconsider how to help deliver enough food to people with fewer dollars to spend and to markets with potentially fewer imported and transported foodstuffs. Just as all industries are reviewing their options to repatriate work and onshore manufacturing for profitable and strategic purposes, so, too, will the political leadership in several countries need to work harder to increase and diversify their food industries' homegrown production and quality.[76]

After all, COVID-19 has changed everything, including the way we eat.

Coda: In an effort to stem the growing hunger crisis caused by the pandemic, President Biden signed an executive order in January 2021 expanding the scope of federal nutrition assistance programs. The order reversed a move by the previous administration to cut federal food benefits. Meat was still on the table.

ENDLESS MIDDLE EAST WARS FUEL ANCIENT PASSIONS

Introduction

In the fight for Libya, Russia and Turkey keep a nineteenth-century war on the front burner. How does the United States keep the region from going up in flames, and the world from getting singed?

Originally published: May 28, 2020

Russia and Turkey just escalated their two-front war over which country will be the big dog in the Middle East. The two rivals have been at this game for a couple of centuries, but it just got a lot more serious this week when Russia introduced jet fighters into the Libyan civil war.[77]

Coronavirus may have shut down Texas beauty parlors and Louisiana bars, stopped international travel and cleared streets across the globe, but hasn't brought war to a halt. Rather, Russia and Turkey are in the midst of a multifront proxy escalation in both Libya and Syria.

Russians have long memories. They recall when Imperial Russia fought Ottoman Turkey in the bloody Crimean War.[78] Ottoman Muslim forces fought Christian Tsarist troops on the Black Sea peninsula, where more fighters fell to the Asiatic cholera epidemic than on the battlefield.

---

76 Purdy, "US Companies Want to Compete in China for the Plant-Based Meat Market."

77 BBC News, "US Says Russia Sent Jets to Libya 'Mercenaries.'"

78 Understanding Uncertainty, "Florence Nightingale and the Crimean War."

Turkey won. Russia today, however, once again occupies Crimea. The 19th-century Crimean War was the crucible in which were forged Russo-Turkish antagonisms and their 21st-century imperial dreams.

Both Russia and Turkey want to take advantage of a dysfunctional and shrinking European Union, a solipsistic America and a China focused on consolidating power in its own neighborhood first. The global pandemic provides an opening for two ambitious nations to both stand their ground and stake new claims.

Syria and Libya may seem like booby prizes, but what happens in Damascus and Tripoli matters. It certainly matters to the victims of indiscriminate killings. People have deeply suffered in Syria, under the brutal Assad regimes and, since 2011, when a Syrian version of the Arab Awakening was quickly quashed.[79] Images of the total destruction of Raqqa and Aleppo look like post-World War II Berlin.[80]

Russians targeted and ran air sorties hitting hospitals,[81] schools and any infrastructure providing solace and survival.[82] Bashar Assad's Russian-supported regime sought total annihilation and rebel capitulation. Most of the nation was brought to its knees by Putin and Assad's one-two punch.

The only hope for normalcy and peace was in Syria's northeast—a predominantly Kurdish region—where until 2018, well-protected American forces had a minimal presence and maximal effect.[83] It was a relatively safe American military investment for an active role in the region's future. The U.S. presence guaranteed the safety and security of the region's toughest anti-ISIS fighters: the Kurds.[84]

What blew-up this accommodation was not a Russian bomb or a Syrian troop incursion. What upset this American humanitarian effort and the fragile balance of power was a single, unexpected and capitulating White House phone call with Turkish President Recep Tayyip Erdoğan. The gist of the conversation? America was pulling out; Turkey could move in.[85]

---

79 Yacoubian, "Syria Timeline."

80 Guardian News, *Syria*.

81 *Miami Herald*, "Turkish Defense Radar Locked on Russian Fighter as It Bombed Syrian Town."

82 McKernan, "Idlib Province Bombing Kills 21 in Single Day."

83 Kounalakis, "Blob's Foreign Policy Experts Get It Right This Time on Kurds."

84 "Prospects for a Deal to Stabilise Syria's North East."

85 Baker and Jakes, "Trump Throws Middle East Policy into Turmoil over Syria."

America's departure was Turkey's invitation to run amok. The cost? Syrian lives, regional stability, American credibility, allies' trust and a seriously messed-up neighborhood with no immediate prospect for lasting peace. Russia and Turkey continue their violent geopolitical game in Syria, testing each other's will to grab what they can and dig in where they must.

Moscow and Ankara, fighting for influence, oil and a bigger Mediterranean footprint, have now also squared off in North Africa. Libya is the new theater for both soldiers of fortune and modern imperial forces. Russia's introduction of advanced fighter planes indicates that things started to go south for Moscow's ally, opposition leader General Khalifa Haftar.[86]

Two major fighting forces act as Turkish and Russian proxies. One, the U.N.-backed Libyan Government of National Accord, is partly underwritten and fully supported by Turkey and is fighting for dear life.[87] The other is Haftar's Russian-tied insurgent group with a base of operations in Benghazi. Haftar claims popular legitimacy, seeks international recognition and, until recently, was rapidly closing in on Libya's capital, Tripoli. The place is a hot mess.

Libyan lawlessness and violence make the country ungovernable. That makes it the perfect place for drug runners, migrant smugglers, arms dealers, oil thieves and marauding men terrorizing innocent citizens.

Meanwhile, Russia and Turkey pump up their respective Libyan teams' sides and pretend to broker ceasefires.[88] Lulls in battle allow the warring factions to regroup and jockey for international advantage and sympathy in this endless on-again, off-again war.

Vladimir Putin longs for the days of the Soviet Union.[89] Erdoğan pines for the Ottoman Empire's lost glory.[90] Both leaders are facing political challenges at home as the coronavirus crisis runs rampant throughout their countries. During these unsettling times at home, there is no better distraction for faltering leaders than a foreign war against a traditional foe[91] Turkey and Russia are just warming up.

Wartime presidents capitalize on national pride and military adventure. The losers of these ill-considered and vain wars invariably are civilians.[92] Last

---

86 BBC News, "Khalifa Haftar: The Libyan General with Big Ambitions."

87 MEE Staff, "UN-Backed Libyan Government Accuses Khalifa Haftar of Staging 'Coup.'"

88 Staff, "Russian, Turkish Foreign Ministers Back Libya Ceasefire in Call."

89 Nemtsova, "Russia's Twin Nostalgias."

90 Pivariu, "Turkey: Erdogan Seeks to Achieve the Dream of the Empire's Rebirth."

91 Tures, "Is Erdogan 'Wagging the Dog' Against the Kurds in Turkey?"

92 Kounalakis, "Women, Children Suffer Most in Conflicts around the World."

weekend reminded us that Memorial Days come and go, but memories of hardship, horror and war inevitably fade— even as global conflicts flare anew.

Coda: A report to the U.N. Security Council published by several news agencies in February 2021 accused American security contractor Erik Prince of violating the arms embargo against Libya.[93] Prince is the founder of the controversial security firm Blackwater and a close ally of ex-President Trump.

WHO KILLED OLOF PALME?

Introduction

The Swedish prime minister's death was as public as the life he lived. Is it really still an open question who murdered him?

Originally published: June 11, 2020

One of the world's most mysterious murders ultimately remains a cold—and now closed—case. In 1986, Sweden's Prime Minister Olof Palme was gunned down on a busy downtown Stockholm street. Investigators just named the only suspect, a guy who committed suicide in 2000. For skeptics and conspiracy theorists, the mystery of who killed Palme lives.

Palme represented a moral Sweden in a messy, immoral world. His global detractors were many. His life was cut down too early, and I miss him.

The first time I saw Palme was in a grocery store in Stockholm's old-town Gamla Stan. It was a weekend, and the prime minister was casually picking up a few staples before waiting in line to pay. Astoundingly, the nation's most recognizable and powerful person was not only out shopping without personal security, he was doing so unhindered—not approached, stopped, acknowledged or greeted by anyone around him. It was as if he was invisible.

My instincts were to go up to him and introduce myself as an American journalist, tell him I knew he graduated from Ohio's Kenyon College and to ask about his critical stance on America's foreign policy—especially Vietnam—that caused a diplomatic rift between the United States and Sweden. The person I was with was horrified that I would dare to brashly assert myself. She dissuaded me from interrupting. Why? "Because it is Saturday and he is going shopping— he is not working right now. Everyone has to respect that."

Everyone did respect that. Swedes in the 1980s had a real and deep understanding of boundaries between public and private lives.

---

93 Axelrod, "UN Report Says Erik Prince Violated Arms Embargo against Libya: Report."

My non-Swedish presumptuousness and American journalistic sensibility meant that I did not view public officials as being entitled to private lives. I felt they lived in the public eye and thrived on attention. Politics was full-time and all-encompassing. It sometimes felt like total war—especially with journalists. That's how I felt when I got to Sweden. Things changed.

After a year at Stockholm University's International Graduate School, I learned a thing or two about the country and its people. One of the most important lessons? Politicians are human. Somehow, during my entire upbringing and throughout my undergraduate years, I failed to understand that politicians are people—not villains, not superhumans. Fallible, emotional, desirous, greedy, complex, loving, silly, funny, egotistical, relatable, stand-offish, simple people.

It sounds trite to write something as simplistic as politicians are people, too, but in this moment in history, the divide between governed and government feels vast and unbridgeable. In a small country of 10 million people, where local democracy felt more direct than representational, the relationship between people and politicians was intimately close.

That's how it felt with Olof Palme. While Palme the politician was a bit aloof and a smarty-pants politico who comfortably traveled the world, criticized powerful nations and walked the United Nations' hallways with authority, he was still a man who could go to the grocery store to pick up provisions like a regular Joe—or Sven. He was normal.

Unfortunately, Swedish normalcy is also what got Palme killed.

Date night with his wife, Lisbet, at the cinema was his undoing. No security. No attempt at anonymity. Just another night out during his off-time to go see a movie. This time, however, someone did pay attention to his movements and possibly understood his patterns. Sweden's relaxed social environment was a weakness, and its authorities were unprepared for and inexperienced with this type of political violence. It happened at night. The movie just let out. A tall man shot Palme twice, point blank in the back with an illegal .357 Magnum handgun. He fell dead, bleeding on a downtown Stockholm sidewalk. There were witnesses, but it was an era without cell phones and incidental video footage. It was also an innocent era.

Palme died, and Sweden lost its innocence. The real world suddenly encroached on that distant, quiet and safe nation. Sweden awoke to a violent modern world that shoved its ugly face into the nation's consciousness. Anyone recalling Palme's murder remembers how everything changed that night.

Palme was a powerful leader cut down in his midlife and early political career. I regularly saw him during my two years as a Radio Sweden journalist.

Generous with his thoughts and cutting in his criticism, he also appreciated an American who understood his country and its global standing. Again, I still miss him.

On Wednesday, Swedish officials gave an unsatisfying answer to who killed Palme. Speculation ranged from Kurdish PKK sympathizers to agents for apartheid South Africa out to silence a harsh and vocal critic. It turns out the blame is put on a lone, dead gunman who took an opportune potshot.[94] The case is now closed, but too many questions remain open.

Coda: In January 2021, the Swedish Social Democratic Party awarded a human rights prize named in honor of Olof Palme to the Black Lives Matter Global Network Foundation. BLM was recognized for its "peaceful civil disobedience against police brutality and racial violence" around the world.[95]

"A CHRISTMAS CAROL"—COURTESY OF THE CHINESE NAVY

Introduction

The ghost of Christmas future may see Beijing reach across the Taiwan Strait to "reunite" the country and find a motherlode of microprocessors.

Originally published: November 3, 2020

What happens when China decides to dominate the world's semiconductor chip production by taking over democratic Taiwan? A look at the not-so-distant Christmas-future…

Christmas Eve, 2020—President Trump is still loudly contesting the November election results in courtrooms and the media. The Electoral College chose Biden–Harris after several red-state electors defected, justified by an overwhelming national popular vote for the Democratic ticket.

The newly elected Democratic Senate is days from taking over, and Mitch McConnell is rushing through last-minute judicial appointments. McConnell is also busy finalizing legislation giving the Executive sweeping policing powers in the face of daily national demonstrations protesting the election outcome.[96] Growing street confrontations are cited as the reason the outgoing president deployed the National Guard to major cities nationwide.

---

94 Duxbury, "Swedish Prosecutor Says Local Man Killed Prime Minister Olof Palme."
95 Business Recorder, "Black Lives Matter Wins Swedish Rights Prize."
96 Skelley, "What If Trump Loses and Won't Leave?"

America is in turmoil and increasingly violent following the deaths of several protestors at the University of California/Berkeley.

The People's Republic of China is monitoring both Fox and CNN, watching the turmoil and feeding the frenzy via its disinformation. Beijing continues cyber operations, testing, and penetrating corporate and defense networks during this confusing moment. COVID's second wave—a tsunami thanks to the flu season's severity—adds new burdens to skeleton staffs at the NSA, CIA, and other national security agencies.

Beijing's Ambassador to Washington sends cables home that suggest this is an opportune moment to make dramatic global moves. His memo references Jimmy Carter and how the Soviet Union used Christmas 1979 as the perfect moment to invade and occupy Afghanistan.[97] The ambassador tells the Communist Party leadership that it's time to initiate Operation "Iceberg's Tip."

"Tip" stands for the "Taiwan invasion plan." The reference to "Iceberg" is to help throw off intercepted signals' intelligence. Expeditionary People's Liberation Army Navy (PLAN) forces feint towards Antarctica.[98] But "Iceberg" is not aimed at asserting Antarctic claims.[99] Instead, "Iceberg" is how Beijing sees democratic Taiwan—a dangerous and independent floating hazard that has broken off from the mainland and threatens the PRC's ship of state.

An impatient Chairman Xi Jinping and a distracted America have set the stage for Beijing.[100] The PRC implements its titanic Taiwan invasion plan.

The world immediately denounces the move, but many nations remorsefully admit that they have long abandoned the Republic of China—aka Taiwan—diplomatically.[101] Multiple nations shuttered their Taipei embassies for the PRC's economic favor and, in the process, recognized Beijing's historical claims and long-term unification ambitions.

Global dependence on trade and nations' financial interdependence with the PRC temper international responses and dampen outrage in the United Nations. Even nations that once loudly objected to Russia's Crimean incursion rationalize their milder stance towards the PRC.

Beijing plays up its geographic and cultural ties to Taiwan. The PRC claims that Taipei's autonomy is a clear and present threat to the mainland. That

---

97 US Department of State, "Milestones: 1977–1980—Office of the Historian."

98 USNI New, "People's Liberation Army Navy Archives."

99 Cortellessa and Kounalakis, "The Only Place in the World Not Yet Rocked by the Virus."

100 Kounalakis, "The Impatience of China's Xi Jinping."

101 Shattuck, "The Race to Zero?"

argument gained popular traction after America supplied Taiwan with new weapons systems.[102] Further, high-level official U.S. visits catalyzed aggressive PLAN military exercises in the Taiwan Strait.[103] From Xi Jinping's nationalist perspective, ongoing U.S. freedom of navigation operations in the South China Sea sparked his Taiwan invasion.[104]

On this night before Christmas, America is domestically paralyzed, uncertain, and unable to act. America's domestic turmoil prevents her from taking decisive action,[105] especially since every Taiwan Strait war game shows devastating losses.[106] American costs would be intolerably high with sunk ships, picked-off warplanes, and dead soldiers. Sixty years after John F. Kennedy and Richard Nixon vowed to defend two tiny Taiwanese islands against mainland aggression, neither American political party is eager to risk war. After a costly, near twenty-year Middle Eastern war, Americans are tired of foreign adventures. Washington allows Taiwan to be absorbed.

The PRC accepts imposed global sanctions, knowing it can easily absorb international condemnation as it did after the 1989 Tiananmen Square massacre. Beijing's leadership simply sees the world's punitive reaction as the cost of doing business.

Interestingly, for all the talk about culture, history, unification, and fraternal unity, the invasion was really spurred on by one strategic goal: the immediate and total appropriation of most of the world's capacity to produce semiconductor computer chips.[107] Geopolitics and processing power are directly related, and America had recently cut off chips to the People's Republic, undermining Huawei and starving Beijing's AI and quantum computing ambitions.

Taking over Taiwan gives the PRC over half the world's chip manufacturing. It offers Beijing dominance over the world's digital lifeblood—the chips that power everything from iPhones to supercomputers. Game over.

Or not.

Like previous "Yet to Come" Christmas tales, the story can change if America heeds the warnings.[108]

---

102 Stone and Zengerle, ""U.S. Pushes Arms Sales Surge to Taiwan, Needling China—Sources."

103 "China Holds Military Drill as US Envoy Visits Taiwan."

104 Grady, "Panel: Pace of Navy Freedom of Navigation Operations Stressing Force."

105 "Defending Taiwan Is Growing Costlier and Deadlier."

106 Bernstein, "The Scary War Game over Taiwan That the U.S. Loses Again and Again."

107 Bloomberg, "The World Is Dangerously Dependent on Taiwan for Semiconductors."

108 Beete, "Ten Things to Know About Charles Dickens' A Christmas Carol."

A decisive, overwhelmingly clear, and uncontestable 2020 presidential election outcome will speak volumes to the world. American elections appear chaotic. They need to be seen instead as just really messy, self-correcting, legitimate democratic processes at work. Show the world elections matter and elections work.

A peaceful transfer of power will allow America to regain a singular voice that declares: We are united at home. Partisanship stops at the water's edge. Back off, Beijing.

Coda: The transfer of power from Donald Trump to Joe Biden was not peaceful. Trump was impeached, albeit not convicted, for instigating a violent insurrection in an effort to block his elected successor from taking office. Nevertheless, the 46th president was inaugurated on January 20, 2021. China continues to maneuver threateningly around Taiwan.

CHAPTER 10

A FREE WORLD

IN CHOOSING FEMALE LEADERS, U.S. TRAILS MANY NATIONS

Introduction

From India to Britain to Israel to Germany to the Philippines to Chile, women have been elected as their nations' leaders. While Hillary Clinton won the 2016 US presidential national popular vote, she did not win the election.

Originally published: April 30, 2016

Every election brings new questions about the qualities and character of national leadership, in the United States and abroad.

In the 2008 presidential election, the big question was whether America could elect a nonwhite man—in this case, an African American—as president. Up until then, all U.S. presidents had been white Christian males of European descent.

But disruption was in the air. France, for example, had selected a Greco-Hungarian of Jewish ancestry as president the year before Barack Hussein Obama's victory.[1]

In 2016, as the country moves through its primary season, U.S. voters are considering making history in other ways. Will they elect a septuagenarian Jewish socialist,[2] a boisterous billionaire political neophyte,[3] a Cuban American

---

1 BBC News, "France's Nicolas Sarkozy: 'Bling' and Legal Woes."

2 Chana, "Will Bernie Sanders Become the First Jewish President?"

3 *Encyclopedia Britannica*, "Donald Trump | Biography, Education, & Facts."

born outside the United States?[4] Or, after a few years of primary female also-rans, finally elect a woman to the highest office in the land?

If the United States does elect a woman, whether Hillary Clinton, a Republican-convention-brokered female candidate (Carly Fiorina? Condoleezza Rice?) or perhaps a write-in third-party contender as president, it would be following the lead not only of the world's most developed nations, but of many countries spanning a broad economic and political spectrum.

Impoverished India, the world's largest democracy, chose Indira Gandhi as prime minister from 1966 to 1977. Next door, India's greatest adversary, Pakistan, also chose a woman, two-term Prime Minister Benazir Bhutto. Both women served, neither was a pushover, and both paid the ultimate price for their service: They were assassinated.

Less violently, America's closest allies, Britain and Israel, have had strong female leaders in Margaret Thatcher and Golda Meir (the latter an American by birth). America's NATO allies in Europe did not think twice when they chose Norwegian Prime Minister Gro Harlem Brundtland to serve three terms, while Germany's Chancellor Angela Merkel initially was appointed in 2005. Merkel also became the European Council's president in 2007, a role once held by Britain's "Iron Lady," Margaret Thatcher.

Prime ministers and chancellors are chosen by their parties, but female leaders have won direct popular elections, too. Iceland's President Vigdís Finnbogadóttir served from 1980 to 1996 and was that country's—and Europe's—first female president and feminist-in-chief.[5]

In Asia, Corazon Aquino eschewed the opulence of the toppled Ferdinand Marcos' regime and the traditional Malacañang Palace during her six-year Philippine presidency. In South America, Michelle Bachelet is serving her second nonconsecutive term as president of Chile. Ireland's former president Mary Robinson is now the U.N. High Commissioner for Human Rights—a task of increasing importance and attention.

Developed and developing states choose women. So do transitioning democratic states, such as Myanmar's Aung San Suu Kyi. When Taiwan decided to play tough with the world's most populous nation, China, it chose Tsai Ing-wen to take office next month.

---

4 Biography, "Ted Cruz."

5 Icelandmag, "First Female Head of State, Vigdís Finnbogadóttir, Elected 35 Years Ago Today."

In Africa, the estimable Ellen Johnson Sirleaf, the Liberian leader and Nobel Prize winner, is a paragon of ethics and leadership, and brings dignity and a reform agenda to a troubled country and continent.

When it comes to leading a country, size does not matter. In teeny-tiny San Marino, 17 women have been heads of state since 1981.

Big or small, there is not a continent on Earth that has failed to elect a woman to lead a nation … well, two: North America (not counting the 132 days that Kim Campbell served as prime minister of Canada in 1993[6]) and Antarctica.

That's not to say that elected, appointed or anointed female heads of state are a panacea for global, or even local, problems. Corruption and failure are gender neutral and an equal-opportunity temptation for all races, religions, creeds and sexes. A look south reveals two embattled Latin American leaders on the brink of trial or impeachment: Argentina's recent former President Cristina Fernández de Kirchner[7] and Brazil's current highest officeholder, Dilma Rousseff.[8]

It took the elevation of Nancy Pelosi to the role of speaker of the U.S. House of Representatives in 2007 to change the North American meaning of "a woman's place is in the house." Around the world, a woman's place is not only in the House leadership, but also as leaders of senates and other representative, administrative and judicial bodies. And here in the United States, it may soon be that a woman's place is in the most important house of all—the White House.

(Disclosure: My wife served as a U.S. ambassador under Secretary of State Hillary Clinton and actively supports her.)

Coda: Kamala Harris was the first woman elected as U.S. vice president on November 3, 2020. She became first in the line of succession and, by tradition, positioned to seek her party's nomination for president at the end of Joe Biden's tenure.

MCCAIN AND THE AMERICAN CENTURY STRUGGLE TO SURVIVE

Introduction

McCain and Trump could not be more different. McCain opposed Trump's evolving world disorder and disdained the president's privileging of autocratic leaders. Honor can play an important role in maintaining freedom.

---

6 Parliament of Canada, "Prime Ministers of Canada."

7 Associated Press, "Cristina Fernández de Kirchner Indicted in Argentina Corruption Case."

8 CBS News, "Brazil's 1st Female President Faces Impeachment."

Originally published: July 5, 2018

Independence Day brings out this country's most patriotic expressions, from marching flag-wavers to parades of fez-wearing Shriners in mini-cars. This year, America celebrates its 242nd birthday, a year when the country actively redefines its concept of greatness.

America's role in the world is rapidly changing, going from being the world's policeman to loutish neighborhood beat cop. No one exemplifies the post-WWII generation of public servants who understood and promoted American global leadership than the now terminally ill U.S. Senator John McCain.

He would be the first to admit that he is an imperfect man, but the last to believe that America's role is obsolete, immoral, or defined strictly by economic interests and presidential whim. He has sacrificed his time and his body to fight against the shrill and the small-minded who argue that America's sins and historic mistakes are anywhere near morally equivalent to the Mao massacres,[9] Stalin scourge[10] or Hitler holocaust.[11]

Fighting Communism was his generation's cause and he believed he was on the front lines in Vietnam to make the world safe and secure from ideological empires that led to totalitarianism and mass murder around the world.

He screwed up when his time came to lead his party and promote his policies. He prevaricated, he postured, he Palin-ed. The personal and professional trade-offs he felt he had to make to turn an anti-maverick GOP into a party that would support a moderate McCain cost him his pride and tarnished his brand. McCain got spanked at the polls by America's first African-American president.

We all figure out how to personally reconcile our mistakes and move-on, but McCain still dwells on his public life's greatest regret[12]—picking Sarah Palin and accelerating the movement towards a populist politics that opened the Oval Office door for Donald J. Trump, historic revisionism, and America's dramatic retreat from friends, allies, and the global stage. Despite McCain's years of service and sacrifice, this one fact will remain a prominent feature of his reputation and remembrances.

McCain lost a presidential election and never got the chance to run foreign policy from the White House. Instead, he remained in the august and deliberative

9 Edwards, "The Legacy of Mao Zedong Is Mass Murder."

10 Lawrence, "A Portrait of Stalin in All His Murderous Contradictions."

11 "Hitler Comes to Power."

12 Hart, "McCain Regrets His Palin Pick for the Wrong Reasons."

Senate where he could advise and consent, but not do much more than taunt and obstruct Trump's inadvisable plans and often unfathomable instincts.

Reckoning a life in politics requires a focus not only on failings. The humane and patriotic contrasts between Senator McCain and the president are notable. McCain opposes Trump's evolving world disorder and disdains the president's privileging of autocratic leaders. Policy and style stand in stark contrast between the two men. Here are a few highlights:

- Children? McCain and his wife, Cindy, adopted into their family a little girl from an orphanage in Bangladesh run by Mother Teresa.
- Putin & Moscow? McCain saved some of his most virulent criticism for the Russian autocratic leader and argued in favor of helping protect persecuted ethnic and religious minorities in the region. His unvarnished and direct style came across clearly when he wrote that "Vladimir Putin is an evil man."[13]
- Military affairs? He is a war hero and Chairman of the Senate Committee on Armed Services.
- Leadership? By example, both as a warrior or prisoner in Vietnam, he led and took that leadership to the Senate floor as, for example, he fought his party leadership to cast the deciding vote on healthcare.[14]

The list goes on but the work is never ending. What does seem to be fading, however, is the role and understanding of patriotic honor in this era. Honor is a worthy goal, though it is losing favor. Honor prefers to show, not tell. His reticence about his military or political achievements speaks volumes.

George H.W. Bush and John McCain are cut from the same cloth. Both U.S. Navy war pilots, they fought for America in the air and on the seas, rose to political prominence, and saw the world with clear vision and a long view. In their estimation, America is great because America is good. Both men are now in their twilight.

McCain always felt the honorable pull and deep need to be near the men and women who fight our fights and defend our freedoms. Since 2003 and up until his brain cancer diagnosis, John McCain spent every Independence Day with American troops in Iraq or Afghanistan. Parts of these remote desert nations might, topographically, remind him of his adopted Arizona, a state he has represented as a congressman or senator since 1982.

---

13 McCain, "'Vladimir Putin Is an Evil Man.'"
14 O'Keefe, "The Night John McCain Killed the GOP's Health-Care Fight."

Arizona is landlocked but preparing for a sea change. Jeff Flake is dropping out of the Senate and John McCain is writing his last chapter. With them will disappear another sign of comity and civility.

Meghan McCain will be around a lot longer to remind us of her father's sacrifice and our country's debt to him. She'll also be around to remind President Trump that harsh rhetoric, humiliation, and disdain both for true patriots and America's partners alone will not revive the American Century, but can singularly work to divide our nation, destroy our reputation, and dissipate our global leadership. She, for one, is "never going to forgive" Donald Trump for his disrespectful attacks on her father.[15] Neither should the rest of us if his spirit and our nation are to endure.

Coda: John McCain passed into history on August 25, 2018. Trump did not attend the funeral.

PRESIDENTIAL CANDIDATES AND FOREIGN POLICY

Introduction

Those running for America's top leadership role are seldom asked questions about international affairs. The conventional wisdom among political consultants is that voters don't care about the rest of the world. A healthy democracy, however, demands an informed public.

Originally published: December 5, 2019

Presidential candidates are rarely judged on their knowledge of foreign policy. They're often governors or from states where engagement in world affairs is limited to the trade promotion of state products or produce. They're both salespeople and promoters of their states' workers, goods and environment, pitching their local and regional corporate interests in global markets.

Given these candidates' limited global exposure and experience, we instead rely on future presidents to be of strong character—leaders whose judgment we trust, with nimble minds and the ability to learn quickly and think critically. If the past is prologue, then we can expect future elected leaders—whether Democrats, Republicans or Independents—to lack real experience with national security, strategic foreign affairs, and global diplomacy.

In this presidential cycle alone, there are only two candidates with real world executive foreign policy experience, both having received intensive

---

15 Meghan McCain, "'Never Going to Forgive' Trump Attacks on Dad."

on-the-job training. One is the current incumbent. The other is Vice President Joe Biden.

Candidates can get some experience and exposure to foreign affairs by serving on congressional or Senate committees, like Armed Services (Warren and Gabbard) or Foreign Relations (Booker). However, executive experience in foreign affairs is available in only one place: The White House.

Given this reality, we need to focus on electing leaders who have two vitally important qualities: good instincts and good intentions. As an electorate, we need to judge these two things well. They are mutually important for successful American foreign policy.

Good instincts alone are not enough. Neither are good intentions. America deserves and should always demand a person who has a selfless abundance of both.

Successful gubernatorial candidates who advance to the presidency are accomplished and decisive individuals who need to deal with a whole set of new global challenges that they rarely come across in their statehouses in Tallahassee or Salem, Juneau or Austin. Senators and congress people who eventually get the Electoral College nod have had an even more narrowly obsessive focus on their district needs or state interests. They are rarely ready to be the world's most powerful person and will be tested by adversaries on Day One.

Paradoxically, the authority that presidents have is near total when it comes to the singular area where they also have the least experience and insight: foreign policy. Courting votes at county fairs while wolfing down corn dogs or stumping at fish frys is not the best training for trading views with Russian leaders who are former KGB officers or deciding to invade a nation based on dodgy intelligence.

Up until the Trump presidency, advisors played a crucial role in bridging the gap for the Commander-in-Chief, providing institutional memory and structural support to foreign policy decision-making. That went out the window immediately after the last inaugural speech focused on "American Carnage" and a POTUS who distrusts and denigrates the CIA and FBI.

Whether the next president follows precedent and brings with him or her a trustworthy team of foreign policy advisors is unclear. The following primer is for future leaders who will undoubtedly rely on their instincts and intentions. It's meant to help hone those instincts before being confronted with the modern equivalent to the Cuban missile crisis, where they're eyeball-to-eyeball with another powerful nation's leader and trying not to blink.

In fact, the lessons are simple. They're things that can be carried from the kiddy classroom to the Oval Office. Everything you need to know about foreign policy you should have learned in Kindergarten or Sunday school:

- **Love thy neighbor**: Look at a map and find Canada and Mexico. These two nations are our neighbors.
- **Honor thy family**: We're always stronger as a cohesive unit and need to respect each other, our beliefs, and strive to understand our differences at home. Like Honest Abe said, "A house divided against itself cannot stand."
- **Protect the vulnerable**: Stand up for your friends and those who can't defend themselves. Stick up for what's right.
- **Play well with others**: You can disagree, but you don't have to be disagreeable. Friends and allies aren't blood-sucking leeches. They sometimes take advantage of America's largesse, but can help achieve our mutual objectives. Be nice, but never cower. When threatened remember Teddy Roosevelt's advice: "Speak softly and carry a big stick."
- **Share**: There are secrets, of course, but not everything needs to go to a personal attorney or a classified server. Sometimes it's better to share.
- **Remember to nap**: Put down the cell phone, put away the social media, and remember to rest and reflect. Big decisions require clear thinking.

Of course, all this holds as true for foreign leaders who come up from the ranks of parliamentarians, military officers, party hacks, academics, comedians, street protesters, or revolutionaries. Foreign affairs is an executive's unique domain and there's no sure way to plan for it. So, dear candidates, be safe and practice playground etiquette and schoolhouse smarts.

    Coda: Rather than engaging in civil discourse on various topics that included foreign affairs, the first debate between Donald Trump and Joe Biden in the 2020 presidential race was marked by chaos. The incumbent frequently interrupted his opponent and exceeded his allotted time. The second scheduled event was canceled because Trump refused to participate in a virtual debate despite his COVID-19 diagnosis. In the third and final debate, the Commission on Presidential Debates imposed microphone controls to prevent either candidate from speaking out of turn.

A PERFECTLY GOOD JOB FOR A MAN—POLITICAL SPOUSE

Introduction

I should know. I'm one of them.

Originally published: December 27, 2019

Women on the world stage are increasingly playing lead roles. Whether New Zealand's Jacinda Ardern, the newest all-female Finnish government's cabinet led by 35-year-old Prime Minister Sanna Marin[16] or the record number of American women who ran and won in the 2018 midterm elections,[17] women are moving on up. Get used to it.

Increasingly, women have elbowed and edged their way into previously male-dominated representative chambers around the world in what were once more smoke-filled men's clubs than curtained lactation stations. As a result, the public, too, should wake up and prepare for a new category of men who will accompany and support these freshly elected women.

Happily, I am one of them. Last year, I became California's "Second Partner" after my wife, Eleni Kounalakis, was elected overwhelmingly the state's first female lieutenant governor.

A friend at a Washington, D.C., think tank now jokingly introduces me as Sacramento's Denis Thatcher, former British Prime Minister Margaret Thatcher's husband and the butt of many jokes.

What do my male cohorts and I share with Sir Thatcher? We all married strong, confident women who neither threaten us nor our masculinity. We don't compete with our spouses either for public affection or attention and we are in mutually respectful and loving relationships. We are supportive. We work as a team bringing up our kids and making financial decisions.

California's "First Partner" Jennifer Newsom argues in Glamour magazine that achieving gender equality requires burden sharing.[18] She says it's imperative that we "stop treating parenting as a mom's burden and a dad's adorable hobby." She's right, and I've done my best over the years. In fact, I enjoy it. So do the other guys I know married to political spouses.

First, we are confident, self-assured men. When I'm with my wife in a political context, my role is not to show others how great I am, it is to highlight her incredible strengths and attributes. To her credit, she always acknowledges me and my support, but knowing what my role is and how to manage it is really important. My colleagues and I try to remain immune to those who needle us about being obedient trailing spouses—their projections and insecurities rarely affect us.

Second, the political spouses I know have satisfying careers and work. Both men and women married to public servants need an avocation or profession outside politics to give them purpose, pride and strength. That can be a career,

---

16 Specia, "Who Is Sanna Marin, Finland's 34-Year-Old Prime Minister?"

17 Rankin and Burnett, "Women Keep up Wins in Trump-Era Political Surge."

18 Newsom, "It's Time to Stop Treating Parenting as a Mom's Burden and a Dad's Adorable Hobby."

taking care of a family, going to school, writing a book. Whatever it is, it must be important to the person and find respect and support at home. It's important to have a life. Thankfully, I have both a wife and a life.

Third, political spouses know that attaining and maintaining public office is a whole family effort. Spouses and their political partners, children and other family members need to understand the job and its personal and professional demands. Politics, as House Speaker Nancy Pelosi reminds her colleagues, "is not for the faint of heart."[19] It requires a strong family structure to weather the political barbs, false narratives, personal attacks and, in the case of women, their inordinate dismissal and devaluation.

If that last part sounds as if women are treated differently in politics and business, welcome to the real world. Unfortunately, women are socially limited in their response options when attacked for their competence, experience or overall qualification. A guy has a broad and forceful palette of societally acceptable responses and actions, but a woman generally is limited to a narrower range of approaches that keep her from being labeled a vicious cur, or, alternatively, weak and indecisive. I've seen it all first-hand.

My family learned how a public-service job works from the days when my wife was U.S. ambassador to Hungary, an old-world country with old-world attitudes. The U.S. State Department was no better, restricting me professionally to academia. No more journalism or jobs. Regardless, our time in Budapest became magical. I helped our two boys grow more socially and culturally aware, despite gaps in my parenting capabilities.

As my wife wrote in "Madam Ambassador," her 2015 memoir, "Markos was a great father, but a so-so mother."[20] But what I lacked in nurturing our sons, I made up for with adventure and intrigue. I grew closer to my boys and together we took three-man international treks with few provisions or clear destinations.

Today, the majority of political spouses around the world remain women. I am studying how they successfully manage their prominent roles while balancing their lives, careers and marriages.

The spousal equation has begun to change as more men join their publicly prominent wives, partners, and husbands while forging new roles and killing off dated and sexist traditions. Don't expect Clarke Gayford,[21] Paul Pelosi,[22] Markus Räikkönen[23] or me to bake cookies anytime soon.

---

19 Zernike, "Nancy Pelosi."

20 Kounalakis, "Madam Ambassador."

21 UNICEF, "Clarke Gayford on the Little Milestones as a Parent."

22 Kindred, "Who Is Speaker Nancy Pelosi's Husband Paul?"

23 Richardson, "A Politician for the Instagram Generation: Meet the World's Youngest Prime Minister Sanna Marin, 34."

Coda: On January 20, 2021, when his wife, Kamala D. Harris, was sworn in as Vice President of the United States, Doug Emhoff became the nation's first "second gentleman"—or "second dude" as he prefers.

RUN, MEGHAN, RUN!

Introduction

Meghan Markle is the disruptor America needs.

Originally published: January 16, 2020

Meghan Markle for president!

Markle is over the age of 35, a resident of the United States for at least 14 years and a natural-born citizen. That's more than we can say about either foreign-born John McCain[24] or Ted Cruz.[25]

President Obama's birth was also questioned, of course. His birth certificate was demanded by his successor, someone rumored to have been born on another planet.

Regardless, Markle meets all the requirements to run for president. She may be looking for a new gig now that she and her husband quit their day jobs in Sussex.

Republicans need look no further than Markle for a young, fresh, future-oriented politico who is going to appeal to their conservative monarchic fantasies, sense of pomp and need for celebrity candidates. Markle is a proven disruptor. Ask Queen Elizabeth II.

Naturally, Markle also happens to be a woman and a person of color. Nikki Haley, eat your heart out.

Bonus points: Markle is the former "Suits" star who can give the "Apprentice" reality lead a run for his money and his ratings. She's already been critical of the 45th president, calling him "divisive" and "misogynistic."[26]

Canada seems to be the current chosen destination for the near-abdicating, quasi-royal couple, but they should think this through a bit before snubbing the United States. After all, Canada is already run by a dynastic prince. Prime Minister Justin Trudeau is the scion of former PM Pierre Trudeau. Trudeau

---

24 Blake, "There Was a Very Real 'Birther' Debate about John McCain."
25 Costa and Rucker, "Trump Says Cruz's Canadian Birth Could Be 'Very Precarious' for GOP."
26 Kounalakis, "Trump Is Looking like a Royal Loser in the U.K."

ʟounger lacks a mean hockey slapshot that would endear him to a broader cross-section of Québécoise. But his snowboarding skills are rad.[27]

The point? Skip Canada.

Come back home, Meghan! Run. Make "Megxit" great again.[28]

If this all seems far-fetched, then imagine that the guy currently running Great Britain is a Big Apple-born mophead who won on promises to build a bigger moat and upgrade[29] British healthcare. Prime Minister Boris Johnson not only was born in New York's Upper East Side, he skipped out on his IRS debts.[30] America and Britain do indeed have a "special relationship."[31]

Meghan, if BoJo can hop the pond to run Britain by winning a stunning majority of parliamentary seats,[32] you can certainly come home and make a splash in D.C. You really have a shot. Your candidacy would also block any ideas Johnson might have about coming back to the United States to run for president himself. A pre-emptive strike, if you will.

Midwestern credentials are pretty key in any American electoral run—and you've got them! Your time at Northwestern University balances out your upbringing in the largest and most elector-rich state of the union—your native California is a good place to pick up convention delegates. Plus, you've got real, hands-on experience in foreign affairs, not only from your time working in a U.S. Embassy in Buenos Aires, but in your recent job representing Britain's national interests abroad.

Healthcare? You used to be on "General Hospital," for goodness sake! You may not have been a real nurse, but you did play one on TV.

The current Dealmaker-in-Chief would also have to contend with a competitor who understands that successful offers and payoffs are often hidden in briefcases. Your time on "Deal or No Deal" gave you on-stage experience in human greed and motivation.[33] You performed under pressure, with grace in the spotlight, and learned to anticipate interested parties' reactions to the artful reveal of the deal.

---

27 Hendricks, "Canada's New Prime Minister, Justin Trudeau, Is a Snowboarder."

28 Day, "Meghan Markle Steps out for First Time since 'Megxit' Announcement."

29 Mason and Proctor, "Boris Johnson Pledges to Prioritise NHS after Election Victory."

30 Croucher, "Britain's New Prime Minister Was a U.S. Citizen for Decades—until the IRS Caught up with Him."

31 Tisdall, "Love, Hate … Indifference."

32 Smith, "Boris Johnson's Conservatives Win Decisive Victory in Crucial Election."

33 CNBC, "Deal or No Deal."

Hey, we are not living in ordinary times. Reality is now often what the electorate perceives reality to be. If a guy calls himself a great feminist, dealmaker, billionaire and "the chosen one"[34] and there are enough people around him willing to validate that narrative, then that pseudo-reality takes on a life of its own. It becomes an acceptable and defensible truth for a large minority of people.[35]

Royalty is already a fairy tale. You have unmasked the more unsavory aspects of it without making it impossible to watch "The Crown" on Netflix.[36] Ultimately, you have the one quality that every voter in America, regardless of gender pronoun, says he or she or they want: Authenticity.

Bring your authenticity back to the United States triumphantly. Use your resources to challenge the Republican incumbent. You were not born for hereditary succession. Neither is your son, Archie.

You have always made your own breaks, followed your own heart, blazed your own path. Use whatever resources, goodwill and experience you have to run in 2020. The worst thing that can happen is that you lose. But only after you make your point, continue your advocacy for human rights and stand your ground.

Meghan Markle, you have the poise and prominence to make a difference. A royal flush is a winning hand in poker and politics.

Coda: Having been formally freed by Buckingham Palace from all further royal responsibilities, the former Duke and Duchess had carte blanche for an exclusive TV interview with America's kingmaker, Oprah Winfrey.

IS KIM DEAD?

Introduction

Rumors of any political leader's demise can have purpose and consequences especially in a dictatorship.

Originally published: April 24, 2020

Remember where you were when you first heard "Paul is dead?" Boomers easily recall the day their beloved mop-top Beatle was missing, declared dead and

---

34 Cillizza, "Yes, Donald Trump Really Believes He Is 'the Chosen One.'"

35 Griswold, "Franklin Graham's Uneasy Alliance with Donald Trump."

36 IMDB, "The Crown (TV Series 2016–)—IMDb."

gone. It was a traumatic moment for many who saw the signs, found the clues and believed the hype. Paul McCartney had clearly passed away.[37]

It was a déjà vu moment this week when international rumors took flight and premature reports came in declaring the near death of Kim Jong Un.[38] North Korea's dictatorial ruler and modern mop-top leader was said to have gone through a medical procedure that rendered him at death's door. As of this writing, these rumors have not been confirmed. What is confirmed is that Kim Jong Un is no Paul McCartney.

In fact, Kim more likely resembles Fidel Castro.

Castro was regularly rumored to be dead. It became a featured meme. James Cason, who later became Coral Gables mayor, served as head of the U.S. Interests Section in Havana between 2002 and 2005 and once said that Castro "must have died 20 times since the time I went to Cuba."[39]

Sensational rumors are started and popularly circulated for many reasons. Self-started rumors, for example, are often launched for publicity purposes, as with Morton Downey Jr. or Jussie Smollett.[40]

For the Beatles, McCartney's rumored death proved a sales coup. The public mourning for him led to headlines, premature obituaries and huge record sales. Americans scoured albums and pictures to find clues—a barefoot Paul walking across Abbey Road or a cryptic Sgt. Pepper's photo with Paul's back turned. Songs played backward supposedly revealed "Paul is dead!"

Except he wasn't.

Enter Kim Jong Un. Why on Earth would this rumor start?

Unlike rumors spread for self-promotion, those spread by others can be weaponized, meant to weaken a target or to test an adversary's resilience and reactions. Kim's leadership and hold on power are constantly being tested. This rumor-mongering may just be the latest installment.

It could be an attempt by the West—or Beijing—to smoke out Kim just to see where he is and if he's willing to come forth and dispel the rumor. This allows adversaries the ability to calculate if and how he responds to foreign pressures. Does he remain out of the public eye? Or does he order and preside

---

37 Sheffield, "Paul McCartney Is Dead: Bizarre Story of Music's Most Notorious Rumor."
38 Finnegan, "How Reports of Kim Jong Un's Health Spread and What They Tell Us about What Comes Next for North Korea."
39 Alvarez, "Rumor Fatigue Sets in at False Alarms of Castro's Death."
40 Harris, "The Jussie Smollett Scandal Recalls the Infamous (And Very Fake) Neo-Nazi Attack on Morton Downey Jr."

over a missile test launch? Each type of response gives the world a clue both to his personality and his grip on power.

The Kim's-dead rumor also provides grist for any surviving and well-hidden North Korean opposition—weak as it may be—to step up and act. Credible rumors of a weakened or dead leader provide pretext and cover for any potential Pyongyang political factions or military leaders to consider a coup d'état.

U.S. intelligence agencies and defense personnel look for troop movements, changed postures, heightened defense preparedness, broadcast messaging, chatter within diplomatic channels, runs on goods and altered daily worker patterns.

Weaponized rumors also are a psychological game played by adversarial nations to test the resilience and response mechanisms of other countries. In nations that have unreliable, usually state-run, news organizations, rumors carry greater weight and credibility than denials. People living in dictatorships rely heavily on rumors and whispered news for their information. No wonder—listening to the regularly broadcast staccatoed exhortations of North Korean TV newscasters[41] praising the "Dear Respected Comrade Leader"[42] is enough to turn a die-hard Socialist worker into a fearful rumor consumer.

At times, when a political leader is presumed critically ill or dead, there is an opportunity to take the temperature of a population toward its leadership. When the wishful thinking and targeted rumors of Castro's death were being floated, there were many who stood anxiously in the Miami and Havana wings, waiting to spring into action and overthrow his regime. In the end, however, Castro outlived most of his island-based opponents. Kim may be unhealthy—he may even actually be taking his last breaths—but at 36 years old, he is younger, seemingly physically fitter and likely to outlive President Donald Trump.

Soviet leaders were often dead and rumored to be alive. The only way the world was ever assured that people like Soviet General Secretary Leonid Brezhnev were really dead[43] was when Moscow's radio stations stopped their regularly scheduled programming and put Tchaikovsky's "Swan Lake" into heavy rotation.[44]

---

41 On Demand News, "North Korea TV Broadcast Says Missile Test Is Warning to South Korea."

42 Staff, "North Korea's Dear Respected Comrade Leader Gets a New Title."

43 Gwertzman, "Brezhnev Rumors Annoy U.S. Aides."

44 Eckel, "From Stalin to Karimov."

Authoritarian states may be uniquely vulnerable to weaponized rumors, but developed, democratic countries with free and independent media and radio stations are also susceptible. Thanks, Facebook![45]

Neither Sir Paul McCartney nor Kim Jong Un seem to be dead quite yet. But one person who definitely is long gone is the great American author and journalist Mark Twain. During his lifetime, Twain was also rumored to be dead. When contacted by an English reporter for the New York Journal, he famously responded, "The reports of my death are greatly exaggerated."[46]

Coda: The Trump presidency met its demise in January 2021. But as a member of Generation X and with no likely challenger, Kim's political longevity could exceed that of Joe Biden and possibly even Kamala Harris.

KAMALA HARRIS ON THE WORLD STAGE

Introduction

On November 3, 2020, Vice President Kamala Harris became the first female, first African American and first South Asian American elected to the nation's second-highest office.

Originally published: October 22, 2020

California is waiting to be welcomed back into the national conversation after four years of disrespect and neglect from the White House. In a Joe Biden–Kamala Harris administration, not only will California's favorite daughter bridge the widened—and widening—federal-state divide, she will team with a President Biden to rebuild America's powerful role in the world.

In fact, Harris could be key to building new strategic global relationships and alliances. (Disclosure: My wife and I are Harris' longtime friends.) While Biden shores up NATO, reaffirms multilateral agreements and Zoom calls his close foreign-leader friends, Harris will also bring unique foreign-policy advantage to the table.

As a globally aware Indo-American, with African-American roots, her heritage opens up possibilities to grow America's relationships in new corners.

---

45 Suciu, "Rumors and Hoaxes Continue to Spread Fast on Social Media, and Why It Is Unlikely to Stop."
46 Petsko, "Reports of Mark Twain's Quote about His Own Death Are Greatly Exaggerated."

Likely receptive nations to future Harris overtures include the ever-important "Quad" partners—in particular, India.[47]

The tightening Quad partnership is made up of four key Indo-Pacific democracies: the United States, Australia, Japan and India. They are working together regionally to defend democracy and free markets where China is a persistent and growing threat.

Presidential campaigns simplify candidate narratives, and the one around Harris focuses on her Black heritage and electoral appeal. Her Oakland-Berkeley upbringing is emphasized, as is her attending Howard University, where she joined the African-American Alpha Kappa Alpha sorority.[48]

There is less public attention and understanding of her potential to expand a dialogue and deepen relations with the world's largest democracy. India is where Harris spent summers as a child. Her mother, Shyamala Gopalan, came from an intellectually achieving and privileged class in Chennai and she came to the United States to work and study.

Harris' personal story means that she viscerally understands and appreciates India. Further, as a Californian, her formative experiences and orientation are westward toward the Pacific Ocean. The Indo-Pacific is home to Harris.

India will always be a reluctant international partner, however. A staunchly independent country, India has rabidly avoided alliances. Since the early days of the post-colonial nation's history, it has asserted its voice and power to lead other non-aligned nations and to navigate deftly between rival superpowers.

In 1983, I met with India's Prime Minister Indira Gandhi in Athens, Greece. We spoke about her nation's tight Soviet relationship and her unwillingness to criticize Moscow's 1979 Afghan invasion or the tragic shooting down of Korean Airliner, KAL 007.[49] She was unapologetic in her defense of the USSR and responded to my pointed questions by attacking American foreign policy. Gandhi was adept at actively using the Cold War's superpower rivalry to balance Soviet ambitions with American interests.

In the 21st century, Moscow no longer is as influential on the Asian subcontinent. Instead, the looming regional threat comes from China. India is actively looking for good, reliable friends to balance strategically against Beijing, especially following a recent border clash that killed Indian soldiers.[50] Further,

---

47 Raleigh News & Observer, "India, Australia, Japan, US 'Quad' Take on China Together."

48 Ellis, "Kamala Harris and Alpha Kappa Alpha."

49 Grier, "The Death of Korean Air Lines Flight 007."

50 BBC News, "India-China Clash: 20 Indian Troops Killed in Ladakh Fighting."

Beijing supports India's main adversary, Pakistan. As China pushes India closer to the Quad, Harris can help pull Delhi closer to America.

American foreign policy is not dictated by our ancestral affiliations, but they do make a difference for the parties seeking to be seen and heard. In the same way that Clinton and Kennedy and Reagan could be heard in Ireland because of their roots there, Harris has access to the cultural and ethnic links that associate her with her ancestral lands. Bill Clinton—who claimed Irish heritage[51]—partnered with legislative lion George Mitchell, a Lebanese Irish-American,[52] to cajole and wrangle warring parties to come to an unprecedented peace accord: the solidly lasting Good Friday Agreement.[53]

Harris, the mixed-race vice-presidential candidate can leverage her Caribbean roots and understanding to improve America's regional presence and leadership. Her time in French-speaking Canada as a high schooler will be a real advantage toward rebuilding the traditionally strong, but recently strained, Washington–Ottawa relationship.[54]

Her grandfather P.V. Gopalan was a high-ranking Indian civil servant in Zambia, where he managed a refugee influx from the south into what was once Northern Rhodesia.[55] Africa, Canada, the Caribbean basin and the Asian subcontinent are integral parts of Harris' person and personality.

A Biden–Harris administration would differentiate itself from the Trump administration in several ways. President Trump prefers one-on-one agreements with nations—bilateral agreements. However, he has had more luck breaking agreements than getting new ones signed and delivered.

Biden and Harris promise to restore respect for multilateral institutions and accords signed by previous presidents. They value global partnerships. The Biden–Harris team shows a strong preference toward building alliances, knowing that America can get more done and is more powerful when it works together with other nations.

What will certainly help America is that Kamala Harris has good friends and admirers not just here at home, but around the world.

---

51 Clinton House Museum, "How Irish Are the Clintons?"

52 de Bréadún, "George Mitchell."

53 Staff, "Bill Clinton Regards Good Friday Agreement as His Greatest Foreign Policy Achievement Says Aide."

54 Bilefsky, "In Canada, Kamala Harris, a Disco-Dancing Teenager, Yearned for Home."

55 Bengali and Mason, "The Progressive Indian Grandfather Who Inspired Kamala Harris."

Coda: Early in her first term, Vice President Harris had policy talks with several world leaders including French President Macron and Canadian Prime Minister Trudeau.

ADDRESSING CHINA'S GLOBAL GOALS

Introduction

China continually finds new battlegrounds to assert its power. One of the most vulnerable arenas for the United States is academia. Beijing's prying eyes may shut down US universities' academic freedoms.

Originally published: June 19, 2020

During the height of the 1950s Red Scare, when there were communists under every bed and spies in every closet, America saw threats to its national security everywhere. Justifiably, there were purges of those who really sought to sneak state secrets to the Soviets. War plans and bomb-making schematics were the most important of those confidential documents. Accusations abounded; not everyone was guilty.

Fast forward to 2020, and the new Red Scare is Beijing, not Moscow. The fear is that China's long reach is not only touching but grabbing some of America's dominant industries, institutions, plans and, of course, people. Scientists and researchers are in the crosshairs. Dr. Charles M. Lieber, the Harvard professor who recently was arrested by U.S. officials for allegedly sending research to China[56]— and lying about it to American authorities—pleaded not guilty on Tuesday.[57]

Lieber was Harvard's chair of Chemistry and Chemical Biology Department and received $15 million in U.S. government research grants. Good work, prestigious position. It turns out Lieber also was working with Wuhan University and a target of China's deeply suspect "Thousand Talents" program, which recruits and nurtures key individuals abroad to tap their expertise, networks, research and intellectual property.[58] Lieber was offered a lot of support by the U.S. government while, it's alleged, he was offering a lot to China. If Lieber is

---

56 "Harvard University Professor and Two Chinese Nationals Charged in Three Separate China Related Cases."

57 Court, "Harvard Professor Pleads Not Guilty to Lying to US Officials about His Ties to Wuhan University."

58 Leonard, "China's Thousand Talents Program Finally Gets the U.S.'s Attention."

found guilty, all universities may undergo greater government scrutiny, research oversight and likely even more restrictions on academic freedom.

America's National Security Strategy identifies this moment as one of great power rivalry between the United States and China (and Russia, too).[59] In an international political environment where Beijing and Moscow are seen as America's strategic competitors, any technological edge they gain is considered a national security threat. Those technological advantages exist in the private sector and at tech companies, of course, but basic R&D is mostly done in America's most open and vulnerable institutions: universities.

Weaknesses in the university system were revealed by the recent Varsity Blues admissions' scandal that ultimately caught actress Lori Loughlin in its net.[60] The scam helped get a large cohort into college via corrupt insiders who showed the moneyed how to make end runs around a relatively fair admissions system.

Like Loughlin, China, too, leverages the inherent weaknesses of America's open, trust-based higher education system, where intellectual freedom reigns supreme and shared research leads to career advancement and generates knowledge. China actively exploits this system, breaking into university-research structures that intertwine higher education with government, society, innovation and capital.

The Trump administration is trying to confront these actions by wholesale blocking some of China's students from sensitive American research labs.[61] Unfortunately, as the administration reverts to Red Scare tactics to prevent the theft of intellectual property and protect secrets on campuses, it is also feeding racist attitudes towards Asians. It should know better. America has a bad history of both anti-Asian racism and red-baiting.[62]

During the height of the 1950s Red Scare and Cold War with the Soviets, Sen. Joe McCarthy saw a communist "fifth column" everywhere he looked.[63] McCarthy's purges destroyed so many individuals and sullied so many more— from actors to playwrights, scientists to politicians. Everyone was suspect and, in McCarthy's estimation, everyone was guilty.[64]

59 Brookings, "Brookings Experts on Trump's National Security Strategy."

60 Sanchez, Morales, and Jorgensen, "Lori Loughlin and Mossimo Giannulli Plead Guilty in College Admissions Scam."

61 Cong, "US Ban on Chinese Students with Military Links Divides Experts on Impact."

62 Frail, "The Injustice of Japanese-American Internment Camps Resonates Strongly to This Day."

63 Powers, "The Nation: Fifth Column; The Evil That Lurks in the Enemy Within."

64 American Masters, "Arthur Miller ~ McCarthyism | American Masters | PBS."

Cold War hysteria led to broad purges but also, at times, to exposing real spies. Julius and Ethel Rosenberg were a New York couple accused of seeking atomic secrets to pass to the Soviets. They went to the gas chamber after a rushed trial tinged with anti-Semitism. A new HBO documentary claims Ethel Rosenberg was innocent,[65] but after the Soviet Union fell, KGB documents revealed the Rosenbergs' guilt.

America is now in the midst of myriad domestic crises and major geopolitical challenges. Societal tensions rise as Washington abdicates responsibility for a sane pandemic response, minimizes real economic fallout and justifies market volatility. The administration's tone-deaf response to America's inherent racial problems adds to domestic strife and opens up new global vulnerabilities. Domestic problems and international challenges set the stage for a politically threatened administration to exploit Americans' real fears. In this environment and during a presidential election year, it is raising the red flag about Red China.

The case against Lieber is about more than just a university professor trying to make a few extra bucks with a foreign side gig. Rather, it will set the tone for how paranoid America and the world are about China's intentions. Does Beijing seek global domination or a peaceful rise? What is China willing to do to achieve this goal? There will be no simple answers.

While Lieber claims his innocence, the trial and popular jury are still out on the bigger question of China's global challenge.

Coda: On January 14, 2021, federal agents arrested M.I.T. Professor Gang Chen and charged him with grant fraud, alleging that he failed to disclose his work for the People's Republic of China to the U.S. Energy Department.[66]

CHINA, RUSSIA NOT PUTTING PLANS TO EXPLOIT ANTARCTICA ON ICE

Introduction

The continent surrounding Earth's South Pole is more than a frozen wasteland. Antarctica has been free from disease and armed conflict. But how will nations treat this continent when the treaty guaranteeing its freedom from unilateral conquest expires?

Originally published: July 10, 2020

---

65 Meeropol, "Bully. Coward. Victim. The Story of Roy Cohn."
66 Barry, "A Scientist Is Arrested, and Academics Push Back."

New York continues to slowly open up after being the nation's hottest of COVID-19 hot spots while the incidence in Brazil spikes, and cases explode in Latin America and South Asia.

There is one place, however, that has been far from infections and safe from the need for serology testing: Antarctica.[67] It's not exactly a holiday destination, but this continent is sparsely inhabited, plays an important global research role and, so far, is safe from nearly every disease known to man. If the hot zone is where disease can break out, the frozen zone of the South Pole is where human disease rarely ventures.

Antarctica, however, also happens to be the least hospitable place on Earth. That doesn't mean that adventurers, researchers and nations stay away. In fact, it is an attractive continent for explorers who care to trek on pristine ice.[68] It's also a perfect laboratory for investigating geologic history, climate change and whales,[69] and for filming cute movies about penguins.[70]

Most important, however, is that it doesn't belong to any one nation. Like outer space, Antarctica does not fall under the jurisdiction of any one country or fly one flag. It is both no one's and everyone's. COVID-19 has been kept off the continent through a joint decision by several nations.[71]

Antarctica is not only free of disease and exploitation of its resources, it is also a fully non-nuclear and demilitarized zone. In fact, there's a 1958 international treaty that guarantees that, "Antarctica shall be used for peaceful purposes only. There shall be prohibited... the establishment of military bases and fortifications, as well as the testing of any type of weapons."[72] The treaty remains in force until 2048. And that is when all hell could break loose.

Treaties sometimes are not worth the paper on which they are written. China signed a 1997 treaty with the United Kingdom to keep Hong Kong free in a one country-two systems status quo until 2047. That treaty just got crushed last week.[73]

---

67 Hardingham, "What It's like to Live in Antarctica during the Pandemic."
68 Soergel, "Polar Adventurer Marks 100th Birthday, 81 Years after His First Expedition to Antarctica."
69 Pyenson, "Spying on Whales."
70 Movieclips, *March of the Penguins Official Trailer #1 - (2005) HD*.
71 BBC News, "Coronavirus: New Zealand Cuts Research in Antarctica to Keep It Virus Free."
72 "The Antarctic Treaty."
73 James, "UK Says China's Security Law Is Serious Violation of Hong Kong Treaty."

Similarly, China and Russia are eying current Antarctic treaty to evaluate the world's willingness to enforce it. Beijing and Moscow are also preparing to build cultural symbols, send personnel, deploy dual-use military hardware and plop down oil and gas extraction rigs on the day the Antarctic treaty lapses. This is a real cause for concern.

Antarctica may look barren, but it is resource rich. Under all that ice lie precious ores and minerals, from gold to uranium. The Ross Sea that abuts Antarctica and has massive untapped energy reserves, according to a U.S. Geological Survey.[74]

The most obvious, plentiful and valuable resource in Antarctica is—wait for it—ice! About 70% of the world's fresh and potable water is trapped in Antarctic ice.[75] Getting to all those valuable resources is the challenge, of course. But time and technology march on, and what seems foreboding today may be easy peasy tomorrow.

Can't the world's major powers just get along, collaborate on shared interests and protect the global commons? If the Antarctic's polar opposite— the Arctic—is any indication, then the answer is *nyet*.

Near the North Pole, the fight over the Arctic's sea lanes, resources and strategic military basing already have heated up.[76] As global warming melts down and opens up a once frozen north, China covets the prospect that a northern sea channel can alter trade routes and dramatically cut shipping times from its ports to Western markets.[77]

Russia, for its part, is way ahead on controlling those sea channels. Moscow's formidable collection of icebreaker navy ships means that it has the technical ability to cut swaths of ice, open lanes, patrol, pilot and free ships.[78] The United States and other Arctic Council nations object to Russia's asserting greater control there, but its presence and plans are bolstered by military might.[79]

From a commercial perspective, the Arctic's climate change story has a silver lining via the opening of new trade routes and allowing access for resource exploitation. There is, however, also a significant downside to warmer climes. Right now, Siberia is on fire, a raging inferno releasing tons of carbon dioxide and on track

---

74 Kingston, *The Undiscovered Oil and Gas of Antarctica*.

75 Cool Australia, "Antarctica."

76 Chorush, "'Prepared to Go Fully Kinetic': How U.S. Leaders Conceptualize China's Threat to Arctic Security."

77 Kounalakis, "Warm Water, Cold Reality, New Frontier for Exploiting Resources."

78 Hambling, "U.S. Seeks Armed Nuclear Icebreakers for Arctic Show of Force."

79 The Arctic Council, "Arctic Council."

to be the largest Arctic fire on record.[80] An unprecedented heatwave has fueled this fire and brought Siberian temperatures to over 100 degrees Fahrenheit.[81] Further, increased Russian commercial activity led to a massive Arctic fuel spill that has an environmental watchdog seeking almost $3 billion in damages.[82]

As in the Arctic, Russia and China would like to lay claim to Antarctica's continental resources as soon as possible to make sure they get and retain access, rights, control and ownership early. Claims are on hold for now, but when Antarctica does open up and nations rush to cash in, is there any doubt that some of the ills that are already plaguing the north will eventually migrate south?

Coda: In December 2020, 36 people at Chile's Antarctic research station tested positive for COVID-19.

WILL BELARUS FINALLY RID ITSELF OF EUROPE'S LAST DICTATOR?

Introduction

In the twentieth century, the Soviet Union had Lenin and Stalin. There was Italy's Mussolini, Franco of Spain, and Tito of Yugoslavia. In fact, there were plenty of European dictators in the twentieth century ... but only one remained: Lukashenko.

Originally published: July 24, 2020

All-star authoritarians are a ruble a dozen in Russia these days. President Vladimir Putin leads the pack, of course, but there are plenty of local and regional tough guys running their neighborhoods and governments like mob bosses. Many of them are direct offshoots of Putin's United Russia party, and some are even worse. Ultra-nationalists in the far east of the country are protesting their inability to run their own government and local syndicates, complaining that Moscow insists on central control over the means of corruption.[83]

Russia is not the only former Soviet state that is stuck with megalomaniacal overlords. Next door and related, Belarus—the country also known as White Russia—is a paragon of parasitic politics. Run by the same guy since 1994,

---

80 Ferreira, "The Arctic Is on Fire Again, and It's Even Worse This Time."

81 Borunda, "What a 100-Degree Day in Siberia, above the Arctic Circle, Really Means."

82 "Russian Watchdog Seeks Nearly $3B in Damages over Arctic Fuel Spill in Siberia."

83 Radio Free Europe, "Thousands in Khabarovsk Protest Arrest of Russian Governor."

Belarus is heading toward "elections" next month where the main opposition candidates have been disqualified or arrested.[84]

A vlogger, a banker and a diplomat were all running against incumbent President Alexander Lukashenko and have dubiously found their way into the political penalty box, or jail. In their stead, their spouses have stepped in to strut their candidacies and keep the erstwhile candidates' messages alive. Surprisingly, there is an early anti-establishment groundswell coalescing around the candidacy of Svetlana Tikhanovskaya, the wife of popular Belarus online journalist vlogger Sergei Tikhanovsky.[85] She been dismissed by Lukashenko, who said the demanding presidential pressures of governing would cause Svetlana to "collapse, poor thing."[86]

Spoiler alert: My prediction is that Lukashenko, a former Soviet collective chicken-farm boss, will triumph with a landslide victory with only a smattering of opposition ballots. If my cynical prediction is right, and the electoral fix is in, then Lukashenko will be heading into his sixth consecutive term as president.

Should he win, Lukashenko's longevity in office will be typical of many ex-Soviet states. Kazakhstan's President Nursultan Nazarbayev, who recently tested positive for COVID-19, kept power from 1990 until last year.[87] Tajikistan's kleptocratic ruler, President Emomali Rahmon, has been in office since 1994, with his latest term running out in 2021, when his son is set up to take over the reins.[88]

Russia and Belarus, too, have had deeply predictable electoral outcomes with incumbents holding their executive titles for multiple terms and a head-spinning number of years. Putin may ultimately break all ruling records. He recently managed to get a Russian national referendum passed that will allow him to remain president until 2036.[89]

Lukashenko has been in office uninterruptedly over the past 26 years. His success rides on his nationalist rhetoric and his oversized persona.[90] He's a burly

---

84 "Belarus Election."

85 "Страна Для Жизни—YouTube."

86 Makhovsky, "Dismissed as 'Poor Things', Three Women Try to Unseat Male President of Belarus."

87 Putz, "Kazakhstan's First President Nursultan Nazarbayev Tests Positive for COVID-19."

88 Staff, "Tajikistan Leader's Son Named Senate Speaker."

89 Neuman, "Referendum in Russia Passes, Allowing Putin to Remain President Until 2036."

90 McKay, "Putin Could Make Move to Absorb Belarus, Europe's 'Last Dictatorship,' Experts Say."

farmer and hockey fan with rough, masculine charisma. Corrupt elections and laws making it illegal to insult him keep him in office, too.

Other than nationalist messages and manufactured pride, Lukashenko has had financial good fortune thanks to Russia. Moscow essentially subsidizes his regime with cheap oil,[91] which keeps inefficient heavy industry chugging and has dramatically lowered the country's poverty rate.[92] Russia's oil exports buy off Belarus to guarantee Minsk and Lukashenko stay in Moscow's orbit. Those subsidies and the outdated state manufacturing plants they support come to an end in 2025.

Successfully feeding his citizenry and delivering a fervent nationalist message to sate proud masses who feed off flag-waving is a winning formula.[93] So is building a constellation of Lukashenko-sponsored hockey rinks around the countryside—the proven "bread and circuses" Roman formula for maintaining public support.

Sometimes Lukashenko needs to confront brother Russia to turn-up the nationalist heat, arguing that Russia wants to absorb Belarus the way it occupies Crimea. When necessary, he tweaks Putin and raises the specter of Russian imperial designs, arguing that Belarus remains a fiercely independent country stuck between East and West. Lukashenko rejects European overtures for stronger ties while also showing he's not Putin's poodle.[94]

Lukashenko tamps down domestic dissent with broad accusations against rivals. His anti-corruption campaign[95] ensnares nearly every opponent. Further, his contrived world is full of enemies and threats—both foreign and domestic, real and imagined. Lukashenko runs a full-court-press propaganda machine and police state that continue to reflexively scare a nation into submission.

Despite financial stability, a monopoly on violence and control of the ballot box, the upcoming election still could have been a real contest. COVID-19 has fed rising discontent with "Europe's last dictator."[96] Like other populist leaders around the world, he dismissed the pandemic. According to Lukashenko, Belarusians' physical constitution required only that citizens drink vodka, visit

---

91 Champion and Kudrytski, "Belarus's Soviet Economy Has Worked Better Than You Think."

92 World Bank, "Poverty Reduction in Belarus."

93 BBC Monitoring, "'It's Better to Be a Dictator than Gay'—Who Is Alexander Lukashenko?"

94 Isachenkov, "Belarus' Leader Warns Russia against Forceful Merger."

95 Makhovsky, "Belarus President Accuses Election Rival of Corruption after Raid."

96 Light, "How Poor Handling of Covid-19 Has Caused Uproar in Belarus."

saunas and go for tractor rides to fortify their already super-tough immune systems.[97]

Vodka does not have the life-saving medical outcomes of remdesivir, but it does have a powerful fogging effect on rational decision-making.[98] Whether this helps Lukashenko at the ballot box will be revealed on Aug. 9.

Regardless, Belarusians will certainly wake-up the next day with a political hangover.

Coda: Lukashenko's 2020 re-election was widely seen as fraudulent. It prompted massive protests across Belarus that continued into 2021. Many governments around the world refused to recognize the results. The dictator responded by arresting journalists who covered the unrest.

THE WORLD IGNORED AMERICA UNDER TRUMP

Introduction

As Americans were distracted by Trump's debate theatrics, the world continued to turn. Political candidates can't forget that international tensions come home to roost.

Originally published: October 1, 2020

The presidential debate Tuesday devolved into a political food fight, where assaulting speech became a verbal pie in the public's face. Lost in the noise was any calm substance or serious questions about foreign policy.

The 21st century debate now produces more heat than light. These exercises allow candidates to target a sliver of Americans in a handful of states who somehow remain undecided. More important, they aim to excite and motivate the majority of already decided voters to go mark their ballots.

Debates are not ideological jousts about America's role in the world. They are mostly focused on domestic challenges. The new twist in 2020? An incumbent president unbecomingly used the platform to launch wild attacks on his opponent instead of telling, for example, Russia's Vladimir Putin to stuff it.[99]

Foreign policy is increasingly important to everyday life in the United States. Most Americans understandably are more concerned right now with fighting

---

97 Meredith, "Belarus' President Dismisses Coronavirus Risk, Encourages Citizens to Drink Vodka and Visit Saunas."

98 Kounalakis, "The U.S. Has Snatched up Global Supplies of Remdesivir."

99 Staff, "Donald Trump Steps Up Wild Attacks on Joe Biden as First Debate Looms."

an invisible virus, getting their kids to school and holding on to jobs. But what happens in Wuhan does not stay in Wuhan.[100] Foreign policy matters.

Americans should, however, take a breath—through their masks—and look through their fogged-up glasses at the various hot spots around the globe.[101] They may end up feeling safer locked up at home, socially distant from troubles near and far.

Latin America provides plenty of fodder, and the usual suspects are hard at work making things tough for their neighbors and their own populations. Cuba[102] and Nicaragua[103] struggle to balance their own shortages and others' sanctions to deliver a modicum of services and security. The Castro successors in Havana[104] and the endless Ortega family business in Nicaragua govern with an iron fist.[105] Political change threatens their power, and they avoid it at all costs.

Scoot down the map a bit to Venezuela to see an ongoing disaster—a Caracas run further into the ground by Nicolás Maduro and his ruling clique.[106] Nothing that has been done during the past four years has moved the leadership in Cuba, Nicaragua or Venezuela closer to the exit door. In fact, the policies of the recent past have further entrenched these dictatorial regimes.

In fact, American actions and rhetoric have made it easier for Havana, Managua and Caracas to jail opposition leaders and drive its victimized citizens into neighboring countries. To add insult to injury, Donald Trump was secretly establishing Havana business ties while courting Cuban Americans with tough anti-Cuba talk, el Nuevo Herald just revealed.[107]

The problems go beyond Latin America. People are on the move from Syria and Libya, desperate humans trying their hardest to escape civil wars. In both countries, civilians are Russian and Turkish pawns caught in punishing proxy wars.

---

100 Vazquez, "Calling COVID-19 the 'Wuhan Virus' or 'China Virus' Is Inaccurate and Xenophobic."

101 Whalen and Kounalakis, "Area 45."

102 Augustin and Robles, "Cuba's Economy Was Hurting. The Pandemic Brought a Food Crisis."

103 Amnesty International, "Nicaragua: Ortega Government Appears to Be Preparing for a New Phase of Repression | Amnesty International."

104 Pedreira, "New Cuban Leadership Reflects a Rebranding of Castro Dictatorship—UPI.Com."

105 Kounalakis, "Nicaragua's 'House of Cards' Stars Another Corrupt and Powerful Couple."

106 Kounalakis, "Florida Could Punish Trump for Failed Latin America Policy."

107 "Donald Trump Registered His Trademark in Cuba."

And now, Armenia and Azerbaijan are waging a hot war. High-tech drones drop out of the sky to smoke dug-in tanks and artillery. Previously unthinkable battles have become phantasmagorical viral videos.[108] This battle, too, is growing into an indirect Russia–Turkey conflict. Ankara sides with the Azeris while Moscow joins its former Soviet sister state, Armenia. France might jump in, too.[109]

The mother of all potential foreign conflicts, however, continues to brew in one of the most volatile regions on Earth—between India and Pakistan.[110] These neighbors always seem on the threshold of open conflict. India and Pakistan have opposing claims of historic autonomy in Kashmir and Jammu.[111] There is also a social, cultural and geopolitical reality that animates these tensions.

Hindu nationalism increasingly drives India's domestic politics, while Pakistan flexes its Muslim muscle and tightens its China ties. With Beijing in the mix, China is both girding and goading Pakistan to rev up its revulsion toward India, especially following China's recent Himalayan border skirmish with the Indian military.[112] It didn't turn out well for either of the two most populous nations on Earth. There was no satisfactory resolution to the military deaths or the dispute along the two nations' Line of Actual Control. Tensions could flare again between nuclear-armed China, India and Pakistan. The good news? Some political theorists believe possessing nukes prevents nations from using them on each other.[113]

Elsewhere, Russia is dallying with Belarus' embattled President Alexander Lukashenko, with Moscow worrying a nearby domino could fall. Turkey continues to troll Greece by testing Athens's resolve and America's support in the Eastern Mediterranean.

Around the world, any cross-border agitation could blow up. U.S. presidential elections are always an opportune moment for foreign trouble-making and inflamed tensions. Elections are exciting, but they are also distracting.

---

108 Sleuth Media, *Video Compilation.*

109 Hovhannisyan and Bagirova, "France and Turkey at Odds as Karabakh Fighting Divides NATO Allies."

110 Osborne, "World War 3 News: Why Nuclear-Armed Pakistan 'Poses Bigger Threat to India than China,'" 3.

111 *The New Indian Express,* "Jammu and Kashmir: Pakistan Violates Ceasefire along LoC in Krishna Ghati Sector."

112 Choudhury, "India China Border Clash: Small Mistakes Can Be Costly, Former NSA Says."

113 Sagan, "The Spread of Nuclear Weapons."

That there was no foreign-policy discussion in the first presidential debate is one sign that America is no longer watching the shop.

Coda: Trump's tactics didn't work: Americans rejected his shenanigans and voted for change. The Biden administration is pursuing a stated policy of diplomatic re-engagement.

AFTERWORD

THE CHALLENGE TO FREEDOM[1]

Ideas are dangerous things. Allow them to spread uncontrollably and they can infect the thinking and behavior of a people. Some ideas can lead to revolutionary acts, as with democracy and the concept that power can accrue to the people instead of deities or despots.

Ideas allow us to question our beliefs, our leaders and our societies. The viral spread of these ideas has been accelerated over the millennia, making an exponential leap in the early 15th century with the invention of the printing press. What Gutenberg's machine did to spread ideas challenging religious hierarchy and ideology of the day was revolutionary and catalyzed the Reformation.

Enter the 21st century. We are now at a point in human history where the spread of ideas is instantaneous, global and ubiquitous. Nearly 600 years after the invention of the printing press, we are in an information environment that envelops us in words, images and sounds that force us to reflect upon and question every aspect of our human condition. Data swirls about us to challenge every form of authority.

Democratic systems and societies are best able to adapt to this changing environment. Those who are less democratic and wish to preserve a power structure try to limit or stop ideas from spreading. They often do this by killing the message, disrupting the Internet or practicing broad censorship.

More perniciously, dictators and theocrats often find ways to intimidate or kill the messenger.

The goal is to achieve what is effectively unattainable today—information sovereignty. What this means is the ability of a nation or a leader to have total control over both the message and the messenger. In a system of information sovereignty, Google, Facebook and Twitter are subversive tools. Foreign correspondents are agents of change. And humor magazines highlight hypocrisy.

---

1 Originally published on January 8, 2015.

anted, not all ideas are worthy or able to ignite the creative and humane imagination in effective or positive ways. Many ideas are stupid. Unfortunately, even stupid ideas are able to find their way into the crevices of a craven cranium.

But faith in the human character and in the critical and adaptive capacity of a community gives us the belief that the answer to bad speech or deleterious ideologies is more speech, not less. That is why allowing all ideas—a tsunami of ideas—to infest our consciousness is important, so that each individual's critical capacities are developed and allowed to discern the difference between the inane and something more worthy.

Kim Jong Un may not have figured out the ridiculous and unthreatening nature of a movie like *The Interview*. Islamic militants have an equally hard time figuring out what is more blasphemous: a crass cartoon depiction of a world religion's prophet, or the perverted use of his teachings to kill and destroy on a mass scale.

The 12 apostles of irreverent humor at the Paris-based magazine *Charlie Hebdo* are now dead, and the only ones who remain laughing are the murderous miscreants who claim blind faith in Mohammed.

The Paris attack on free speech and open societies is a perverse warning to our way of life, a threat to our civil liberties and a provocation of our leaders. We can survive both the assault and the threat by doubling down on our institutions of free speech and by following the 1939 British dictum that has now become part of popular culture: "Keep Calm and Carry On."

Our leaders need to keep a cool head, too, because the emotional reactions that such attacks are intended to engender are tempting and hard to fight. Resolve and resilience should outweigh revenge and retribution.

Bring the culpable individuals to justice, but do not overreact by waging a reckless or wanton war in a far-off land without forethought to the end game or an exit strategy. Failing to do so would be playing into the hands of those forces that are taunting us. Lowering our societal goals to get involved in a brawl would cheapen the West's superior ideas of *liberté, égalité, fraternité*.

ACKNOWLEDGMENTS

Freedom is not free and the required support for any writing project, including this one, is not automatic and cannot be taken for granted. Friends, family, and colleagues all played an active role in helping to nurture and develop this work. They have done so over many years, in varied ways and in disparate contexts. What has been a constant, however, is my recognition and gratitude for their moral and material support. Thank you to all those who are listed below and to the few who either asked that I keep them anonymous or whom I inadvertently left off this page of personal appreciation.

HOOVER INSTITUTION

Dave Brady, David Berkey, Chris Dauer, Larry Diamond, Mike McFaul, Liz Economy, Jim Mattis, Jim Ellis, George P. Shultz, Jim Timbie, John Taylor, John Cogan, Michael Boskin, David Fedor, Abe Sofaer, Lucy Shapiro, Tom Stephenson, Joe Felter, James Goodby, Arye Carmon, Gary Roughead, Adele Hayutin, Glenn Tiffert, Condoleezza Rice, Eric Wakin, Jim Hoagland, H.R. McMaster, Misha Auslin, Amy Zegart, Niall Ferguson, Dan Kessler, Denise Elson, Shana Farley, Don Meyer, Kharis Templeman, Kori Schake, Victor Davis Hanson, Barbara Arellano, Mandy MacCalla, Jacquelyn Johnstone, Jeff Marschner, and Kathy Campitelli.

CENTRAL EUROPEAN UNIVERSITY

Erin Jenne, Matteo Fumagalli, Ellen Hume, Eva Bognar, Kate Coyer, Fruszi Kacsko, Phil Howard, John Shattuck, Ellen Hume, Marius Dragomir, Amy Brouillette, Judit Szakacs, Istvan Rev, Michael Ignatieff, and George Soros.

WASHINGTON MONTHLY

Matt Cooper, Paul Glastris, Kukula Glastris, Eric Cortellessa, Jim Fallows, Nick Lemann, Nick Confessore, Nick Thompson, Ben Wallace-Wells, Josh Green, Christina Larson, Amy Sullivan, Diane Strauss, Claire & Carl Iseli, Kevin Drum, Josh Marshall, Stephanie Mencimer, Bill Moyers, and Charlie Peters.

JOURNALISM COLLEAGUES

Rod Nordland, Pia Hinckle, Kristin Roberts, Dan Morain, Foon Rhee, Gary Reed, Shawn Hubler, Luisa Yanez, Colleen Nelson, Hannah Bloch, Doug Menuez, Drew Banks, Pascal Privat, Karen Nazor, Don Shanor, Judith Crist, Geoff Cowan, Murray Fromson, Ed Reingold, Rachael Myers Lowe, George Wood, Glenn Ruffenach, Willow Bay, Jana Stefačkova, Tim Grieve, and Bernard Ohanian.

The McClatchy organization and, in particular, The Sacramento Bee and Miami Herald, gave me the popular platform and the developed distribution network to get my work read. The print and digital weekly work created an active and interactive feedback loop of comments that allowed me to build a new vocabulary and greater respect for an intrinsically engaged, vastly diverse, and often very vocal readership.

Over the course of my professional career, I have served and continue to serve on the advisory or governing boards of the following organizations. The extraordinary people with whom I've shared board duties continue to inform my ever-broadening perspective on democratic governance and individual freedom: The Annenberg Foundation Trust at Sunnylands, The Asia Foundation, Internews, The World Affairs Council of Northern California, Common Cause, Center for National Policy, Fulbright Foreign Scholarship Board, USC's Center on Public Diplomacy, Georgetown College, Columbia Graduate School of Journalism, Wilson Center, Western Policy Center, and the Annenberg School of Journalism and Communication at USC.

ANTHEM PRESS

Kudos and thanks go to Megan Greiving and her team for shepherding through this project. I extend that gratitude to the peer reviewers—who remain anonymous to me—for their invaluable insights and comments.

SPECIAL THANKS

Peter Laufer for the introduction to Anthem Press and so much more. Thank you for your professional counsel and ongoing encouragement and collaboration.

Terry Phillips for editorial support during the original column writing, project managing this book, and his good friendship and support during our time together through wars and revolutions from Eastern Europe to the USSR to Afghanistan. Thank you for everything, *Koumbare*.

Josh Ober for expanding my understanding of the roots of Athenian democracy and its lessons for the contemporary world. Our family friend, Mike McFaul, remains in the global fight for democracy and is a model professor, public intellectual, and policy practitioner. Ober, McFaul, and Larry Diamond (known around our household as the "doctor of democracy"), are all three scholars who have devoted a lifetime of inquiry and advocacy to teach and promote the blessings of democratic governance.

FRIENDS AND FAMILY

There are two sustaining categories of people who make anything possible. Friends and family. In the friend category, I want to thank Mark Bauman, Peter Kaufman, David Streitfeld, Amanda Jones, Susan Burks, Christine Pelosi, Heidi Bradner, Randy Fry, Vicki Liviakis, Bill Antholis, Alexi Papahelas, Marguerite Holloway, Achileas and Constantza, Kosti and Rena, and Christo & Marina Constantakopoulos, Cleon and Efi Papadopoulos, Sofia Kolokotronis, Jim McKee, Barney Jones, David Carrillo, Susanne Biedenkopf-Kuerten, Jeff Levine, David Lane, Kathleen Doherty, Jeff Phillips, Christian Catomeris, Ann Simmons, Tom Ginsberg, Jojo Schroeder, George Marcus, Rick Belluzzo, Orville Schell, Mary Kay Magistad, Steve and Vicki Mavromihalis, Ernest J. Wilson III, and Jay Wang.

On the family side of the equation sit firmly my father-in-law Angelo K. Tsakopoulos and his family as well as my sister, Diane Kounalakis and her family. I deeply appreciate their love, devotion, and support.

This book, however, is dedicated to my immediate family, for whom I have unbounded gratitude, love and respect: Neo, Eon, and my wife, California Lt. Governor Eleni Kounalakis. You are the most important people in my life. You make everything both possible and enjoyable. Thank you.

San Francisco
May 2021

BIBLIOGRAPHY

"1951 Convention Relating to the Status of Refugees." Accessed February 23, 2021. https://www.unhcr.org/afr/3b73b0d63.pdf.

ABC News. "As Virus Infections Dwindle, Hong Kong Protests Gain Steam." ABC News. Accessed February 23, 2021. https://abcnews.go.com/International/wireStory/virus-infections-dwindle-hong-kong-protests-gain-steam-70400711.

Acton Institute. "Lord Acton Quote Archive." Accessed February 23, 2021. https://www.acton.org/research/lord-acton-quote-archive.

Adalian, Rouben Paul. "Ambassador Henry Morgenthau, Sr., and the Armenian Genocide." Armenian National Institute. Accessed February 22, 2021. https://www.armenian-genocide.org/morgenthau.html.

Adam, Nina, and Andrea Thomas. "U.S. Criticizes Germany's Export-Led Policies." *Wall Street Journal*, January 8, 2014. https://www.wsj.com/articles/SB10001424052702303393804579307722825726640.

AFAR. "Castle of Mytilene." AFAR, May 27, 2015. https://www.afar.com/places/castle-of-mytilene-mitilini.

AFP and SCMP. "Great Firewall 'upgrade' Hits Internet Users as China Prepares Crackdown." *South China Morning Post*, December 21, 2012. https://www.scmp.com/news/china/article/1109755/great-firewall-upgrade-hits-internet-users-china-prepares-crackdown.

"AG Barr Letter to Hon. Priti Patel." Office of the Attorney General, August 18, 2020. Accessed January 29, 2021. https://www.govexec.com/media/ag_barr_letter-aug-2020.pdf.

Agence France-Presse. "Anti-Putin Activist Ruslan Shaveddinov 'Forcibly Conscripted' and Sent to Arctic." *Guardian*, December 26, 2019. http://www.theguardian.com/world/2019/dec/26/anti-putin-activist-ruslan-shaveddinov-forcibly-conscripted-and-sent-to-arctic.

———. "Jamal Khashoggi Murder: Saudi Court Overturns Five Death Sentences." *Guardian*, September 7, 2020. http://www.theguardian.com/world/2020/sep/07/jamal-khashoggi-saudi-court-overturns-five-death-sentences.

Ahmed, Hamid Ould. "Algeria Bans Street Marches due to Virus; Some Protesters Unswayed." Reuters, March 17, 2020. https://www.reuters.com/article/us-health-coronavirus-algeria-protests-idUSKBN2143UH.

"Al Qaeda Associates Charged in Attack on USS Cole, Attempted Attack on Another U.S. Naval Vessel." Department of Justice. Accessed February 23, 2021. https://www.justice.gov/archive/opa/pr/2003/May/03_crm_298.htm.

All about History. "The Dangers of Royal Inbreeding." History Answers. Accessed February 24, 2021. http://www.historyanswers.co.uk/kings-queens/the-dangers-of-royal-inbreeding/.

———. "Spanish Flu: The Deadliest Pandemic in History." Livescience. Accessed February 25, 2021. https://www.livescience.com/spanish-flu.html.

Alvarez, Lizette. "Rumor Fatigue Sets in at False Alarms of Castro's Death." *New York Times*, January 9, 2015. https://www.nytimes.com/2015/01/10/us/rumor-fatigue-sets-in-at-false-alarms-of-fidel-castros-death.html.

American Civil Liberties Union. "Living with the Muslim Ban." ACLU. Accessed February 23, 2021. https://www.aclu.org/issues/immigrants-rights/living-muslim-ban.

American Masters. "McCarthy: Power Feeds on Fear," August 23, 2006. https://www.pbs.org/wnet/americanmasters/arthur-miller-mccarthyism/484/.

Amnesty International. "Death Penalty in 2019: Facts and Figures." Accessed February 23, 2021. https://www.amnesty.org/en/latest/news/2020/04/death-penalty-in-2019-facts-and-figures/.

———. "Nicaragua: Ortega Government Appears to Be Preparing for a New Phase of Repression." Accessed February 25, 2021. https://www.amnesty.org/en/latest/news/2020/09/nicaragua-gobierno-pareciera-preparar-nueva-fase-represion/.

ANCA. "Over 100 U.S. Representatives Press President Trump to Properly Commemorate Armenian Genocide." *Armenian Weekly*, April 21, 2018. https://armenianweekly.com/2018/04/21/over-100-u-s-representatives-press-president-trump-to-properly-commemorate-armenian-genocide/.

Anderson, Jon Lee. "Juan Carlos's Fall from Grace in Spain and the Precarious Future of the World's Monarchies." *New Yorker*, August 25, 2020. https://www.newyorker.com/news/daily-comment/juan-carloss-fall-from-grace-in-spain-and-the-precarious-future-of-the-worlds-monarchies.

Ant, Onur, and Ghaith Shennib. "Saudis Are After the Muslim Brotherhood, and Turkey's in the Way." Bloomberg, July 2, 2017. https://www.bloomberg.com/news/articles/2017-07-03/saudis-are-after-the-muslim-brotherhood-and-turkey-s-in-the-way.

Antarctic Treaty. "The Antarctic Treaty." Accessed February 25, 2021. https://www.ats.aq/e/antarctictreaty.html.

Antetokounmpo, Giannis. "Giannis Shares His Inspiring Story on 60 Minutes." NBA.com. Accessed February 23, 2021. https://www.nba.com/bucks/features/giannis-shares-inspiring-story-60-minutes.

AOL Staff. "AG Nominee Barr 'Can Conceive' of Jailing Journalists 'as a Last Resort.'" Accessed February 23, 2021. https://www.aol.com/news/barr-can-conceive-jailing-journalists-last-resort-194811931.html.

Applebaum, Anne. "How the Use of a Nerve Agent on British Soil Exposes the UK's Isolation." *NZ Herald*, March 13, 2018. https://www.nzherald.co.nz/world/how-the-use-of-a-nerve-agent-on-british-soil-exposes-the-uks-isolation/JVZYWH3DZMRAUOW43FVCVOUE54/.

Appelbaum, Yoni. "Trump's Claim: 'I Alone Can Fix It.'" *Atlantic*, July 22, 2016. https://www.theatlantic.com/politics/archive/2016/07/trump-rnc-speech-alone-fix-it/492557/.

Arango, Tim. "A Century after Armenian Genocide, Turkey's Denial Only Deepens." *New York Times*, April 17, 2015. https://www.nytimes.com/2015/04/17/world/eur ope/turkeys-century-of-denial-about-an-armenian-genocide.html.

Arce, Luis. "Bolivia's Morales Calls for Calm after Protesters Demand Junta." Yahoo News, October 27, 2020. https://news.yahoo.com/bolivias-morales-calls-calm-pro testers-200626572.html.

Arciga, Julia. "Marianne Williamson's First Act in Office: Call New Zealand PM and Say 'Girlfriend, You Are So On.'" *Daily Beast*, June 28, 2019. https://www.thedai lybeast.com/2020-democratic-debate-marianne-williamson-says-first-act-as-presid ent-would-be-call-to-new-zealand-pm.

The Arctic Council. "Arctic Council." Accessed February 25, 2021. https://arctic-coun cil.org/en/.

"As Trump Fiddles on Climate, the World Goes Californian." *Sacramento Bee*. Accessed February 23, 2021. https://www.sacbee.com/opinion/editorials/article153669 384.html.

Associated Press. "AT&T under Pressure to Defy Maduro's Censors." AP News, January 17, 2020. https://apnews.com/article/e5247995bc15a8b6bf479bf5a f42f411.

———. "Cristina Fernández de Kirchner Indicted in Argentina Corruption Case." *Guardian*, December 27, 2016. http://www.theguardian.com/world/2016/dec/27/ cristina-fernandez-de-kirchner-indicted-corruption-argentina.

———. "Despite Campaign Vow, Obama Declines to Call Massacre of Armenians 'Genocide.'" *New York Times*, April 23, 2016, sec. World. https://www.nytimes.com/ 2016/04/23/world/europe/despite-campaign-vow-obama-declines-to-call-massa cre-of-armenians-genocide.html.

Atwood, Kylie. "Trump Fires Steve Goldstein, a Top Tillerson Deputy, in State Department Shake-Up." CBS News. Accessed February 23, 2021. https://www.cbsn ews.com/news/trump-fires-top-tillerson-deputy-in-state-department-shake-up/.

Augustin, Ed, and Frances Robles. "Cuba's Economy Was Hurting. The Pandemic Brought a Food Crisis." *New York Times*, September 20, 2020. https://www.nytimes. com/2020/09/20/world/americas/cuba-economy.html.

Axelrod, Tal. "UN Report Says Erik Prince Violated Arms Embargo against Libya: Report." *Hill*, February 19, 2021. https://thehill.com/policy/international/ 539697-un-report-says-erik-prince-violated-arms-embargo-against-libya-report.

Aydintasbas, Asli. "It's Time for a New Peace Process between Turkey and the Kurds." *Washington Post*, September 27, 2016. https://www-washingtonpost-com.stanford. idm.oclc.org/news/global-opinions/wp/2016/09/27/its-time-for-a-new-peace-process-between-turkey-and-the-kurds/?utm_term=.5440a3342e12.

Bacon, John. "President Donald Trump on Kim Jong Un: 'We Fell in Love' over 'Beautiful Letters.'" *USA Today*. Accessed February 23, 2021. https://www.usatoday. com/story/news/politics/2018/09/30/trump-north-koreas-kim-love-beautiful-lett ers/1478834002/.

Baker, Peter, and Lara Jakes. "Trump Throws Middle East Policy into Turmoil over Syria." *New York Times*, October 7, 2019. https://www.nytimes.com/2019/10/07/us/politics/turkey-syria-trump.html.

Baker, Peter, and David E. Sanger. "Trump Says Tillerson Is 'Wasting His Time' on North Korea." *New York Times*, October 1, 2017. https://www.nytimes.com/2017/10/01/us/politics/trump-tillerson-north-korea.html.

Baldwin, Robert E. "The Political Economy of Trade Policy." *Journal of Economic Perspectives* 3, no. 4 (1989): 119–35. DOI: 10.1257/jep.3.4.119.

Bannink, Dirk. "Contaminated Foodstuffs Dumped on World Market." Wise International, May 4, 1991. https://www.wiseinternational.org/nuclear-monitor/349-350/contaminated-foodstuffs-dumped-world-market.

Bar'el, Zvi. "Erdoğan Wields Powerful Weapon in Battle with European Union." Haaretz.com, November 22, 2016. http://www.haaretz.com/middle-east-news/turkey/erdogan-wields-powerful-weapon-in-battle-with-european-union-1.5464546.

Barnard, Anne, and Michael R. Gordon. "Worst Chemical Attack in Years in Syria; U.S. Blames Assad." *New York Times*, April 4, 2017. https://www.nytimes.com/2017/04/04/world/middleeast/syria-gas-attack.html.

Barnes, Julian E., Eric Schmitt, and David D. Kirkpatrick. "'Tell Your Boss': Recording Is Seen to Link Saudi Crown Prince More Strongly to Khashoggi Killing." *New York Times*, November 12, 2018, sec. World. https://www.nytimes.com/2018/11/12/world/middleeast/jamal-khashoggi-killing-saudi-arabia.html.

Barry, Ellen. "A Scientist Is Arrested, and Academics Push Back." *New York Times*, January 26, 2021. https://www.nytimes.com/2021/01/26/us/mit-scientist-charges.html.

Battiata, Mary. "Pope Begins Visit to Czechoslovakia." *Washington Post*, April 22, 1990. https://www-washingtonpost-com.stanford.idm.oclc.org/archive/politics/1990/04/22/pope-begins-visit-to-czechoslovakia/07447909-4c0e-4954-879e-e6ef62c54d66/?utm_term=.d198e6819ea6.

BBC Monitoring. "'It's Better to Be a Dictator than Gay'—Who Is Alexander Lukashenko?" 2019. https://www.youtube.com/watch?v=fY8UJAFN7eY&ab_channel=BBCMonitoring.

BBC News. "Coronavirus: New Zealand Cuts Research in Antarctica to Keep It Virus Free." June 9, 2020. https://www.bbc.com/news/world-asia-52975134.

———. "Data Leak Reveals How China 'Brainwashes' Uighurs in Prison Camps." November 24, 2019. https://www.bbc.com/news/world-asia-china-50511063.

———. "France's Nicolas Sarkozy: 'Bling' and Legal Woes." March 1, 2021. https://www.bbc.com/news/world-europe-11576712.

———. "India-China Clash: 20 Indian Troops Killed in Ladakh Fighting." June 16, 2020. https://www.bbc.com/news/world-asia-53061476.

———. "Khalifa Haftar: The Libyan General with Big Ambitions." April 8, 2010. https://www.bbc.com/news/world-africa-27492354.

———. "Libya: US, UK and France Attack Gaddafi Forces." March 20, 2011. https://www.bbc.com/news/world-africa-12796972.

———. "Trump Says Western Civilisation at Stake in Warsaw Speech," July 6, 2017. https://www.bbc.com/news/world-europe-40515329.

———. "US Says Russia Sent Jets to Libya 'Mercenaries.'" May 26, 2020. https://www.bbc.com/news/world-africa-52811093.

Beauchamp, Zack. "Hungary Just Passed a 'Stop Soros' Law That Makes It Illegal to Help Undocumented Migrants." Vox, June 22, 2018. https://www.vox.com/policy-and-politics/2018/6/22/17493070/hungary-stop-soros-orban.

———. "Steve Bannon in Europe: A Dubious Plan for the 2019 EU Parliament Vote." Vox, July 25, 2018. https://www.vox.com/policy-and-politics/2018/7/25/17611 982/steve-bannon-europe-eu-parliament-the-movement.

Bedard, Paul. "Congress Warned North Korean EMP Attack Would Kill '90% of All Americans.'" *Washington Examiner*, October 12, 2017. https://www.washingtonexami ner.com/congress-warned-north-korean-emp-attack-would-kill-90-of-all-americans.

Beeman, Richard R. "Perspectives on the Constitution: A Republic, if You Can Keep It—National Constitution Center." National Constitution Center—constitutioncenter. org. Accessed February 24, 2021. https://constitutioncenter.org/learn/educatio nal-resources/historical-documents/perspectives-on-the-constitution-a-repub lic-if-you-can-keep-it.

Beete, Paulette. "Ten Things to Know about Charles Dickens' A Christmas Carol." National Endowment for the Arts, December 4, 2020. https://www.arts.gov/stor ies/blog/2020/ten-things-know-about-charles-dickens-christmas-carol.

Beirich, Heidi. "David Duke Tossed out of Another European Country." Southern Poverty Law Center, December 6, 2013. https://www.splcenter.org/hatewatch/ 2013/12/06/david-duke-tossed-out-another-european-country.

"Belarus Election: Hundreds Protest after Lukashenko's Rivals Barred." BBC News, July 14, 2020, sec. Europe. https://www.bbc.com/news/world-europe-53411735.

Bellamy, Alex J. "Kosovo and the Advent of Sovereignty as Responsibility." *Journal of Intervention and Statebuilding* 3, no. 2 (June 24, 2009). https://www-tandfonline-com. stanford.idm.oclc.org/doi/abs/10.1080/17502970902829952.

Bengali, Shashank, and Melanie Mason. "The Progressive Indian Grandfather Who Inspired Kamala Harris." *Los Angeles Times*, October 25, 2019. https://www.lati mes.com/politics/story/2019-10-25/how-kamala-harris-indian-family-shaped-her-political-career.

Benoit, Bertrand. "German City Becomes Rallying Point for Anti-Immigration Protests." *Wall Street Journal*, August 30, 2018. https://www.wsj.com/articles/german-police-brace-for-more-protests-over-immigration-1535639150.

Berman, James. "The Three Essential Warren Buffett Quotes to Live By." *Forbes*. Accessed February 23, 2021. https://www.forbes.com/sites/jamesberman/2014/04/20/the-three-essential-warren-buffett-quotes-to-live-by/.

Bernstein, Carl. "Cover Story: The Holy Alliance." *Time*, June 24, 2001. http://content. time.com/time/magazine/article/0,9171,159069,00.html.

Bernstein, Richard. "The Scary War Game over Taiwan That the U.S. Loses Again and again." RealClearInvestigations, August 17, 2020. https://www.realclearinvestigati ons.com/articles/2020/08/17/the_scary_war_game_over_taiwan_that_the_us_l oses_again_and_again_124836.html.

Bershidsky, Leonid. "The Yellow Rubber Duck Is a Potent Protest Symbol." Bloomberg, March 28, 2017. https://www.bloomberg.com/opinion/articles/2017-03-28/the-yellow-rubber-duck-is-a-potent-protest-symbol.

Beyoncé. "Beyoncé—Formation (Official Video), 2016." YouTube. https://www.yout ube.com/watch?v=WDZJPJV__bQ&ab_channel=Beyonc%C3%A9VEVO.

Beyoncé. "Beyoncé: Tours." Accessed February 21, 2021. https://www.beyonce.com/tour/.

Bickerton, James. "World War Three: Putin Russia Has 80,000 Troops in Ukraine Crimea Says Petro Poroshenko." *Express*, December 3, 2018. https://www.express.co.uk/news/world/1053463/World-war-three-Putin-Russia-troops-Ukraine-Crimea-Petro-Poroshenko.

Bilefsky, Dan. "In Canada, Kamala Harris, a Disco-Dancing Teenager, Yearned for Home." *New York Times*. Accessed February 25, 2021. https://www.nytimes.com/2020/10/05/world/canada/kamala-harris-montreal.html.

Bill Kirk. *Casablanca Bogart Round Up the Usual Suspects*, 2014. https://www.youtube.com/watch?v=NRKGblpzhZQ&ab_channel=BillKirk.

Biography. "Ted Cruz." February 3, 2016. https://www.biography.com/political-figure/ted-cruz.

Birnbaum, Ben. "Statue in Budapest's Liberty Square Credits Reagan for Freedom." *Washington Times*, June 29, 2011. https://www.washingtontimes.com/news/2011/jun/29/statue-in-budapests-liberty-square-credits-reagan-/.

Birnbaum, Michael. "A Town That Expels Migrants and Celebrates with Cake Wants to Be a Model for Italy." *Washington Post*, March 3, 2018. Accessed February 23, 2021. http://www.washingtonpost.com/world/europe/a-town-that-expels-migrants-and-celebrates-with-cake-wants-to-be-a-model-for-italy/2018/03/02/5300294e-1cb1-11e8-98f5-ceecfa8741b6_story.html.

Blake, Aaron. "There Was a Very Real 'Birther' Debate about John McCain." *Washington Post*, January 7, 2016. Accessed February 25, 2021. http://www.washingtonpost.com/news/the-fix/wp/2016/01/07/there-was-a-very-real-birther-debate-about-john-mccain/.

Blakemore, Erin. "California Slaughtered 16,000 Native Americans. The State Finally Apologized For the Genocide." History. Accessed February 23, 2021. https://www.history.com/news/native-american-genocide-california-apology.

Blinken, Antony. "On the Extension of the New START Treaty with the Russian Federation." United States Department of State, February 3, 2021. https://www.state.gov/on-the-extension-of-the-new-start-treaty-with-the-russian-federation/.

Blocker, Joel. "'Le Monde' Editor Says Anti-Americanism Has Ceased to Be Relevant." Radio Free Europe/Radio Liberty, April 12, 2002. https://www.rferl.org/a/1099388.html.

Bloomberg. "The World Is Dangerously Dependent on Taiwan for Semiconductors." Accessed February 25, 2021. https://www.bloomberg.com/news/features/2021-01-25/the-world-is-dangerously-dependent-on-taiwan-for-semiconductors.

Bogage, Jacob. "Chiefs' War Chant and Tomahawk Chop Hits the Super Bowl Stage." *Washington Post*, January 27, 2020. https://www-washingtonpost-com.stanford.idm.oclc.org/sports/2020/01/27/tomahawk-chop-kansas-city-chiefs/.

Borger, Julian. "A Blunt, Fearful Rant: Trump's UN Speech Left Presidential Norms in the Dust." *Guardian*, September 19, 2017. http://www.theguardian.com/us-news/2017/sep/19/donald-trump-un-speech-analysis-north-korea.

———. "US Intelligence Fears Iran Duped Hawks into Iraq War." *Guardian*, May 25, 2004. http://www.theguardian.com/world/2004/may/25/usa.iraq10.

Borger, Julian, and Dan Sabbagh. "Lapse of US-Russia Arms Treaty Will Heighten Missile Threat, Says UN." *Guardian*, August 2, 2019. http://www.theguardian.com/world/2019/aug/01/inf-treaty-us-russia-arms-control-to-end.

Borunda, Alejandra. "What a 100-Degree Day in Siberia, above the Arctic Circle, Really Means." National Geographic, June 23, 2020. https://www.nationalgeographic.com/science/article/what-100-degree-day-siberia-means-climate-change.

Bougon, Francois. "Inside the Mind of Xi Jinping." HURST, September 2018. https://www.hurstpublishers.com/book/inside-the-mind-of-xi-jinping/.

Bradford, Alina. "Smallpox: The World's First Eradicated Disease." livescience.com, April 24, 2019. https://www.livescience.com/65304-smallpox.html.

Bradsher, Keith, and Ailin Tang. "China Responds Slowly, and a Pig Disease Becomes a Lethal Epidemic." *New York Times*, December 17, 2019, sec. Business. https://www.nytimes.com/2019/12/17/business/china-pigs-african-swine-fever.html.

Braswell, Sean. "How Herbert Hoover Saved Belgium." OZY, March 19, 2016. https://www.ozy.com/true-and-stories/how-herbert-hoover-saved-belgium/35372/.

Bréadún, Deaglán de. "George Mitchell: A Keystone of the Good Friday Agreement." *Irish America*, May 1999. https://irishamerica.com/2018/04/irish-american-of-the-year-george-mitchell/.

Brean, Henry. "Spontaneous New York-New York 9/11 Shrine Lives on at UNLV as Historical Collection." *Las Vegas Review Journal*, September 11, 2016. https://www.reviewjournal.com/local/local-las-vegas/spontaneous-new-york-new-york-911-shrine-lives-on-at-unlv-as-historical-collection/.

Brice-Saddler, Michael. "While Bemoaning Mueller Probe, Trump Falsely Says the Constitution Gives Him 'the Right to Do Whatever I Want.'" *Washington Post*, July 23, 2019. http://www.washingtonpost.com/politics/2019/07/23/trump-falsely-tells-auditorium-full-teens-constitution-gives-him-right-do-whatever-i-want/.

Broder, John. "U.S. Reaches Accord with Manila, Will Leave Clark Air Base: Philippines: Volcano Causes Abandonment of Field. But Americans Will Keep Subic Naval Base for 10 Years." *Los Angeles Times*, July 18, 1991. https://www.latimes.com/archives/la-xpm-1991-07-18-mn-3381-story.html.

Broich, John. "The Real Reason Charles Dickens Wrote 'A Christmas Carol.'" *Time*, December 13, 2016. https://time.com/4597964/history-charles-dickens-christmas-carol/.

Brookings. "Brookings Experts on Trump's National Security Strategy." December 21, 2017. https://www.brookings.edu/research/brookings-experts-on-trumps-national-security-strategy/.

Brown, Chad, and Melina Kolb. "Trump's Trade War Timeline: An Up-to-Date Guide." PIIE, April 16, 2018. https://www.piie.com/blogs/trade-investment-policy-watch/trump-trade-war-china-date-guide.

Brown, Stephen. "Sweden Freaks Out." Politico, July 11, 2018. https://www.politico.eu/article/sweden-joins-the-club-far-right-democrats-jimmie-akesson-stefan-lofven-general-election/.

Brown University. "Understanding the Iran-Contra Affairs—The Legal Aftermath." Accessed February 23, 2021. https://www.brown.edu/Research/Understanding_the_Iran_Contra_Affair/profile-shultz.php.

Brownstein, Ronald. "Nancy Pelosi's Predictions for Impeachment." *Atlantic*, October 30, 2019. https://www.theatlantic.com/politics/archive/2019/10/nancy-pelosis-pred ictions-impeachment/601081/.

Brumfiel, Geoff. "The North Korean Electromagnetic Pulse Threat, or Lack Thereof." NPR.org, April 27, 2017. https://www.npr.org/2017/04/27/525833275/the-north-korean-electromagnetic-pulse-threat-or-lack-thereof.

Bugh, Gary. "Public Figures and Officials." MTSU. Accessed February 23, 2021. https:// www.mtsu.edu/first-amendment/article/1010/public-figures-and-officials.

Burginger, Lyndsay. "Wendy's Removes Burgers from 1,000 Locations Due to Meat Shortage." Wide Open Eats, May 5, 2020. https://www.wideopeneats.com/wen dys-removes-burgers/.

Business Recorder. "Black Lives Matter Wins Swedish Rights Prize." January 30, 2021. https://www.brecorder.com/news/40057895.

Callamard, Agnes. "The Targeted Killing of General Soleimani: Its Lawfulness and Why It Matters." Just Security, January 8, 2020. https://www.justsecurity.org/67949/the-targeted-killing-of-general-soleimani-its-lawfulness-and-why-it-matters/.

"Campaigning While Female." *New York Times*, July 9, 2018, sec. U.S. https:// www.nytimes.com/interactive/2021/uri/embeddedinteractive/415320c5-226c-5523-aba8-07d6544832fc?

Campbell, John. "Brexit: What Are the Backstop Options?" BBC News, October 16, 2019, sec. N. Ireland Politics. https://www.bbc.com/news/uk-northern-ireland-politics-44615404.

Carroll, Rory. "Former Bus Driver Nicolás Maduro Clings to Wheel in Venezuela." *Guardian*, April 30, 2019. http://www.theguardian.com/world/2019/apr/30/for mer-bus-driver-nicolas-maduro-clings-to-wheel-in-venezuela.

Cassidy, Megan. "Family, SF Leaders Plead with Community for Help in Solving Slaying of 6-Year-Old Boy." *San Francisco Chronicle*, July 8, 2020. https://www.sfchronicle.com/crime/article/Justice-for-Jace-Family-SF-mayor-police-15392 519.php.

"Castle of Mytilene." *Wikipedia*, February 20, 2021. https://en.wikipedia.org/w/index. php?title=Castle_of_Mytilene&oldid=1007930604.

Cato Institute. "Precision-Guided Munitions and the Neutron Bomb." August 26, 1982. https://www.cato.org/policy-analysis/precision-guided-munitions-neutron-bomb.

CBC News: The National. "Iranians Arrested for Pharrell Williams' 'Happy' Tribute Video, 2014." YouTube. https://www.youtube.com/watch?v=lL2BvpOav_w&ab_ channel=CBCNews%3ATheNational.

———. "Russian Watchdog Seeks Nearly $3B in Damages over Arctic Fuel Spill in Siberia." July 8, 2020. https://www.cbc.ca/news/canada/north/russian-watchdog-arctic-fuel-spill-1.5641278.

CBS News. "Brazil's 1st Female President Faces Impeachment." May 12, 2016. https:// www.cbsnews.com/news/brazil-president-dilma-rousseff-impeached-in-senate-vote/.

Centers for Disease Control. "Bovine Spongiform Encephalopathy (BSE) | Prions Diseases." CDC, February 1, 2019. https://www.cdc.gov/prions/bse/index.html.

———. "CDC—Chemical Weapons Elimination." CDC, December 19, 2019. https:// www.cdc.gov/nceh/demil/default.htm.

CGP Grey. "The Trouble with Tumbleweed, 2020." YouTube. https://www.youtube.com/watch?v=hsWr_JWTZss&feature=youtu.be&ab_channel=CGPGrey.

"CGTN (TV Channel)." *Wikipedia*, February 22, 2021. https://en.wikipedia.org/w/index.php?title=CGTN_(TV_channel)&oldid=1008268827.

Chadwick, Paul. "Journalism Has a Vital Role in a Constitutional Democracy." *Guardian*, October 6, 2019. http://www.theguardian.com/commentisfree/2019/oct/06/journalism-media-boris-johnson-uk-government-supreme-court-brexitcourt.

Champion, Marc, and Aliaksandr Kudrytski. "Belarus's Soviet Economy Has Worked Better than You Think." Bloomberg, November 26, 2019. https://www.bloomberg.com/news/articles/2019-11-27/belarus-s-soviet-economy-has-worked-better-than-you-think.

Chana, Jas. "Will Bernie Sanders Become the First Jewish President?" *Tablet Magazine*, August 20, 2015. https://www.tabletmag.com/sections/news/articles/bernie-sanders-story.

"The Changing Story of Russia's 'Little Green Men' Invasion." Radio Free Europe/Radio Liberty. Accessed February 23, 2021. https://www.rferl.org/a/russia-ukraine-crimea/29790037.html.

Chappell, Bill. "Trump Hosts Russian Foreign Minister Lavrov and Ambassador Kislyak at White House." NPR.org, May 10, 2017. https://www.npr.org/sections/thetwo-way/2017/05/10/527755991/trump-meets-with-russias-lavrov-at-the-white-house-today.

The Charlotte Observer. "Donald Trump's Lies Have Consequences. We're Seeing Them Now." Accessed February 25, 2021. https://www.charlotteobserver.com/opinion/editorials/article165203842.html.

Chesser, Preston. "The Burning of the Library of Alexandria." eHISTORY. Accessed February 21, 2021. https://ehistory.osu.edu/articles/burning-library-alexandria.

Cheung, Karen. "Returned Bookseller Says He Believes Others Will Be Released after Colleague's Sentencing Later This Year." Hong Kong Free Press HKFP, July 12, 2016. https://hongkongfp.com/2016/07/12/returned-bookseller-says-he-believes-others-will-be-released-after-colleagues-sentencing-later-this-year/.

"China Holds Military Drill as US Envoy Visits Taiwan." BBC News, September 18, 2020, sec. Asia. https://www.bbc.com/news/world-asia-54200913.

Chorush, Jacquelyn Andrea. "'Prepared to Go Fully Kinetic': How U.S. Leaders Conceptualize China's Threat to Arctic Security." Arctic Institute, June 6, 2020. https://www.thearcticinstitute.org/prepared-kinetic-us-leaders-conceptualize-china-threat-arctic-security/.

Choudhury, Saheli Roy. "India China Border Clash: Small Mistakes Can Be Costly, Former NSA Says." CNBC, September 2020. https://www.cnbc.com/2020/09/09/india-china-border-clash-small-mistakes-can-be-costly-former-nsa-says.html.

Chugani, Michael. "Chinese Who Cry Racial Abuse amid the Coronavirus Epidemic Forget They Are as Bad as the Rest of Us." *South China Morning Post*, March 5, 2020. https://www.scmp.com/comment/opinion/article/3064963/chinese-who-cry-racial-abuse-amid-coronavirus-epidemic-forget-they.

Cillizza, Chris. "Yes, Donald Trump Really Believes He Is 'the Chosen One.'" CNN Politics, August 24, 2019. https://www.cnn.com/2019/08/21/politics/donald-trump-chosen-one/index.html.

"Clinic Study Finds Evidence of Genocide in Myanmar." Accessed February 24, 2021. https://law.yale.edu/yls-today/news/clinic-study-finds-evidence-genocide-myanmar.

Clinton House Museum. "How Irish Are the Clintons?" March 11, 2020. https://clinton housemuseum.org/how-irish-are-the-clintons/.

CNBC. "Deal or No Deal." CNBC, May 16, 2018. https://dealornodeal.cnbc.com/deal-or-no-deal-homepage/.

CNN. "The Story behind Clinton's Trip to North Korea." CNN. Accessed February 22, 2021. https://www.cnn.com/2009/US/08/05/nkorea.journalists.background/.

CNN Business. "Zuckerberg: Internet for the World Is Good for Democracy, 2017." CNN. https://www.youtube.com/watch?v=nAcy2qwpby8&ab_channel=CNNB usiness.

CNN Editorial Research. "Death of Osama Bin Laden Fast Facts." CNN, September 9, 2013. https://www.cnn.com/2013/09/09/world/death-of-osama-bin-laden-fast-facts/index.html.

———. "USS Cole Bombing Fast Facts." CNN. Accessed February 23, 2021. https://www.cnn.com/2013/09/18/world/meast/uss-cole-bombing-fast-facts/index.html.

Cohen, Howard. "Agency Wants More Python Hunters in the Florida Everglades." *Miami Herald*, September 11, 2019. https://www.miamiherald.com/news/local/environm ent/article234964692.html.

Cohen, Roberta. "China's Repatriation of North Korean Refugees." *Brookings* (blog), November 30, 1AD. https://www.brookings.edu/testimonies/chinas-repatriation-of-north-korean-refugees/.

Cold War Sites. "The 'Graveyard to Fallen Monuments', Moscow." Accessed February 23, 2021. https://coldwarsites.net/country/russia/the-graveyard-to-fallen-monume nts-moscow/.

Coleman, Justine. "20 House Dems Call on Trump to Issue Two-Week, Nationwide Shelter-in-Place Order." *Hill*, March 24, 2020. https://thehill.com/homenews/house/489276-democratic-lawmakers-call-on-trump-to-issue-2-week-nationwide-shelter-in-place.

Collins, Michael. "Trump Jokes He Might Leave Country If He Loses to Joe Biden in Nov. 3 Election." USA TODAY. Accessed February 23, 2021. https://www.usatoday.com/story/news/politics/elections/2020/10/16/trump-jokes-he-might-leave-coun try-if-he-loses-joe-biden/3688173001/.

Committee to Protect Journalists. "Record Number of Journalists Jailed as Turkey, China, Egypt Pay Scant Price for Repression." Accessed February 22, 2021. https://cpj.org/reports/2017/12/journalists-prison-jail-record-number-turkey-china-egypt/.

Conan, Neil, and Jared Diamond. "Understanding History with 'Guns, Germs, and Steel.'" NPR.org, September 8, 2011. https://www.npr.org/2011/09/08/140297 259/understanding-history-with-guns-germs-and-steel.

Cong, Forest. "US Ban on Chinese Students with Military Links Divides Experts on Impact." Voice of America, June 4, 2020. https://www.voanews.com/usa/us-ban-chinese-students-military-links-divides-experts-impact.

"Constantine II of Greece." *Wikipedia*, February 21, 2021. https://en.wikipedia.org/w/index.php?title=Constantine_II_of_Greece&oldid=1008093539.

Constitutional Rights Foundation. "Constitutional Rights Foundation." Accessed February 25, 2021. https://www.crf-usa.org/bill-of-rights-in-action/bria-24-1-b-upton-sinclairs-the-jungle-muckraking-the-meat-packing-industry.html.

Cool Australia. "Antarctica." Accessed February 25, 2021. https://www.coolaustralia. org/antarctica-secondary/.

Coronel, Sheila, Mariel Padilla, and David Mora. "The Uncounted Dead of Duterte's Drug War." *Atlantic*. Accessed February 24, 2021. https://www.theatlantic.com/international/archive/2019/08/philippines-dead-rodrigo-duterte-drug-war/595978/.

Correll, John T. "The Neutron Bomb." *Air Force Magazine*, October 30, 2017. Accessed February 23, 2021. https://www.airforcemag.com/article/the-neutron-bomb/.

Cortellessa, Eric, and Markos Kounalakis. "The Only Place in the World Not Yet Rocked by the Virus." *Washington Monthly—Politics* (blog), July 15, 2020. https://washington monthly.com/2020/07/15/the-only-place-in-the-world-not-yet-rocked-by-the-virus/.

Costa, Robert, and Philip Rucker. "Trump Says Cruz's Canadian Birth Could Be 'Very Precarious' for GOP." *Washington Post*, January 5, 2016. https://www-washingtonp ost-com.stanford.idm.oclc.org/politics/trump-says-cruzs-canadian-birth-could-be-very-precarious-for-gop/2016/01/05/5ce69764-b3f8-11e5-9388-466021d971de_st ory.html.

Court, Andrew. "Harvard Professor Pleads Not Guilty to Lying to US Officials about His Ties to Wuhan University." *Daily Mail* Online, June 16, 2020. https://www.dailym ail.co.uk/news/article-8427909/Harvard-professor-pleads-not-guilty-U-S-lying-China-ties.html.

Cox, Mary-Lea. "Author Hochschild Recounts Lost History of Horror in the Belgian Congo." Wilson Center, October 14, 1999. https://www.wilsoncenter.org/article/author-hochschild-recounts-lost-history-horror-the-belgian-congo.

Crook, Jordan. "Steve Jobs Memorial Statue Unveiled in Budapest." TechCrunch, December 12, 2011. https://techcrunch.com/2011/12/21/steve-jobs-memorial-sta tue-unveiled-in-budapest/.

Croucher, Shane. "Britain's New Prime Minister Was a U.S. Citizen for Decades—until the IRS Caught up with Him." *Newsweek*, July 23, 2019. https://www.newsweek. com/boris-johnson-us-citizen-irs-born-new-york-1449974.

Current Trends in Consumption of Animal Products. Designing Foods: Animal Product Options in the Marketplace. National Academies Press (US), 1988. https://www.ncbi.nlm.nih.gov/books/NBK218176/.

Cybersecurity & Infrastructure Security Agency. "Guidance on the Essential Critical Infrastructure Workforce." Accessed February 22, 2021. https://www.cisa.gov/publ ication/guidance-essential-critical-infrastructure-workforce.

Dalton, Matthew, and Lingling Wei. "How China Skirts America's Antidumping Tariffs on Steel." *Wall Street Journal*, June 4, 2018. https://www.wsj.com/articles/how-china-skirts-americas-antidumping-tariffs-on-steel-1528124339.

Daly, Robert. "A Rise without Shine: The Global Weakness of Chinese Culture [渠成水不到]." Wilson Center, September 13, 2016. https://www.wilsoncenter.org/article/rise-without-shine-the-global-weakness-chinese-culture-qu-cheng-shui-bu-dao.

The Daring Gourmet. "Ultimate Bangers and Mash Recipe." October 31, 2019. https://www.daringgourmet.com/bangers-and-mash-recipe/.

Daugherty, Alex, and Tara Copp. "Florida Lawmaker Wants U.S. Military to Help Juan Guaido." *Miami Herald*, April 30, 2019. https://www.miamiherald.com/news/nation-world/world/americas/venezuela/article229845414.html.

Davis, Rebecca. "China's Internet Censorship Law Sets Out Content Rules." Variety, January 3, 2020. https://variety.com/2020/digital/news/china-censorship-law-bytedance-1203455740/.

Day, Nate. "Meghan Markle Steps Out for First Time since 'Megxit' Announcement." Fox News, January 15, 2020. https://www.foxnews.com/entertainment/meghan-markle-first-time-since-megxit-announcement.

De Clercq, Geert, and Marine Pennetier. "More French Protests See Roads Blocked, Trains Disrupted and Scuffles in Paris." Reuters, December 7, 2019. https://www.reuters.com/article/us-france-protests-idUSKBN1YB0DF.

"Deal or No Deal—Home | CNBC Prime." Accessed February 25, 2021. https://dealornodeal.cnbc.com/.

Death Penalty Information Center. "Execution List 2020." Accessed February 23, 2021. https://deathpenaltyinfo.org/executions/2020.

Debusmann, Bernd, Special Correspondent. "Nicaraguans See First Lady as Power behind Throne." Reuters, January 29, 2007. https://www.reuters.com/article/us-nicaragua-wife-idUSN2632184220070129.

"Defending Taiwan Is Growing Costlier and Deadlier." *Economist*, October 8, 2020. http://www.economist.com/asia/2020/10/08/defending-taiwan-is-growing-costlier-and-deadlier.

Denial, Architects of. *Watch Architects of Denial Online | Vimeo On Demand*, 2017. https://vimeo.com/ondemand/architectsofdenial.

Denyer, Simon. "China's Scary Lesson to the World: Censoring the Internet Works." *Washington Post*, May 23, 2016. https://www-washingtonpost-com.stanford.idm.oclc.org/world/asia_pacific/chinas-scary-lesson-to-the-world-censoring-the-internet-works/2016/05/23/413afe78-fff3-11e5-8bb1-f124a43f84dc_story.html?utm_term=.05e5a40a4f08.

Desta, Yohana. "Troy: The Secret Impact of Brad Pitt's Sword-and-Sandal Epic." Vanity Fair. Accessed February 22, 2021. https://www.vanityfair.com/hollywood/2019/05/troy-movie-anniversary-brad-pitt.

Dettmer, Jamie. "Orban Presses on with Illiberal Democracy." Voice of America, April 10, 2019. https://www.voanews.com/europe/orban-presses-illiberal-democracy.

Deutsche Welle. "NATO Commander: Russia Uses Syrian Refugees as 'weapon' against West." February 3, 2016. https://www.dw.com/en/nato-commander-russia-uses-syrian-refugees-as-weapon-against-west/a-19086285.

———. "Trial of Cumhuriyet Journalists Resumes in Turkey." 2018. https://www.dw.com/en/trial-of-cumhuriyet-journalists-resumes-in-turkey/a-42906423.

———. "Xi Jinping and the 'Chinese Dream.'" Accessed February 23, 2021. https://www.dw.com/en/xi-jinping-and-the-chinese-dream/a-43685630.

DeYoung, Karen, Josh Dawsey, and Paul Sonne. "Venezuela's Opposition Put Together a Serious Plan. For Now, It Appears to Have Failed." *Washington Post*, May 1, 2019.

https://www-washingtonpost-com.stanford.idm.oclc.org/world/national-security/venezuelas-opposition-put-together-a-serious-plan-for-now-it-appears-to-have-failed/2019/05/01/7df68fe0-6c19-11e9-be3a-33217240a539_story.html?utm_term=.9c5b81bf30b6.

Diamond, Jared. "Guns Germs & Steel: Variables. Smallpox." PBS. Accessed February 25, 2021. https://www.pbs.org/gunsgermssteel/variables/smallpox.html.

Diamond, Larry. "Saving American Democracy." Stanford University. Accessed February 24, 2021. https://diamond-democracy.stanford.edu/events/saving-american-democracy.

Doubek, James. "Trump Meets North Korea's Kim Jong Un and Says Nuclear Negotiations Will Resume." NPR.org, June 30, 2019. https://www.npr.org/2019/06/30/737365074/trump-to-meet-kim-jong-un-at-dmz.

Doucette, Siobhan K. "Mightier than the Sword: Polish Independent Publishing, 1976–1989. A Dissertation Submitted to the Faculty of the Graduate School of Arts and Sciences of Georgetown University in Partial Fulfillment of the Requirements for the Degree of Doctor of Philosophy in History." April 11, 2013, 429pp., https://repository.library.georgetown.edu/bitstream/handle/10822/559491/Doucette_georgetown_0076D_12356.pdf.

Dri, Karwan Faidhi. "Kurdish Force Makes Appeal after Female Fighter Captured Alive by Turkey-Backed Militia." Rudaw, October 26, 2019. https://www.rudaw.net/english/middleeast/syria/251020192.

Duxbury, Charlie. "Swedish Prosecutor Says Local Man Killed Prime Minister Olof Palme." *POLITICO* (blog), June 10, 2020. https://www.politico.eu/article/sweden-olof-palme-killed-by-local-man/.

Dwyer, Colin. "Donald Trump: 'I Could … Shoot Somebody, And I Wouldn't Lose Any Voters.'" NPR.org, January 23, 2016. https://www.npr.org/sections/thetwo-way/2016/01/23/464129029/donald-trump-i-could-shoot-somebody-and-i-wouldnt-lose-any-voters.

Dyer, Emily. "Is China Afraid of the Next Miss World?" *The Daily Beast*, November 11, 2015, sec. world. https://www.thedailybeast.com/articles/2015/11/11/is-china-afraid-of-the-next-miss-world.

Eckel, Mike. "From Stalin to Karimov: What Happens When Dictators Die?" Radio Free Europe/Radio Liberty, August 12, 2019. https://www.rferl.org/a/authoritarian-leaders-deaths-cult-personality-niyazov-karimov-stalin-brezhnev-andropov-chernenko/30106267.html.

Eckstein, Megan. "Navy Will Perform Unprecedented 21-Fighter Flyover for Bush Funeral." USNI News, December 4, 2018. https://news.usni.org/2018/12/04/navy-jets-depart-for-texas-ahead-of-unprecedented-21-aircraft-flyover-for-bush-funeral.

The Economist. "HEMP-Induced Anxiety—America's Utilities Prepare for a Nuclear Threat to the Grid | Business." September 9, 2017. https://www-economist-com.stanford.idm.oclc.org/business/2017/09/09/americas-utilities-prepare-for-a-nuclear-threat-to-the-grid.

Economist Intelligence Unit. "Democracy Index 2020." Accessed February 22, 2021. https://www.eiu.com/n/campaigns/democracy-index-2020/.

EDIAZ. "Banned Book FAQ." Advocacy, Legislation & Issues, October 25, 2016. http://www.ala.org/advocacy/bbooks/banned-books-qa.

Editors. "Chinese Immigrants and the Gold Rush." WGBH. Accessed February 23, 2021. https://www.pbs.org/wgbh/americanexperience/features/goldrush-chinese-immigrants/.

———. "*DAMN.*, by Kendrick Lamar." The Pulitzer Prize, 2021. https://www.pulitzer.org/winners/kendrick-lamar.

———. "Environmentalists Cleared from Protest Camp in Turkey While Mining Operations Continue." Morning Star. Accessed February 23, 2021. https://morningstaronline.co.uk/article/environmentalists-cleared-protest-camp-turkey-while-mining-operations-continue.

———. "George III." History. Accessed February 24, 2021. https://www.history.com/topics/british-history/george-iii.

———. "John Paul II." Biography. Accessed February 22, 2021. https://www.biography.com/religious-figure/john-paul-ii.

———. "Reaction to 9/11." History, August 13, 2010. https://www.history.com/topics/21st-century/reaction-to-9-11.

———. "Third Rome." Encyclopedia.com. Accessed February 22, 2021. https://www.encyclopedia.com/philosophy-and-religion/christianity/christianity-general/third-rome.

———. "Was My Lai Just One of Many Massacres in Vietnam War?" BBC News, August 28, 2013, sec. Asia. https://www.bbc.com/news/world-asia-23427726.

Edwards, Benji. "Remembering EWorld, Apple's Forgotten Online Service." MacWorld, June 8, 2014. https://www.macworld.com/article/2202091/remembering-eworld-apples-forgotten-online-service.html.

Edwards, Lee. "The Legacy of Mao Zedong Is Mass Murder." Heritage Foundation. Accessed February 25, 2021. https://www.heritage.org/asia/commentary/the-legacy-mao-zedong-mass-murder.

Effron, Lauren. "California City Sees COVID-19 Outbreaks at 9 Facilities, Including Food Processing Plants." ABC News, May 25, 2020. https://abcnews.go.com/US/california-city-sees-covid-19-outbreaks-facilities-including/story?id=70871509.

Ellis, Nicquel Terry. "Kamala Harris and Alpha Kappa Alpha: Black Sorority Was a Source for Life Lessons, Sisterhood." *USA Today.* Accessed February 25, 2021. https://www.usatoday.com/story/news/nation/2019/07/20/can-kamala-harris-secure-black-vote-help-her-sorority/1639638001/.

Encyclopedia Britannica. "Donald Trump | Biography, Education, & Facts." Accessed February 25, 2021. https://www.britannica.com/biography/Donald-Trump.

ESPN Staff. "In the Twilight, Manu Ginobili Is Argentina's Shining Example." ESPN.com, May 22, 2018. https://www.espn.com/nba/story/_/id/23570563/in-twilight-san-antonio-spurs-manu-ginobili-argentina-bright-star.

Essa, Azad. "China Is Buying African Media's Silence." *Foreign Policy* (blog). Accessed February 25, 2021. http://foreignpolicy.com/2018/09/14/china-is-buying-african-medias-silence/.

Estonian History Museum. "Permanent Exhibitions." Accessed February 23, 2021. https://www.ajaloomuuseum.ee/exhibitions/permanent-exhibitions/noukogude-aegsete-monumentide-valinaitus.

EURACTIV. *Obama's Prague Speech on Disarmament*, 2009. https://www.youtube.com/watch?v=uYcAr0ZDSlg&ab_channel=EURACTIV.

Euronews. "Iran Immediately Knew Its Missile Downed Ukrainian Plane—Leaked Recording." February 4, 2020. https://www.euronews.com/2020/02/04/iran-immediately-knew-its-missile-downed-ukrainian-plane-leaked-recording.

Fabian, Jordan, and Brooke Saipel. "Trump to Cops: 'Don't Be Too Nice'." *HIll,* July 28, 2017. https://thehill.com/homenews/administration/344364-trump-encoura ges-cops-to-be-rough-with-suspects.

———. "From Spain, Top Dissident Vows to Fight for a Free Venezuela." *Los Angeles Times,* October 27, 2020. https://www.latimes.com/world-nation/story/2020-10-27/from-spain-top-dissident-vows-to-fight-for-free-venezuela.

Faidell, Sarah, and Bex Wright. "New Zealand's Parliament Votes 119-1 to Change Gun Laws after Christchurch Massacre." CNN, April 10, 2019. https://www.cnn.com/2019/04/10/asia/new-zealand-gun-law-reform-intl/index.html.

Failed Architecture. "Hungary's Identity Crisis Fought in Concrete and Bronze." *Failed Architecture* (blog). Accessed February 23, 2021. https://failedarchitecture.com/budapest-freedom-square/.

Fandos, Nicholas, and Christopher Mele. "Erdogan Security Forces Launch 'Brutal Attack' on Washington Protesters, Officials Say." *New York Times,* May 17, 2017. https://www.nytimes.com/2017/05/17/us/turkish-embassy-protest-dc.html.

FDR Library. "FDR and the Four Freedoms Speech." Accessed February 23, 2021. https://www.fdrlibrary.org/four-freedoms.

"Federal Government to Resume Capital Punishment After Nearly Two Decade Lapse." Department of Justice, July 25, 2019. https://www.justice.gov/opa/pr/federal-gov ernment-resume-capital-punishment-after-nearly-two-decade-lapse.

Feng, Emily, and Scott Neuman. "China Expels 3 'Wall Street Journal' Reporters, Citing 'Racist' Headline." NPR.org, February 19, 2020. https://www.npr.org/2020/02/19/807294777/china-expels-3-wall-street-journal-reporters-citing-racist-editorial.

Fernandez, Marisa. "All the Trump Associates Convicted or Sentenced in the Mueller Investigation." Axios. Accessed February 22, 2021. https://www.axios.com/trump-associates-convicted-mueller-investigations-206295a1-5abc-4573-be25-4da19d9ad cc9.html.

Ferreira, Becky. "The Arctic Is on Fire Again, and It's Even Worse This Time." VICE News, July 7, 2020. https://www.vice.com/en/article/qj43n3/the-arc tic-is-on-fire-again-and-its-even-worse-this-time.

Filkins, Dexter. "John Bolton on the Warpath." *New Yorker,* April 29, 2019. https://www.newyorker.com/magazine/2019/05/06/john-bolton-on-the-warpath.

Finnegan, Conor. "Hours after Being Fired, Emotional Tillerson Tells His Side of the Story." ABC News, March 13, 2018. https://abcnews.go.com/Politics/hours-fired-emotional-tillerson-tells-side-story/story?id=53715748.

———. "How Reports of Kim Jong Un's Health Spread and What They Tell Us about What Comes Next for North Korea." ABC News, April 21, 2020. https://abcnews.go.com/Politics/reports-kim-jong-uns-health-spread-us-north/story?id=70264333.

———. "Pushing Human Rights Abroad 'Creates Obstacles' to US Interests." ABC News, May 3, 2017. https://abcnews.go.com/Politics/tillerson-pushing-human-rig hts-abroad-creates-obstacles/story?id=47190743.

Fitzgibbon, Will. "New Panama Papers Leak Reveals Mossack Fonseca's Chaotic Scramble." International Consortium of Investigative Journalists, June 20, 2018.

https://www.icij.org/investigations/panama-papers/new-panama-papers-leak-reve als-mossack-fonsecas-chaotic-scramble/.

Flatley, Tighe. "The Convenient Alliance: President Reagan and Pope John Paul II, Cold Warriors." Senior Honors Projects, May 1, 2007. https://digitalcommons.uri.edu/ srhonorsprog/48.

"Florida, Texas and California Account for about One-Fifth of the World's New Coronavirus Cases." Accessed February 23, 2021. https://www.nbcnews.com/news/ us-news/florida-texas-california-account-about-one-fifth-world-s-new-n1233793.

Fortune, Aidan. "US Beef Industry Sets Out Japan Trade Goals." foodnavigator-usa. com. Accessed February 25, 2021. https://www.foodnavigator-usa.com/Article/ 2018/12/13/Trade-barriers-for-US-beef-in-Japan.

Foster, Peter. "Populist Duo Viktor Orban and Matteo Salvini Call for Deportation of Migrants from Europe." *The Telegraph.* Accessed February 23, 2021. https://www. telegraph.co.uk/news/2018/08/28/populist-duo-viktor-orban-matteo-salvini-call- deportation-migrants/.

Frail, T. A. "The Injustice of Japanese-American Internment Camps Resonates Strongly to This Day." *Smithsonian Magazine,* February 2017. https://www.smithsonianmag. com/history/injustice-japanese-americans-internment-camps-resonates-strongly- 180961422/.

France 24. "Macron Accepts Orban, Salvini Challenge: 'I Will Yield Nothing to Nationalists,'" August 29, 2018. https://www.france24.com/en/20180829-macron- orban-salvini-migrants-europe.

Franck, Jeffrey. "How F.D.R.'s Death Changed the Vice-Presidency." *New Yorker,* April 17, 2015. https://www.newyorker.com/news/daily-comment/how-f-d-r-s-death-chan ged-the-vice-presidency.

Franck, Thomas. "Trump Says White House Asked China for Plan to Reduce US Trade Deficit with Country by $1 Billion." CNBC, March 7, 2018. https://www.cnbc. com/2018/03/07/trump-says-white-house-asked-china-for-plan-to-reduce-us- trade-deficit-with-country-by-1-billion.html.

Frayer, Lauren. "If Britain Leaves the EU, What Happens to the 'Polish Plumber?'" NPR. org. Accessed February 23, 2021. https://www.npr.org/sections/parallels/2016/ 05/14/477685487/if-britain-leaves-the-eu-what-happens-to-the-polish-plumber.

"The Fresno Bee." Accessed February 22, 2021. https://account.fresnobee.com/payw all/registration?resume=209737409.

Fullerton, Maryellen. "Trump, Turmoil, and Terrorism: The US Immigration and Refugee Ban." *International Journal of Refugee Law* 29, no. 2 (June 1, 2017): 327–38. https://doi.org/10.1093/ijrl/eex021.

Gall, Carlotta, and Mark Landler. "Turkish President Snubs Bolton over Comments That Turkey Must Protect Kurds." *New York Times,* January 8, 2019. https://www.nytimes. com/2019/01/08/world/middleeast/erdogan-bolton-turkey-syria-kurds.html.

Ganley, Elaine. "Bannon to French Far-Right Party: 'Let Them Call You Racist … Wear It as a Badge of Honor.'" *Chicago Tribune,* March 10, 2018. https://www.chicago tribune.com/nation-world/ct-bannon-france-far-right-speech-20180310-story.html.

Gao, Charlotte. "On Rohingya Issue, Both China and India Back Myanmar Government." *The Diplomat,* September 2017. https://thediplomat.com/2017/09/ on-rohingya-issue-both-china-and-india-back-myanmar-government/.

Garrett, Laurie. "The Coming Plague." Accessed February 25, 2021. https://www.laurie garrett.com/the-coming-plague.

Gelder, Lawrence Van. "John A. Scali, 77, ABC Reporter Who Helped Ease Missile Crisis." *New York Times*, October 10, 1995, sec. U.S. https://www.nytimes.com/1995/10/10/us/john-a-scali-77-abc-reporter-who-helped-ease-missile-crisis.html.

Gellene, Denise. "Fergie Takes On a Heavy Load as Spokeswoman." *Los Angeles Times*, January 16, 1997. https://www.latimes.com/archives/la-xpm-1997-01-16-fi-19032-story.html.

Genç, Kaya. "Turkey's Glorious Hat Revolution." Los Angeles Review of Books. Accessed February 22, 2021. https://lareviewofbooks.org/article/turkeys-glorious-hat-revolution/.

Gessen, Keith. "How Did Amazon End Up as Literary Enemy No. 1?" Vanity Fair. Accessed February 21, 2021. https://www.vanityfair.com/news/business/2014/12/amazon-hachette-ebook-publishing.

Gittleson, Ben. "Biden Talks Cuomo, Putin, Migrants, Vaccine in ABC News Exclusive Interview." ABC News, March 27, 2021. https://abcnews.go.com/Politics/biden-talks-cuomo-putin-migrants-vaccine-abc-news/story?id=76490303.

Goldfarb, Ronald. "State Secrets? Let the Courts Weigh In." *Washington Post*, February 22, 2009. http://www.washingtonpost.com/wp-dyn/content/article/2009/02/20/AR2009022002167.html.

Goldstein, Gary. "Review: 'Architects of Denial' a Powerful Look at the Armenian Genocide." *Los Angeles Times*, October 5, 2017. https://www.latimes.com/entertainment/movies/la-et-mn-capsule-architects-of-denial-review-20171005-story.html.

Goodman, Amy. "U.S. Mercenaries Captured in Venezuela After Failed Coup Attempt Compared to a 'Bad Rambo Movie.'" Democracy Now!, May 6, 2020. https://www.democracynow.org/2020/5/6/venezuela_coup_attempt_miguel_tinker_salas.

Goodman, Joshua. "AP Exclusive: AT&T under Pressure to Defy Maduro's Censors." AP News, January 17, 2020. https://apnews.com/article/media-miami-caribbean-ap-top-news-venezuela-e5247995bc15a8b6bf479bf5af42f411.

Google Docs. "What's Up Down Under." Accessed February 23, 2021. https://docs.google.com/document/d/1n280CijL4lnPioNOyoupKH1zZTbW1Wly3Lxlm9eYmtY/edit?ouid=110480983717726574666&usp=docs_home&ths=true&usp=embed_facebook.

Grady, John. "Panel: Pace of Navy Freedom of Navigation Operations Stressing Force." USNI News, October 9, 2020. https://news.usni.org/2020/10/09/panel-pace-of-navy-freedom-of-navigation-operations-stressing-force.

Graham, Bryan Armen. "Enes Kanter Calls Turkey's Erdoğan 'Hitler of Our Century' after Airport Detainment." *Guardian*, May 22, 2017. http://www.theguardian.com/sport/2017/may/22/enes-kanter-airport-detainment-romania-turkey-passport-nba.

Graham-McLay, Charlotte. "Ardern Warns New Zealanders against Covid-19 Complacency." *Guardian*, July 15, 2020. http://www.theguardian.com/world/2020/jul/15/ardern-warns-new-zealanders-against-covid-19-complacency.

Graham-McLay, Charlotte, and Eleanor Ainge Roy. "Christchurch Gunman Pleads Guilty to New Zealand Mosque Attacks That Killed 51." *Guardian*, March 25, 2020.

https://www.theguardian.com/world/2020/mar/26/christchurch-shooting-bren
ton-tarrant-pleads-guilty-to-new-zealand-mosque-attacks-that-killed-51.

Green, Joshua. "Inside the Secret, Strange Origins of Steve Bannon's Nationalist
Fantasia." *Vanity Fair.* Accessed February 23, 2021. https://www.vanityfair.com/
news/2017/07/the-strange-origins-of-steve-bannons-nationalist-fantasia.

Grier, Peter. "The Death of Korean Air Lines Flight 007." *Air Force Magazine* (blog),
January 1, 2013. https://www.airforcemag.com/article/0113korean/.

Griswold, Elisa. "Franklin Graham's Uneasy Alliance with Donald Trump." *New Yorker*,
September 11, 2018. https://www.newyorker.com/news/dispatch/franklin-grah
ams-uneasy-alliance-with-donald-trump.

Guardian News. *Syria: Devastation in Former Isis Stronghold Revealed—Drone Video*, 2017.
https://www.youtube.com/watch?v=bItsSjLHL6M&feature=youtu.be&ab_chan
nel=GuardianNews.

———. "Kanye West Hurls Himself into Lake on Armenian Genocide Anniversary
Trip—Video." April 13, 2015. https://www.theguardian.com/music/video/2015/
apr/13/kanye-west-armenia-lake-genocide-video.

———. "Saudi Arabia Criticised for 48 Beheadings in Four Months of 2018." April 26,
2018. https://www.theguardian.com/world/2018/apr/26/saudi-arabia-criticised-
over-executions-for-drug-offences.

GuelphMercury.com. "U.S. Finally Joins Effort to Eradicate Landmines." Accessed
February 24, 2021. https://www.guelphmercury.com/opinion-story/4900435-u-s-
finally-joins-effort-to-eradicate-landmines/.

Gwertzman, Bernard. "Brezhnev Rumors Annoy U.S. Aides." *New York Times*, January
9, 1975, sec. Archives. https://www.nytimes.com/1975/01/09/archives/brezhnev-
rumors-annoy-us-aides-report-that-soviet-leader-has.html.

Haaretz. "Meet Mike Pompeo, Trump's Likely Next Secretary of State Who Wants
Snowden Executed," November 30, 2017. Accessed February 23, 2021. https://
www-haaretz-com.stanford.idm.oclc.org/us-news/meet-mike-pompeo-trump-s-
reported-new-hardliner-secretary-of-state-1.5627393.

———. "Turkey, Russia Ties Grow Stronger as U.S. Gets Elbowed Out of the Middle
East," April 4, 2018. Accessed February 22, 2021. http://www.haaretz.com/
middle-east-news/turkey-russia-ties-grow-stronger-as-u-s-out-of-the-middle-east-
1.5975136.

Hagiu, Andrei, and Simon Rothman. "Network Effects Aren't Enough." *Harvard Business
Review*, April 1, 2016. https://hbr.org/2016/04/network-effects-arent-enough.

Hakim, Danny. "Beyond Volkswagen, Europe's Diesels Flunked a Pollution Test."
New York Times, February 7, 2016, sec. Business. https://www.nytimes.com/2016/
02/08/business/international/no-matter-the-brand-europes-diesels-flunked-a-
pollution-test.html.

Hambling, David. "U.S. Seeks Armed Nuclear Icebreakers for Arctic Show of Force."
Forbes, June 12, 2020. https://www.forbes.com/sites/davidhambling/2020/06/12/
us-seeks-armed-nuclear-icebreakers-for-arctic-show-of-force/?sh=16abc19375ff.

Hardin, Garrett. "Lifeboat Ethics: The Case against Helping the Poor." The Garrett
Hardin Society, September 1974. http://www.garretthardinsociety.org/articles/art_
lifeboat_ethics_case_against_helping_poor.html.

Hardingham, Tamara. "What It's Like to Live in Antarctica during the Pandemic." CNN Travel, May 7, 2020. https://www.cnn.com/travel/article/life-in-antarctica-during-the-pandemic/index.html.

Harper, Jim. "The New National ID Systems." Cato Institute, January 30, 2018. https://www.cato.org/policy-analysis/new-national-id-systems.

Harrington, Walt. "Shock of Combat Changed George H.W. Bush's Life." HistoryNet, December 1, 2018. https://www.historynet.com/george-h-w-bush-shock-of-combat.htm.

Harris, Will. "The Jussie Smollett Scandal Recalls the Infamous (And Very Fake) Neo-Nazi Attack on Morton Downey Jr." Decider, February 26, 2019. https://decider.com/2019/02/26/morton-downey-jr-jussie-smollett/.

Harrup, Anthony. "Bolivia Expels Mexican and Spanish Diplomats." *Wall Street Journal*, December 30, 2019, sec. World. https://www.wsj.com/articles/bolivia-expels-mexican-and-spanish-diplomats-11577727172.

Hart, Benjamin. "McCain Regrets His Palin Pick for the Wrong Reasons." *Intelligencer*, May 5, 2018. https://nymag.com/intelligencer/2018/05/mccain-regrets-palin-pick-wrong-reasons.html.

"Harvard University Professor and Two Chinese Nationals Charged in Three Separate China Related Cases." US Department of Justice, January 28, 2020. https://www.justice.gov/opa/pr/harvard-university-professor-and-two-chinese-nationals-charged-three-separate-china-related.

Harvey, Fiona. "Paris Climate Change Agreement: The World's Greatest Diplomatic Success." *Guardian*, December 14, 2015. http://www.theguardian.com/environment/2015/dec/13/paris-climate-deal-cop-diplomacy-developing-united-nations.

Hayes, Christof. "Donald Trump Invites Russian President Vladimir Putin to Washington." USA Today. Accessed February 22, 2021. https://www.usatoday.com/story/news/politics/2018/10/26/donald-trump-invites-russian-president-vladimir-putin-washington/1781611002/.

Hendricks, Heather. "Canada's New Prime Minister, Justin Trudeau, Is a Snowboarder." *SNOWBOARDER Magazine* (blog), October 20, 2015. https://www.snowboarder.com/transworld-snowboarding-archive/snowboarding-news/canadas-new-prime-minister-justin-trudeau-is-a-snowboarder/.

Hermann, Peter. "D.C. Police Issue Warrant for 12 on Turkish Security Team in May Brawl." *Washington Post*, June 15, 2017. https://www-washingtonpost-com.stanford.idm.oclc.org/local/public-safety/dc-police-issue-warrant-for-12-turkish-security-personnel-involved-in-embassy-brawl/2017/06/15/4472fae6-51be-11e7-b064-828ba60fbb98_story.html?utm_term=.351d8886015c.

Hersh, Seymour M. "Torture at Abu Ghraib." *New Yorker*, May 10, 2004. https://www.newyorker.com/magazine/2004/05/10/torture-at-abu-ghraib.

Herszenhorn, David M. "Putin and Biden Confirm Extension of New START Treaty." Politico, January 27, 2021. https://www.politico.eu/article/putin-and-biden-confirm-extension-of-new-start-treaty/.

———. "Sergey Lavrov on Spy Attack in UK: 'We Have Nothing to Do with This.'" Politico, March 13, 2018. https://www.politico.eu/article/sergei-skripal-russian-foreign-ministry-summons-uk-ambassador/.

"HHRG-115-HM09-Wstate-PryP-20171012.Pdf." Accessed February 25, 2021. https://docs.house.gov/meetings/HM/HM09/20171012/106467/HHRG-115-HM09-Wstate-PryP-20171012.pdf.

The Hill. "Tillerson: Iran in 'Technical Compliance' with Nuclear Deal." Accessed February 25, 2021. https://thehill.com/policy/international/351677-tillerson-iran-in-technical-compliance-with-nuclear-deal.

Hill, Evan, Ainara Tiefenthäler, Christiaan Triebert, Drew Jordan, Haley Willis, and Robin Stein. "How George Floyd Was Killed in Police Custody." *New York Times,* June 1, 2020, sec. U.S. https://www.nytimes.com/2020/05/31/us/george-floyd-investigation.html.

Hincks, Joseph. "A Brief History of U.S.-Philippine Relations." *Time,* October 26, 2016. https://time.com/4543996/history-of-us-philippine-relations/.

HistoryNet. "California Gold Rush." Accessed February 23, 2021. https://www.history net.com/california-gold-rush.

"Hitler Comes to Power." Encyclopedia, Accessed February 25, 2021. https://encyclope dia.ushmm.org/content/en/article/hitler-comes-to-power.

"Hitman: Agent 47 (2015)." IMDb. Accessed February 24, 2021. https://www.imdb. com/title/tt2679042/.

Hodder, Nate. "Wirtschaftswunder: A Study into the Causes and Catalysts of the German Economic Miracle." *Senior Honors Theses,* March 31, 2019. https://digitalcommons. liberty.edu/honors/872.

Holmes, Oliver. "Philippines President Rodrigo Duterte Says He Personally Killed Criminals." *Guardian,* December 14, 2016. https://www.theguardian.com/world/2016/dec/14/philippines-president-rodrigo-duterte-personally-killed-criminals.

Holmes, Oliver, and Tom Phillips. "Gui Minhai: The Strange Disappearance of a Publisher Who Riled China's Elite." *Guardian,* December 8, 2015, sec. World News. https://www.theguardian.com/world/2015/dec/08/gui-minhai-the-strange-disappearance-of-a-publisher-who-riled-chinas-elite.

Hoodbhoy, Pervez. "The New Coronavirus Has Reminded Us of Our Debt to Darwin." *Wire Science,* November 4, 2020. https://science.thewire.in/the-sciences/novel-coro navirus-vaccines-drugs-evolution-charles-darwin/.

Hopkins, Caroline. "Coronavirus: Medical Workers Are 'Desperate' for Masks as Trump Fails to Act." Vox, March 22, 2020. https://www.vox.com/2020/3/22/21189896/coronavirus-in-us-masks-n95-respirator-doctors-nurses-shortage-ppe.

Hovhannisyan, Nvard, and Nailia Bagirova. "France and Turkey at Odds as Karabakh Fighting Divides NATO Allies." Reuters, October 1, 2020. https://www.reuters. com/article/us-armenia-azerbaijan-idUSKBN26L106.

Huaxia. "China Promotes Large Pig Farms to Ensure Stable Pork Supply." XinhuaNet, September 28, 2019. http://www.xinhuanet.com/english/2019-09/28/c_138431 378.htm.

Hubbard, Ben. "Saudi Death Sentences in Khashoggi Killing Fail to Dispel Questions." *New York Times,* December 23, 2019. https://www.nytimes.com/2019/12/23/world/middleeast/jamal-khashoggi-murder-sentence.html.

Hudson Institute. Vice President Mike Pence's Remarks on the Administration's Policy towards China, 2018. https://www.youtube.com/watch?v=aeVrMniBjSc&ab_chan nel=HudsonInstitute.

Human Rights Watch. "The Philippines' Duterte Incites Vigilante Violence." April 19, 2017. https://www.hrw.org/news/2017/04/19/philippines-duterte-incites-vigilante-violence.

———. "World Report 2018: Rights Trends in China." January 9, 2018. https://www.hrw.org/world-report/2018/country-chapters/china-and-tibet.

Hussey, Tom, and Dan Haygarth. "Harry and Meghan to Be 'Ditched' by Prince Charles in New Monarchy Plans." Cambridgeshire Live, April 25, 2021. https://www.cambridge-news.co.uk/news/uk-world-news/harry-meghan-to-ditched-prince-20460872.

Icelandmag. "First Female Head of State, Vigdís Finnbogadóttir, Elected 35 Years Ago Today." June 29, 2015. https://icelandmag.is/article/first-female-head-state-vigdis-finnbogadottir-elected-35-years-ago-today.

Illing, Sean. "Are We in a Constitutional Crisis Yet?" Vox, October 9, 2019. https://www.vox.com/policy-and-politics/2019/10/9/20905503/trump-white-house-letter-democrats-impeachment.

IMDB. "The Crown" (TV Series 2016–). IMDb. Accessed February 25, 2021. https://www.imdb.com/title/tt4786824/.

Institute of National Remembrance. "'The Pope from Behind the Iron Curtain'—Cracow-Budapest." Institute of National Remembrance. Accessed February 22, 2021. https://ipn.gov.pl/en/news/1390,The-Pope-from-Behind-the-Iron-Curtain-Cracow-Budapest.html.

International Crisis Group. "Prospects for a Deal to Stabilise Syria's North East." September 5, 2018. https://www.crisisgroup.org/middle-east-north-africa/eastern-mediterranean/syria/190-prospects-deal-stabilise-syrias-north-east.

Internet Archive. "Digital Library of Free & Borrowable Books, Movies, Music & Wayback Machine." Accessed February 20, 2021. https://archive.org/.

Interpol. "About Red Notices." Accessed February 23, 2021. https://www.interpol.int/How-we-work/Notices/Red-Notices.

"Iran Plane Downing: Person Who Filmed Video 'Arrested.'" BBC News, January 14, 2020, sec. Middle East. https://www.bbc.com/news/world-middle-east-51114945.

Isachenkov, Vladimir. "Belarus' Leader Warns Russia against Forceful Merger." AP News, December 24, 2019. https://apnews.com/article/0ef06c716e331bd4411441a8b4b63af7.

"ISIS 'Beatles' Will Not Face Death Penalty in US." BBC News, August 20, 2020, sec. UK. https://www.bbc.com/news/uk-53837724.

Jackson, David. "On Syria, Donald Trump Cites 'My Great and Unmatched Wisdom'—Others Say No Way." USA Today. Accessed February 24, 2021. https://www.usatoday.com/story/news/politics/2019/10/07/donald-trump-unmatched-wisdom-syria-tweet/3898498002/.

Jacobs, Sarah. "15 Photos of Former US Presidents Hanging Out Together." Business Insider, August 25, 2018. https://www.businessinsider.com/us-presidents-hanging-out-together-photos-2018-2.

JFK Library. "Cuban Missile Crisis." Accessed February 22, 2021. https://www.jfklibrary.org/learn/about-jfk/jfk-in-history/cuban-missile-crisis.

Jakes, Lara, and Steven Lee Myers. "U.S. Designates China's Official Media as Operatives of the Communist State." *New York Times*, February 18, 2020, sec. World. https://www.nytimes.com/2020/02/18/world/asia/china-media-trump.html.

James, William. "UK Says China's Security Law Is Serious Violation of Hong Kong Treaty." Reuters, July 1, 2020. https://www.reuters.com/article/us-hongkong-prote sts-britain-idUSKBN2425LL.

JAY-Z. "JAY-Z—Show Me What You Got, 2009." https://www.youtube.com/watch?v= FS4U-HAHwps&ab_channel=JayZVEVO.

———. "JAY-Z—The Story of O.J., 2017." https://www.youtube.com/watch?v=RM7l w0Ovzq0&ab_channel=JayZVEVO.

Jewish Virtual Library. "Refusniks." Accessed February 23, 2021. https://www.jewishvir tuallibrary.org/refusniks.

"John Paul II." Accessed February 22, 2021. http://www.vatican.va/content/john-paul-ii/en.html.

Jones, Dorian. "Turkey Imposes Sanctions for French Genocide Bill." Voice of America, December 21, 2011. https://www.voanews.com/europe/turkey-imposes-sanctions-french-genocide-bill.

Joseph, Elizabeth, and Katie Hunt. "Missing Hong Kong Bookseller: I Was Kidnapped." CNN, June 16, 2016. https://www.cnn.com/2016/06/16/asia/china-hong-kong-booksellers/.

Kalan, Dariusz. "Poland's New Populism." Foreign Policy, October 5, 2018. https:// foreignpolicy-com.stanford.idm.oclc.org/2018/10/05/polands-new-populism-pis/.

Kanter, Enes. "Turkey's Erdogan Wants Me Back in His Country So He Can Silence Me." *Washington Post*, January 15, 2019. https://www-washingtonpost-com.stanford. idm.oclc.org/opinions/enes-kanter-anyone-who-speaks-out-against-erdogan-is-a-target-that-includes-me/2019/01/15/dea79a90-1846-11e9-88fe-f9f77a3bcb6c_st ory.html?utm_term=.346d03d55a33.

Kaplan, Fred M. "Enhanced-Radiation Weapons." *Scientific American* 238, no. 5 (1978): 44–51.

Kappler, Maija. "Women on TikTok in Egypt Are Being Arrested for 'Indecent' Videos." *HuffingtonPost*, August 5, 2020. https://www.huffingtonpost.ca/entry/egypt-tiktok-arrests_ca_5f2ad9bdc5b6b9cff7ebdf71.

Kardas, Umit. "Insulting the Turkish President: Article 299 and Why Europe Says Its Illegal." Ahval, November 16, 2018. https://ahvalnews.com/turkey-democracy/insulting-turkish-president-article-299-and-why-europe-says-its-illegal.

Karimi, Nasser, and Aya Batrawy. "Iran Announces Arrests over Downing of Plane That Killed 176." AP News, January 14, 2020. https://apnews.com/article/40f1b9bd4 75d23bd5d2977ff2e473d7b.

Karimi, Nasser, and Jon Gambrell. "Iran Shoots down US Surveillance Drone, Heightening Tensions." AP News, June 20, 2019. https://apnews.com/article/ e4316eb989d5499c9828350de8524963.

Keller, Jared. "The Key to Bridging the Civil-Military Divide, According to Mattis." *Task & Purpose* (blog), December 4, 2018. https://taskandpurpose.com/analysis/civil-military-divide-mattis/.

Kelley, Michael B., and Rob Wile. "America's Robber Barons." Business Insider, March 20, 2012. https://www.businessinsider.com/americas-robber-barons-2012-3.

Kelly, John, and Pierre Thomas. "Disaster in Motion: Where Flights from Coronavirus-Ravaged Countries Landed in US." ABC News, April 7, 2020. https://abcnews. go.com/Health/disaster-motion-flights-coronavirus-ravaged-countries-landed-us/ story?id=70025470.

Kelly, Mary Louise. "American University CEU Kicked Out of Hungary, Says It Will Move to Vienna." December 6, 2018. NPR. Accessed February 24, 2021. https://www.npr.org/2018/12/06/674310948/american-university-ces-kicked-out-of-hungary-says-it-will-move-to-vienna.

Kester, John. "The Trump Administration Has No Plan for Dealing with a North Korean EMP Attack." Foreign Policy, October 15, 2017. https://foreignpolicy.com/2017/10/16/the-trump-administration-has-no-plan-for-dealing-with-a-north-korean-emp-attack/.

Kieschnick, Clara. "Caroline Kushel '21 Chosen as New Stanford Tree." *Stanford Daily*, March 13, 2019. https://www.stanforddaily.com/2019/03/13/caroline-kushel-21-chosen-as-new-stanford-tree/.

Kindred, Alahna. "Who Is Speaker Nancy Pelosi's Husband Paul?" *Scottish Sun*, February 9, 2019. https://www.thescottishsun.co.uk/news/3708570/nancy-pelosi-husband-paul-venture-capitalist-married/.

King, Neil. "'The KKK Is Active Here in Germany'." Deutsche Welle. Accessed February 23, 2021. https://www.dw.com/en/the-kkk-is-active-here-in-germany/a-37668846.

Kingsley, Patrick. "How a Liberal Dissident Became a Far-Right Hero, in Hungary and Beyond." *New York Times*, April 6, 2018. https://www.nytimes.com/2018/04/06/world/europe/viktor-orban-hungary-politics.html.

Kingston, John. *The Undiscovered Oil and Gas of Antarctica.* Open-File Report. Dept. of the Interior, U.S. Geological Survey, 1991. https://doi.org/10.3133/ofr91597.

Kirchick, James. "Hungary's Ugly State-Sponsored Holocaust Revisionism." *Tablet Magazine*, March 14, 2017. https://www.tabletmag.com/sections/news/articles/hungary-kirchick-end-of-europe.

Knight, Will. "China Flexes Its Soft Power With 'Covid Diplomacy.'" Wired, April 2, 2020. https://www.wired.com/story/china-flexes-soft-power-covid-diplomacy/.

Kolodny, Lora. "California Health Corps Site Scored 25,000 Sign-Ups in Its First Day, Governor Newsom Says." CNBC, March 31, 2020. https://www.cnbc.com/2020/03/31/california-health-corps-site-scored-25000-sign-ups-in-its-first-day.html.

Koppel, Ted. *Lights Out: A Cyberattack, a Nation Unprepared, Surviving the Aftermath.* Crown, 2015.

Kounalakis, Eleni. "Madam Ambassador." The New Press. Accessed February 25, 2021. https://thenewpress.com/books/madam-ambassador.

Kounalakis, Markos. "Adding to America's Rogues' List of Unsavory but Friendly Leaders." *Sacramento Bee*, November 7, 2015. https://www.sacbee.com/opinion/op-ed/soapbox/article43491471.html.

———. "Blob's Foreign Policy Experts Get It Right This Time on Kurds." *Miami Herald.* Accessed February 25, 2021. https://www.miamiherald.com/opinion/op-ed/article235998818.html.

———. "China's Position on International Intervention: A Media and Journalism Critical Discourse Analysis of Its Case for 'Sovereignty' versus 'Responsibility to Protect' Principles in Syria." *Global Media and China* 1, no. 3 (September 1, 2016): 149–67. https://doi.org/10.1177/2059436416654918.

———. "Chinese Agents Posed as Journalists in US. And the US Just Did Something about It." McClatchy Washington Bureau. Accessed February 22, 2021. https://www.mcclatchydc.com/opinion/article218805365.html.

———. "Death Penalty in the U.S. Protects Edward Snowden." *Fort Worth Star-Telegram.* Accessed February 23, 2021. https://www.star-telegram.com/opinion/article3842 156.html.

———. "Florida Could Punish Trump for Failed Latin America Policy." *Miami Herald.* Accessed February 25, 2021. https://www.miamiherald.com/opinion/op-ed/artic le237362379.html.

———. "Goodnight Mao." Hoover Institution. Accessed February 21, 2021. https:// www.hoover.org/research/goodnight-mao.

———. "Home Sweet Palace." *Sacramento Bee.* Accessed February 23, 2021. https:// www.sacbee.com/opinion/op-ed/markos-kounalakis/article9456599.html.

———. "Malls, Dying in America, Have Been Revived by Protesters in Hong Kong." *Miami Herald.* Accessed February 23, 2021. https://www.miamiherald.com/opin ion/op-ed/article235261012.html.

———. "Nicaragua's 'House of Cards' Stars Another Corrupt and Powerful Couple." *Miami Herald.* Accessed February 25, 2021. https://www.miamiherald.com/opin ion/op-ed/article222373075.html.

———. "Opinion: Hostile Turkey Aims to Sideline Washington, the West." The News & Observer, January 18, 2018. https://www.newsobserver.com/opinion/article19 5202884.html.

———. "Rohingya Attacks Are the Murderous Version of Trump's Muslim Ban." McClatchy Washington Bureau. Accessed February 23, 2021. https://www.mcclatch ydc.com/opinion/article174427831.html.

———. "Secretary of State Rex Tillerson Handled Venezuela Deftly—Until He Fumbled." *Miami Herald,* February 9, 2018. https://www.miamiherald.com/opin ion/op-ed/article199460219.html.

———. "Skripal Attack Forces US, UK to Punish Russia or Risk Other Attacks." *Miami Herald.* Accessed February 23, 2021. https://www.miamiherald.com/article205153 454.html.

———. "Spin Wars and Spy Games." Hoover Institution. Accessed February 22, 2021. https://www.hoover.org/research/spin-wars-and-spy-games.

———. *Spin Wars and Spy Games: Global Media and Intelligence Gathering.* Hoover Institution Press, Stanford University, 2018.

———. "The Conversation: America's International Broadcasters Are Losing the Air Wars." *Sacramento Bee,* June 22, 2014. https://www.sacbee.com/opinion/the-conve rsation/article2601683.html.

———. "The Impatience of China's Xi Jinping." Medium, October 28, 2018. https:// medium.com/@KounalakisM/the-impatience-of-chinas-xi-jinping-44e0ef772d2e.

———. "The Tension Is High in Venezuela's Standoff, but No One Can Afford to Shoot First." *Miami Herald,* March 7, 2019. https://www.miamiherald.com/opinion/op-ed/article227248354.html.

———. "The U.S. Has Snatched Up Global Supplies of Remdesivir." *Miami Herald.* Accessed February 25, 2021. https://www.miamiherald.com/opinion/op-ed/artic le243971337.html.

———. "Trump Is Looking Like a Royal Loser in the U.K." *Sacramento Bee.* Accessed February 25, 2021. https://www.sacbee.com/opinion/california-forum/article18 7177323.html.

———. "Under Trump's 'Sovereignty Doctrine,' Foreign Tyrants Have Nothing to Worry About." *Miami Herald*. Accessed February 24, 2021. https://www.miamiher ald.com/opinion/op-ed/article220974935.html.

———. "U.S. Takes Significant Steps Rid World of Land Mines." *Sacramento Bee*. Accessed February 24, 2021. https://www.sacbee.com/opinion/california-forum/ article2618972.html.

———. "Warm Water, Cold Reality, New Frontier for Exploiting Resources." *Sacramento Bee*, April 20, 2014. https://www.sacbee.com/opinion/op-ed/article 2595988.html.

———. "Women, Children Suffer Most in Conflicts around the World." *Miami Herald*. Accessed February 25, 2021. https://www.miamiherald.com/opinion/op-ed/artic le236864258.html.

Kramer, Jane. "Matteo Renzi's Agenda for Italy." *New Yorker*, June 22, 2015. https://www. newyorker.com/magazine/2015/06/29/the-demolition-man.

Krever, Mick. "Marie Colvin Was Deliberately Targeted by Assad Regime, Sister Says." CNN, April 10, 2018. https://www.cnn.com/2018/04/10/world/marie-colvin-cat-colvin-amanpour-intl/index.html.

Kroft, Steve. "Ex-British Spy on Leading a 'Double Life' as a Famous Author." CBS News, January 21, 2018. https://www.cbsnews.com/news/john-le-carre-ex-british-spys-double-life-as-a-famous-author-1/.

Kuo, Lily. "'The New Normal': China's Excessive Coronavirus Public Monitoring Could Be Here to Stay." *Guardian*, March 9, 2020. http://www.theguardian.com/ world/2020/mar/09/the-new-normal-chinas-excessive-coronavirus-public-monitor ing-could-be-here-to-stay.

LII / Legal Information Institute. "Article I." Accessed February 24, 2021. https://www. law.cornell.edu/constitution/articlei.

Labott, Elise. "CIA Concludes Saudi Crown Prince Ordered Jamal Khashoggi's Death, Sources Say." CNN, November 17, 2018. https://www.cnn.com/2018/11/16/polit ics/cia-assessment-khashoggi-assassination-saudi-arabia/index.html.

Lagunina, Irina. "Gorbachev Remembers Pope John Paul II." Radio Free Europe/Radio Liberty, April 8, 2005. https://www.rferl.org/a/1058353.html.

Larter, David B. "US Navy Moves toward Unleashing Killer Robot Ships on the World's Oceans." Defense News, January 15, 2019. https://www.defensenews.com/naval/ 2019/01/15/the-us-navy-moves-toward-unleashing-killer-robot-ships-on-the-wor lds-oceans/.

"Las Vegas Strip Hotel." New York New York. Accessed February 22, 2021. https:// newyorknewyork.mgmresorts.com/en.html?

Lawler, Dave. "China's Coronavirus Cover-up Was among Worst in History, Congressman Says." Axios. Accessed February 25, 2021. https://www.axios.com/china-coronavi rus-cover-up-wuhan-pandemic-fa894bb8-998d-494b-8e7a-e834f86d2ea9.html.

Lawless, Jill. "It's Final: Harry and Meghan Won't Return as Working Royals." AP News, February 19, 2021. https://apnews.com/article/prince-harry-meghan-royal-duties-f4b38611a4ba8e1a611efec0bc6ecd65.

Lawrence, Mark Atwood. "A Portrait of Stalin in All His Murderous Contradictions." *New York Times*, October 19, 2017, sec. Books. https://www.nytimes.com/2017/10/ 19/books/review/stephen-kotkin-stalin-biography.html.

Lazarus, Sarah. "Women. Life. Freedom. Female Fighters of Kurdistan." CNN, January 27, 2019. https://www.cnn.com/2019/01/27/homepage2/kurdish-female-fight ers/index.html.

Lederman, Daniel. "The Pandemic Roadmap: How New Zealand Beat COVID-19." FIU News. Accessed February 23, 2021. https://news.fiu.edu/2020/the-pandemic-roadmap-how-new-zealand-beat-covid-19.

Lee, Matthew. "After Meet on Iran Nuke Deal, Tillerson Says Iran Complying but Violating Spirit." *Times of Israel*, September 21, 2017. https://www.timesofisrael. com/after-meet-on-iran-nuke-deal-tillerson-says-iran-complying-but-violating-spirit/.

Lee, Spike. *BlacKkKlansman*. Biography, Comedy, Crime, Drama. Focus Features, Legendary Entertainment, Perfect World Pictures, 2018.

Leiber, Nick. "Foreign Students Sour on America, Jeopardizing a $39 Billion Industry." Bloomberg, January 17, 2019. https://www.bloomberg.com/news/articles/2019-01-17/foreign-students-are-a-39-billion-industry-trump-is-scaring-them-off.

Leigh, Henry. "5 Things Tiger King Doesn't Explain about Captive Tigers." World Wildlife Fund, March 31, 2020. https://www.worldwildlife.org/stories/5-things-tiger-king-doesn-t-explain-about-captive-tigers.

Lemann, Nicholas. "Hating on Herbert Hoover." *New Yorker*, October 16, 2017. https://www.newyorker.com/magazine/2017/10/23/hating-on-herbert-hoover.

Leonard, Jenny. "China's Thousand Talents Program Finally Gets the U.S.'s Attention." Bloomberg, December 12, 2019. https://www.bloomberg.com/news/articles/2019-12-12/china-s-thousand-talents-program-finally-gets-the-u-s-s-attention.

Leopold, Jason. "High-Profile Russian Death in Washington Was No—It Was Murder, Officials Say." BuzzFeed News, July 28, 2017. https://www.buzzfeednews.com/arti cle/jasonleopold/putins-media-czar-was-murdered-just-before-meeting-feds.

"Lese-Majeste Explained: How Thailand Forbids Insult of Its Royalty." BBC News, October 6, 2017, sec. Asia. https://www.bbc.com/news/world-asia-29628191.

Lewis, David. "President Trump Claims the FBI Is Tainted and Its Reputation in Tatters. This Graph Shows He's Wrong." *Washington Post*, December 16, 2017. https://www-washingtonpost-com.stanford.idm.oclc.org/news/monkey-cage/wp/2017/12/16/president-trump-claims-the-fbi-is-tainted-and-its-reputation-in-tatters-this-graph-shows-hes-wrong/.

Lewis, John. "John Lewis: Together, You Can Redeem the Soul of Our Nation." *New York Times*, July 30, 2020, sec. Opinion. https://www.nytimes.com/2020/07/30/opin ion/john-lewis-civil-rights-america.html.

Library of Congress. "The Religion Clauses: Historical Background | Constitution Annotated." Accessed February 22, 2021. https://constitution.congress.gov/bro wse/essay/amdt1_1_1/.

Light, Felix. "How Poor Handling of Covid-19 Has Caused Uproar in Belarus." *New Statesman*, June 24, 2020. https://www.newstatesman.com/world/europe/2020/06/how-poor-handling-covid-19-has-caused-uproar-belarus.

Lim, Darren, and Victor Ferguson. "In Beef over Barley, Chinese Economic Coercion Cuts against the Grain." *The Interpreter*, May 13, 2020. https://www.lowyinstit ute.org/the-interpreter/barney-over-beef-chinese-economic-coercion-cuts-agai nst-grain.

Lim, Louisa. "China's Top 5 Censored Posts in 2015." *Foreign Policy* (blog). Accessed February 22, 2021. http://foreignpolicy.com/2015/12/31/china-top-5-censored-posts-2015-censorship-communist-party-xi-jinping-explosion-pooh/.

Lim, Louisa, and Julia Bergin. "Inside China's Audacious Global Propaganda Campaign." *Guardian*, December 7, 2018, sec. News. https://www.theguardian.com/news/2018/dec/07/china-plan-for-global-media-dominance-propaganda-xi-jinping.

Lim, Michael Martina, and Benjamin Kang. "China's Xi Anointed 'core' Leader, on Par with Mao, Deng." Reuters, October 27, 2016. https://www.reuters.com/article/us-china-politics-idUSKCN12R1CK.

Lister, Tim. "Attack on Saudi Oil Field a Game-Changer in Gulf Confrontation." CNN, September 15, 2019. https://www.cnn.com/2019/09/15/middleeast/saudi-oil-attack-lister-analysis-intl/index.html.

The Local. "Four Ku Klux Klan Groups Active in Germany, Says Govt." Accessed February 23, 2021. https://www.thelocal.de/20161025/four-ku-klux-klan-groups-in-germany-report-kkk.

Locke, Sarina. "$66m African Swine Fever Detection Boost at Sydney and Melbourne Airports, Mail Centres." ABC News Australia, December 10, 2019. https://www.abc.net.au/news/rural/2019-12-11/funding-boost-quarantine-to-prevent-african-swine-fever-arrival/11787948.

Los Angeles Times. "'I Didn't Want This Baby': Rohingya Rape Survivors Face a Harrowing Choice." Accessed February 23, 2021. https://www.latimes.com/world/la-fg-myanmar-rohingya-rape-20180601-story.html.

Loveluck, Louisa. "The Battle for Aleppo, Explained." *Washington Post*, Novmeber 24, 2016. https://www.washingtonpost.com/news/worldviews/wp/2016/11/24/the-battle-for-aleppo-explained/.

Mackintosh, Eliza. "'Trump Baby' Balloon Takes Flight in London Protests—CNN." CNN, July 13, 2018. https://www.cnn.com/2018/07/13/uk/trump-baby-blimp-to-fly-over-uk-parliament-intl/index.html.

Macmillan Dictionary. "IRL (Abbreviation) American English Definition and Synonyms." Accessed February 23, 2021. https://www.macmillandictionary.com/us/dictionary/american/irl.

Madison, Lucy. "Ron Paul Fears NSA Leaker Assassination." CBS News, June 12, 2013. https://www.cbsnews.com/news/ron-paul-fears-nsa-leaker-assassination/.

Magical Magnus. "Hamilton—King George—All Three Songs, 2016." YouTube. https://www.youtube.com/watch?v=1NOjkmkanrc&ab_channel=MagicalMagnus.

Main, Douglas. "'Murder Hornets' Have Arrived in the U.S.—Here's What You Should Know." National Geographic, May 4, 2020. https://www.nationalgeographic.com/animals/article/asian-giant-hornets-arrive-united-states.

Makhovsky, Andrei. "Belarus President Accuses Election Rival of Corruption after Raid." Reuters, June 12, 2020. https://www.reuters.com/article/us-belarus-election-idUSKBN23J2R1.

———. "Dismissed as 'Poor Things', Three Women Try to Unseat Male President of Belarus." Reuters, July 22, 2020. https://www.reuters.com/article/us-belarus-election-opposition-idUSKCN24N1PT.

Maremont, Mark, and Nick Kostov. "Behind Ghosn's Escape, an Ex-Green Beret with a Beef about His Own Time in Jail—WSJ." *Wall Street Journal*, June 18, 2020.

https://www.wsj.com/articles/behind-ghosns-escape-an-ex-green-beret-with-a-beef-about-his-own-time-in-jail-11579323661.

Marines.com. "History of the Marine Corps." Accessed February 23, 2021. https://www.marines.com/about-the-marine-corps/who-are-the-marines/history.html.

Mark, Jason. "Toward a Moral Case for Meat Eating | Sierra Club." Sierra Club, February 24, 2017. https://www.sierraclub.org/sierra/green-life/toward-moral-case-for-meat-eating.

Markos Kounalakis. The War Prayer, 2011. https://www.youtube.com/watch?v=IRVo d4PwQHs&ab_channel=MarkosKounalakis%2CPhD.

Maslin, Janet. "The Knotty Ties Binding America's Ex-Leaders." *New York Times*, April 17, 2012, sec. Books. https://www.nytimes.com/2012/04/18/books/the-preside nts-club-by-nancy-gibbs-and-michael-duffy.html.

Mason, Rowena, and Kate Proctor. "Boris Johnson Pledges to Prioritise NHS after Election Victory." *Guardian*, December 13, 2019. https://www.theguardian.com/politics/2019/dec/13/boris-johnson-pledges-to-prioritise-nhs-after-election-victory.

McCain, John. "'Vladimir Putin Is an Evil Man.'" *Wall Street Journal*, May 11, 2018. https://www.wsj.com/articles/john-mccain-vladimir-putin-is-an-evil-man-152 5964549.

McCain, Meghan. "'Never Going to Forgive' Trump Attacks on Dad." *Time*. Accessed February 25, 2021. https://time.com/5327550/meghan-mccain-donald-trump-atta cks-john-mccain/.

McDonnell, Tim. "Turkey's Invasion of Syria Worsens a Humanitarian Crisis." NPR. org, October 11, 2019. https://www.npr.org/sections/goatsandsoda/2019/10/11/769445696/turkeys-invasion-of-syria-worsens-a-humanitarian-crisis.

McKay, Hollie. "Putin Could Make Move to Absorb Belarus, Europe's 'Last Dictatorship,' Experts Say." Fox News, March 2, 2020. https://www.foxnews.com/world/inside-europes-last-dictatorship-the-soviet-styled-belarus.

McKernan, Bethan. "Idlib Province Bombing Kills 21 in Single Day." *Guardian*, February 26, 2020. http://www.theguardian.com/world/2020/feb/26/syria-21-dead-targ ets-including-schools-and-nurseries-bombed-in-idlib.

McLaughlin, Timothy. "A U.S. Ally Is Turning to China to 'Build, Build, Build.'" *Atlantic*, May 8, 2019. https://www.theatlantic.com/international/archive/2019/05/phil ippines-us-ally-china-investment/588829/.

McNish, Jacquie. "Huawei Executive's Extradition Hearing in Canada Begins." *Wall Street Journal*, January 20, 2020, sec. World. https://www.wsj.com/articles/huawei-executives-extradition-hearing-in-canada-begins-11579561125.

MEE Staff. "UN-Backed Libyan Government Accuses Khalifa Haftar of Staging 'Coup.'" Middle East Eye, April 28, 2020. https://www.middleeasteye.net/news/un-backed-libyan-government-accuses-khalifa-haftar-staging-coup.

Meeropol, Ivy. "Bully. Coward. Victim. The Story of Roy Cohn." HBO. Accessed February 25, 2021. https://www.hbo.com/documentaries/bully-coward-vic tim-the-story-of-roy-cohn.

"Meet the Author: Markos Kounalakis." USC Center on Public Diplomacy. Accessed February 25, 2021. https://uscpublicdiplomacy.org/story/meet-author-markos-kou nalakis.

"Mehriban Əliyeva—Azərbaycanın Birinci Xanımı—Biography Site—the First Lady of Azerbaijan." Accessed February 23, 2021. https://mehriban-aliyeva.az/en/site/biography.

"Memento Park Budapest | Communist Statues and Ghosts of Communist Dictatorship." Accessed February 23, 2021. http://www.mementopark.hu/.

Menon, Praveen. "Ardern Dances for Joy after New Zealand Eliminates Coronavirus." Reuters, June 8, 2020. https://www.reuters.com/article/us-health-coronavirus-new zealand-idUSKBN23F0B5.

Meredith, Sam. "Belarus' President Dismisses Coronavirus Risk, Encourages Citizens to Drink Vodka and Visit Saunas." CNBC, March 31, 2020. https://www.cnbc.com/2020/03/31/coronavirus-belarus-urges-citizens-to-drink-vodka-visit-saunas.html.

Meyer, Eric. "With Oil and Gas Pipelines, China Takes a Shortcut through Myanmar." *Forbes.* Accessed February 24, 2021. https://www.forbes.com/sites/ericrmeyer/2015/02/09/oil-and-gas-china-takes-a-shortcut/.

Meyers, Jessica. "China Once Welcomed Refugees, but Its Policies Now Make Trump Look Lenient." *Los Angeles Times*, October 18, 2017. https://www.latimes.com/world/asia/la-fg-china-forgotten-refugees-2017108-story.html.

"Miami Herald." Accessed February 25, 2021. https://account.miamiherald.com/payw all/stop?resume=220659675.

Miami Herald. "Chinese Pork Production Beset by African Swine Fever." Accessed February 25, 2021. https://www.miamiherald.com/opinion/op-ed/article241142286.html.

———. "Donald Trump Registered His Trademark in Cuba." Accessed February 25, 2021. https://www.miamiherald.com/news/nation-world/world/americas/cuba/article245902870.html.

———. "President Trump Weighs Pardoning 'Tiger King' Joe Exotic." Accessed February 25, 2021. https://www.miamiherald.com/news/nation-world/national/article241877621.html.

———. "Rubio and Enes Kanter Discuss Free-Speech Erosion in Turkey." Accessed February 23, 2021. https://www.miamiherald.com/news/politics-government/article224565050.html.

———. "Turkish Defense Radar Locked on Russian Fighter as It Bombed Syrian Town." Accessed February 25, 2021. https://www.miamiherald.com/news/nation-world/national/article37743798.html.

Miller, Johnny. "S.F. Schools Boss Orders Lowell High Mascot Change." SFGate, December 5, 2013. https://www.sfgate.com/entertainment/article/S-F-schools-boss-orders-Lowell-High-mascot-change-5039721.php.

Minder, Raphael, and Elian Pelitier. "Coronavirus in Europe: Thousands of Health Workers Out of Action." The New York Times, March 24, 2020. https://www.nyti mes.com/2020/03/24/world/europe/coronavirus-europe-covid-19.html.

Ming, Yao. "The Naismith Memorial Basketball Hall of Fame: Yao Ming." Basketball Hall of Fame. Accessed February 23, 2021. https://www.hoophall.com/hall-of-fam ers/yao-ming/.

Moens, Barbara, and Camille Gijs. "Of Race and Royalty: How the King Surprised Belgium." Politico, July 3, 2020. https://www.politico.eu/article/of-race-and-roya lty-how-the-king-philippe-surprised-belgium-leopold-statue-black-lives-matter-fland ers-wallonia/.

Montalbano, William. "For Jews, a 500-Year Turkish Haven: Sanctuary: In 1492, 60,000 of Them Driven from Spain Were Welcomed in Istanbul, Where They Have Flourished." Los Angeles Times. Accessed February 22, 2021. https://www.latimes. com/archives/la-xpm-1991-11-02-mn-704-story.html.

Moody, John. "Why Trump Can Envy, but Not Imitate, China." Fox News, January 3, 2018. https://www.foxnews.com/opinion/why-trump-can-envy-but-not-imit ate-china.

Moran, Michael. "Frantically, the Army Tries to Armor Humvees." NBC News, April 15, 2004. https://www.nbcnews.com/id/wbna4731185.

Moscaritolo, Angela. "Facebook Has a New Mission." Entrepreneur, June 23, 2017. https://www.entrepreneur.com/article/296302.

Movieclips. March of the Penguins Official Trailer #1 - (2005) HD, 2011. https://www. youtube.com/watch?v=L7tWNwhSocE&ab_channel=Movieclips.

Mozur, Paul. "Drone Maker D.J.I. May Be Sending Data to China, U.S. Officials Say." *New York Times*, November 29, 2017. https://www.nytimes.com/2017/11/29/tec hnology/dji-china-data-drones.html?_r=1.

Natarajan, Sridhar, and Tom Schoenberg. "Venezuelan Oil Official Flees to U.S. with Intel on Maduro's Inner Circle." WorldOil.com, August 31, 2020. https://www. worldoil.com/news/2020/8/31/venezuelan-oil-official-flees-to-us-with-intel-on-maduro-s-inner-circle.

Nations, United. "404." United Nations. United Nations. Accessed February 23, 2021. https://www.un.org/en/genocideprevention/about-responsibility-to-protect.html.

"NATO—Topic: Collective Defence—Article 5." Accessed February 25, 2021. https:// www.nato.int/cps/en/natohq/topics_110496.htm.

The Nature Conservancy. "Invasive Species in Florida." Accessed February 25, 2021. https://www.nature.org/en-us/about-us/where-we-work/united-states/florida/ stories-in-florida/combating-invasive-species-in-florida/.

Navrozov, Andrei. "The Saxon Soul." *Chronicles*, September 17, 2014. https://www.chr oniclesmagazine.org/article/the-saxon-soul/.

Nebehay, Stephanie. "U.N. Calls on China to Free Uighurs from Alleged Re-Education Camps." Reuters, August 31, 2018. https://www.reuters.com/article/us-china-rig hts-un-idUSKCN1LF1D6.

Needham, Kirsty. "Australia Rejects Chinese 'Economic Coercion' Threat Amid Planned Coronavirus Probe." Reuters, April 27, 2020. https://www.reuters.com/article/us-health-coronavirus-australia-china-idUSKCN2290Z6.

Nelson, Craig, and Ehsanullah Amiri. "Taliban Release Two Western Hostages in Exchange for Militants." *Wall Street Journal*, November 19, 2019. https://www.wsj.com/articles/ taliban-prisoners-in-doha-ahead-of-swap-for-u-s-hostages-11574149286.

Nelson, Steven. "Trump Sticks to Easter Reopening despite Skepticism." *New York Post*, March 25, 2020. https://nypost.com/2020/03/25/trump-sticks-to-easter-reopen ing-despite-skepticism/.

Nemtsova, Anna. "A Bloodless Uprising in Armenia Just Forced the Leader to Resign: Will New Peaceful Revolutions Follow?" *Daily Beast*, April 24, 2018. https://www.thedai lybeast.com/a-bloodless-uprising-in-armenia-just-forced-the-president-to-resign-will-new-peaceful-revolutions-follow.

————. "Russia's Twin Nostalgias." *Atlantic*, December 7, 2019. https://www.theatlan tic.com/international/archive/2019/12/vladimir-putin-russia-nostalgia-soviet-union/603079/.

"NETSurveillance WEB." Accessed May 18, 2021. http://192.168.1.81/.

Neuman, Scott. "Referendum in Russia Passes, Allowing Putin to Remain President until 2036." NPR.org, July 1, 2020. https://www.npr.org/2020/07/01/886440694/ref erendum-in-russia-passes-allowing-putin-to-remain-president-until-2036.

Neuman, Scott, and Rob Schmitz. "Despite the End of China's One-Child Policy, Births Are Still Lagging." NPR.org, July 16, 2018. https://www.npr.org/2018/07/16/ 629361870/despite-the-end-of-chinas-one-child-policy-births-are-still-lagging.

"New Start Extended Deal—Google Search." Accessed February 25, 2021. https:// www.google.com/search?q=new+start+extended+deal&rlz=1C5CHFA_enUS8 98US898&oq=new+start+extended+deal&aqs=chrome..69i57.6843j0j4&sourc eid=chrome&ie=UTF-8.

Newman, Lily Hay. "Russia Takes a Big Step toward Internet Isolation." WIRED, January 5, 2020. https://www.wired.com/story/russia-internet-control-disconnect-censorship/.

Newsom, Jennifer Siebel. "It's Time to Stop Treating Parenting as a Mom's Burden and a Dad's Adorable Hobby." Glamour. Accessed February 25, 2021. https:// www.glamour.com/story/jennifer-siebel-newsom-gavin-newsom-parenthood-part nership.

The New Indian Express. "Jammu and Kashmir: Pakistan Violates Ceasefire along LoC in Krishna Ghati Sector." *New Indian Express*, September 30, 2020. https://www. newindianexpress.com/nation/2020/sep/30/jammu-and-kashmir-pakistan-viola tes-ceasefire-along-loc-in-krishna-ghati-sector-2204068.html.

The New York Times. "Why Referendums Aren't as Democratic as They Seem." October 5, 2016. https://www.nytimes.com/2016/10/05/world/americas/colombia-brexit-referendum-farc-cameron-santos.html.

————. "Upton Sinclair, Whose Muckraking Changed the Meat Industry." Accessed February 25, 2021. https://www.nytimes.com/interactive/projects/cp/obituaries/ archives/upton-sinclair-meat-industry.

Nichols, Michelle. "Exclusive: Bangladesh PM Says Expects No Help from Trump on Refugees Fleeing Myanmar." Reuters, September 19, 2017. https://www.reuters. com/article/us-myanmar-rohingya-bangladesh-trump-exc-idUSKCN1BU07C.

Nicholson, Alisdair. "Suspicion Creeps into the Five Eyes." *Interpreter*, August 30, 2019. https://www.lowyinstitute.org/the-interpreter/suspicion-creeps-five-eyes.

Noack, Rick. "A Foiled Assassination Plot in Denmark May Have Just Cost Iran a Partner against Trump." *Washington Post*, October 31, 2018. https://www-washingtonpost-com.stanford.idm.oclc.org/2018/10/31/foiled-assassination-plot-denmark-may-just-have-cost-iran-partner-against-trump/?utm_term=.c5e48d1b3790.

NobelPrize.org. "The Nobel Peace Prize 2013." Accessed February 23, 2021. https:// www.nobelprize.org/prizes/peace/2013/summary/.

Nordland, Rod, and Nesar Azadzoi. "3 U.S. Soldiers Died in Afghanistan: Why This Fight Drags On." *New York Times*, November 27, 2018. https://www.nytimes.com/ 2018/11/27/world/asia/us-soldiers-killed-afghanistan.html.

Norton, Marcy. "Sacred Gifts, Profane Pleasures." Accessed February 25, 2021. https://
www.goodreads.com/work/best_book/4506264-sacred-gifts-profane-pleasures-a-
history-of-tobacco-and-chocolate-in-t.

Nozizwe, Lena. "Pulse: Armenian Rapper." Deutsche Welle, April 22, 2016. https://
www.dw.com/en/pulse-armenian-rapper/av-19207698.

NPR.org. "Notorious Drug Lord 'El Chapo' Pleads Not Guilty to Federal Charges."
Accessed February 23, 2021. https://www.npr.org/sections/thetwo-way/2017/01/
20/510776930/feds-announce-charges-against-notorious-drug-lord-el-chapo.

———. "Trump Meets North Korea's Kim Jong Un and Says Nuclear Negotiations Will
Resume." June 30, 2019. Accessed February 24, 2021. https://www.npr.org/2019/
06/30/737365074/trump-to-meet-kim-jong-un-at-dmz.

Nuclear Threat Initiative. "United States | Countries | NTI." Accessed February 23,
2021. https://www.nti.org/learn/countries/united-states/.

Oakland Museum of California. "Gold Fever Law, Order, and Justice for Some—
Discrimination." Accessed February 23, 2021. http://explore.museumca.org/goldr
ush/fever16-di.html.

Ober, Josiah, and Brook Manville. "Beyond Empowerment: Building a Company of
Citizens." *Harvard Business Review*, January 2003. https://hbr.org/2003/01/beyond-
empowerment-building-a-company-of-citizens.

The Ocean Conference, United Nations, New York, June 5-9, 2017. Accessed February
23, 2021. https://www.un.org/sustainabledevelopment/wp-content/uploads/
2017/05/Ocean-fact-sheet-package.pdf.

O'Connor. *Virginia v. Black* (Opinion of the Court), 538 U.S. 343 (U.S. Supreme Court
2003).

Ohlheiser, Abby. "How Kanye West Became a Hero of the Pro-Trump Internet: A
Step-by-Step Guide." *Washington Post*, April 25, 2018. https://www-washingtonpost-
com.stanford.idm.oclc.org/news/the-intersect/wp/2018/04/23/a-step-by-step-
guide-to-how-kanye-west-became-a-hero-of-the-pro-trump-internet/?noredirect=
on&utm_term=.707f88f1d583.

O'Keefe, Ed. "The Night John McCain Killed the GOP's Health-Care Fight."
Washington Post, July 28, 2017. https://www-washingtonpost-com.stanford.idm.
oclc.org/powerpost/the-night-john-mccain-killed-the-gops-health-care-fight/
2017/07/28/f5acce58-7361-11e7-8f39-eeb7d3a2d304_story.html?utm_term=
.0682faf8a006.

O'Keeffe, Kate, and Aruna Viswanatha. "Chinese State Media Giant CGTN Registers
as Foreign Agent in U.S." *Wall Street Journal*, February 5, 2019. https://www.wsj.
com/articles/chinese-state-media-giant-cgtn-registers-as-foreign-agent-in-u-s-1154
9387532.

Olkowski, Tyler S. B. "Former NBA Star Lays Out Philanthropic Goals for Democratic
Republic of Congo." *Harvard Crimson*, October 24, 2014. https://www.thecrimson.
com/article/2014/10/24/NBA-player-talks-philanthropy/.

On Demand News. "North Korea TV Broadcast Says Missile Test Is Warning to South
Korea." 2019. https://www.youtube.com/watch?v=Hsa-3oK4GSc&ab_channel=
OnDemandNews.

O'Neil, Rachelle. "Congressman John Lewis Dancing to Pharrell Williams'
'Happy': 'Nothing Can Bring Me Down,'" 2014. https://www.youtube.com/
watch?v=4QchDC9FaiI&ab_channel=RachelleO%27Neil.

Oppenheim, Maya. "Neo-Nazi Richard Spencer 'Banned from 26 European Countries.'" *The Independent*, November 23, 2017. https://www.independent.co.uk/news/world/americas/richard-spencer-ban-european-countries-alt-right-white-supremacist-neo-nazi-eu-a8071971.html.

OPCW. "Organisation for the Prohibition of Chemical Weapons." Accessed February 23, 2021. https://www.opcw.org/node/2632.

Osborne, Simon. "World War 3 News: Why Nuclear-Armed Pakistan 'Poses Bigger Threat to India than China.'" Express, September 24, 2020. https://www.express.co.uk/news/world/1339602/world-war-3-news-pakistan-india-china-nuclear-weapons-nuclear-war-kashmir-latest.

Ouellette, Jennifer. "Attack of the Murder Hornets Is a Nature Doc Shot through Horror/Sci-Fi Lens." Ars Technica, February 23, 2021. https://arstechnica.com/science/2021/02/attack-of-the-murder-hornets-is-a-nature-doc-shot-through-horror-sci-fi-lens/.

Parker, Ashley, David Nakamura, and Dan Lamothe. "'Horrible' Pictures of Suffering Moved Trump to Action on Syria." *Washington Post*, April 7, 2017. https://www-washingtonpost-com.stanford.idm.oclc.org/politics/horrible-pictures-of-suffering-moved-trump-to-action-on-syria/2017/04/07/9aa9fcc8-1bce-11e7-8003-f55b4c1cfae2_story.html?utm_term=.cdc9aae49979.

Parliament of Canada. "Prime Ministers of Canada." Accessed February 25, 2021. https://lop.parl.ca/sites/ParlInfo/default/en_CA/People/primeMinisters.

Parry, Ryan. "We Expose Vile Racist Biker as British Leader of the Ku Klux Klan." *Mirror*, October 19, 2011. https://www.mirror.co.uk/news/uk-news/we-expose-vile-racist-biker-as-british-86445.

PBS. "The Iran-Contra Affair." Accessed February 23, 2021. https://www.pbs.org/wgbh/americanexperience/features/reagan-iran/.

PBS NewsHour. "Tillerson Says Poisoning of Ex-Spy in Britain 'clearly Came from Russia' and 'Will Trigger a Response,'" March 12, 2018. https://www.pbs.org/newshour/world/tillerson-says-poisoning-of-ex-spy-in-britain-clearly-came-from-russia-and-will-trigger-a-response.

Peck, Michael. "Britain Is Sending Its Special Forces to Fight Russian 'Little Green Men.'" The National Interest. June 22, 2019. https://nationalinterest.org/blog/buzz/britain-sending-its-special-forces-fight-russian-%E2%80%9Clittle-green-men%E2%80%9D-63622.

Pedreira, Daniel I. "New Cuban Leadership Reflects a Rebranding of Castro Dictatorship—UPI.Com." UPI, October 4, 2019. https://www.upi.com/Top_News/Voices/2019/10/04/New-Cuban-leadership-reflects-a-rebranding-of-Castro-dictatorship/2661570190990/.

Pengelly, Martin. "'We Don't Have a King': Trump and Cuomo in Bizarre Exchange over Covid-19 Response." *Guardian*, April 14, 2020. http://www.theguardian.com/us-news/2020/apr/14/trump-coronavirus-reopen-us-cuomo.

Peter, Laurence. "What Makes Russia's New Spy Ship Yantar Special?" BBC News, January 3, 2018, sec. Europe. https://www.bbc.com/news/world-europe-42543712.

Peterson, Scott. "In Turkey, Erdoğan Fans an Islamic Nationalism to Build Ottoman-Style Influence." *Christian Science Monitor*, February 22, 2017. https://www.csmonitor.com/World/Middle-East/2017/0222/In-Turkey-Erdogan-fans-an-Islamic-nationalism-to-build-Ottoman-style-influence.

Petsko, Emily. "Reports of Mark Twain's Quote about His Own Death Are Greatly Exaggerated." *Mental Floss*, November 2, 2018. https://www.mentalfloss.com/article/562400/reports-mark-twains-quote-about-mark-twains-death-are-greatly-exaggerated.

Pham, Sherisse. "How Oracle Ended Up with TikTok." CNN, September 14, 2020. https://www.cnn.com/2020/09/14/tech/oracle-tiktok-us-china-intl-hnk/index.html.

Phillips, Amber. "'Do Not Despair of Our Present Difficulties:' John McCain's Last Statement, Annotated." *Washington Post*. Accessed February 23, 2021. http://www.washingtonpost.com/news/the-fix/wp/2018/08/27/do-not-despair-of-our-present-difficulties-john-mccains-last-words-annotated/.

Phillips, Macon. "The Clinton Bush Haiti Fund." whitehouse.gov, January 16, 2010. https://obamawhitehouse.archives.gov/blog/2010/01/16/clinton-bush-haiti-fund.

Pierini, Marc. "The 2018 Turkey Regress Report." Carnegie Europe. Accessed February 22, 2021. https://carnegieeurope.eu/2018/03/14/2018-turkey-regress-report-pub-75794.

Pierson, Brendan. "'El Chapo' Paid Former Mexican President $100 Million Bribe: Trial Witness." Reuters, January 25, 2019. https://www.reuters.com/article/us-usa-mexico-el-chapo/el-chapo-paid-former-mexican-president-100-million-bribe-trial-witness-idUSKCN1P92OS.

Pifer, Steven. "The Budapest Memorandum and U.S. Obligations." *Brookings* (blog), November 30, 1AD. https://www.brookings.edu/blog/up-front/2014/12/04/the-budapest-memorandum-and-u-s-obligations/.

The Pig Site. "China's ASF Woes Could Linger in 2021." January 27, 2021. https://www.thepigsite.com/news/2021/01/chinas-asf-woes-could-linger-in-2021.

Pilkington, Ed. "Unprepared America Wakes Up to Coronavirus, Gradually Then All at Once." *Guardian*, March 13, 2020. http://www.theguardian.com/world/2020/mar/13/us-coronavirus-impact-shutdowns-unprepared-america-wakes-up.

Piper, Kelsey. "The Rise of Meatless Meat, Explained." Vox, May 28, 2019. https://www.vox.com/2019/5/28/18626859/meatless-meat-explained-vegan-impossible-burger.

Pivariu, Corneliu. "Turkey: Erdogan Seeks to Achieve the Dream of the Empire's Rebirth." Ifimes, February 10, 2020. https://www.ifimes.org/en/9767.

Plucinska, Joanna. "Italy and Poland Want 'New Spring' in Europe: Salvini." Reuters, January 9, 2019. https://www.reuters.com/article/us-eu-poland-italy-salvini-idUSKCN1P318E.

Plumer, Brad. "A Simple Guide to CRISPR, One of the Biggest Science Stories of the Decade." Vox, July 23, 2018. https://www.vox.com/2018/7/23/17594864/crispr-cas9-gene-editing.

Poe, Marshall. "Moscow, the Third Rome: The Origins and Transformations of a 'Pivotal Moment.'" *Jahrbücher Für Geschichte Osteuropas* 49, no. 3 (2001): 412–29.

Polansek, Jeff, and Tom Mason. "Trump Orders U.S. Meat-Processing Plants to Stay Open despite Coronavirus Fears." Reuters, April 29, 2020. https://www.reuters.com/article/us-health-coronavirus-trump-liability-idUSKCN22A2OB.

Politico. "Harris: 'We Do Have 2 Systems of Justice in America.'" Accessed February 23, 2021. https://www.politico.com/news/2020/09/06/kamala-harris-police-justice-law-order-409387.

Politico. "DOJ: No Death Penalty for Snowden." Accessed February 23, 2021. https://www.politico.com/story/2013/07/eric-holder-edward-snowden-russia-death-penalty-094803.

Popovski, Vesselin. "Can the U.N. Adapt to Donald Trump?" US News & World Report, February 16, 2017. https://www.usnews.com/news/best-countries/articles/2017-02-16/can-the-united-nations-adapt-to-donald-trump.

"The Power of Xi Jinping." *The Economist*, September 18, 2014. http://www.economist.com/china/2014/09/18/the-power-of-xi-jinping.

Powers, Richard Gid. "The Nation: Fifth Column; The Evil That Lurks in the Enemy Within." *New York Times*, June 16, 2002. https://www.nytimes.com/2002/06/16/weekinreview/the-nation-fifth-column-the-evil-that-lurks-in-the-enemy-within.html.

Pratik. "Pirates Are Kidnapping More Seafarers off West Africa, IMB Reports." Accessed February 23, 2021. https://www.icc-ccs.org/index.php/1298-pirates-are-kidnapping-more-seafarers-off-west-africa-imb-reports.

"Preserving Sacramento's Historic City Cemetery." Accessed February 25, 2021. https://historicoldcitycemetery.org/.

Purdy, Chase. "US Companies Want to Compete in China for the Plant-Based Meat Market." Quartz. Accessed February 25, 2021. https://qz.com/1784465/the-plant-based-meat-wars-are-going-to-china/.

Putz, Catherine. "Kazakhstan's First President Nursultan Nazarbayev Tests Positive for COVID-19." *Diplomat*. Accessed February 25, 2021. https://thediplomat.com/2020/06/kazakhstans-first-president-nursultan-nazarbayev-tests-positive-for-covid-19/.

Pyenson, Nick. "Spying on Whales." Penguin-Random House, June 25, 2019. https://www.penguinrandomhouse.com/books/556686/spying-on-whales-by-nick-pyenson/.

Radio Free Europe/Radio Liberty. "Thousands in Khabarovsk Protest Arrest of Russian Governor." July 18, 2020. https://www.rferl.org/a/russia-khabarovsk-thouands-protest-arrest-governor-furgal/30734564.html.

Radio, Sveriges. "Radio Sweden." Accessed February 22, 2021. https://sverigesradio.se/radiosweden.

Raleigh News & Observer. "India, Australia, Japan, US 'Quad' Take on China Together." Accessed February 25, 2021. https://www.newsobserver.com/opinion/article246320670.html.

Ramishvili, Levan. *Reagan Jokes: American & Russian Arguing About Freedom in Their Countries*, 2013. https://www.youtube.com/watch?v=9qh-1_tXeuQ&ab_channel=LevanRamishvili.

Rankin, Sarah, and Sara Burnett. "Women Keep up Wins in Trump-Era Political Surge." AP NEWS, November 7, 2019. https://apnews.com/article/1fb70dd6a7b04c24858c5b414d976d1a.

Ratner, Paul. "Liberty or Death? The Coronavirus Attacks the Soul of America." Big Think, April 15, 2020. https://bigthink.com/politics-current-affairs/liberty-or-death-the-coronavirus-attacks-the-soul-of-america?rebelltitem=1#rebelltitem1?rebelltitem=1.

Reality Check Team. "Trade War: How Reliant Are US Colleges on Chinese Students?" BBC News, June 11, 2019, sec. Asia. https://www.bbc.com/news/world-asia-48542913.

Rees, Matt. "Where's Arafat's Money?" *Time*, November 14, 2004. http://content.time.com/time/magazine/article/0,9171,782141,00.html.

"Refusenik." *Wikipedia*, December 25, 2020. https://en.wikipedia.org/w/index.php?title=Refusenik&oldid=996193329.

Richardson, Hayley. "A Politician for the Instagram Generation: Meet the World's Youngest Prime Minister Sanna Marin, 34." *Daily Mail* Online, December 9, 2019. https://www.dailymail.co.uk/femail/article-7771821/A-politician-Instagram-generation-Meet-worlds-youngest-prime-minister-Sanna-Marin-34.html.

Rodrigo, Chris Mills. "Critics Fear Facebook Fact-Checkers Losing Misinformation Fight." *Hill*, January 20, 2020. https://thehill.com/policy/technology/478896-critics-fear-facebook-fact-checkers-losing-misinformation-fight.

Rodriguez, Peter. "Playing the Long Game." Jones Graduate School of Business at Rice University. Accessed February 22, 2021. https://business.rice.edu/wisdom/expert-opinion/why-president-george-hw-bush-went-bat-nafta.

Ronca, Debra. "Why Do Shriners Drive Those Little Cars?" HowStuffWorks, August 6, 2015. https://money.howstuffworks.com/why-do-shriners-drive-little-cars.htm.

Roosevelt, Franklin D. "'A Date Which Will Live in Infamy': FDR Asks for a Declaration of War." Accessed February 25, 2021. http://historymatters.gmu.edu/d/5166/.

Ros-Lehtinen, Ileana. "Nicaragua Human Rights and Anticorruption Act of 2018." Webpage, December 20, 2018. 2017/2018. https://www.congress.gov/bill/115th-congress/house-bill/1918.

Roxborough, Scott. "Germany, after Recep Tayyip Erdoğan Case, Drops Law against Insulting Foreign Leaders." Hollywood Reporter, January 26, 2017. https://www.hollywoodreporter.com/news/germany-dropping-law-mocking-foreign-leaders-968834.

Rudolph, Josh. "Sensitive Words: Xi to Ascend His Throne." China Digital Times (CDT), February 26, 2018. https://chinadigitaltimes.net/2018/02/sensitive-words-emperor-xi-jinping-ascend-throne/.

Rupar, Aaron. "Trump Is Running on Criminal Justice Reform but Just Praised China's Execution of Drug Dealers." Vox, February 10, 2020. https://www.vox.com/2020/2/10/21131863/trump-china-executions-drug-dealers.

"Russian Spy: What Happened to Sergei and Yulia Skripal?" BBC News, September 27, 2018, sec. UK. https://www.bbc.com/news/uk-43643025.

The Sacramento Bee. "Jerry Brown Says Donald Trump's Position on Climate Change Is Backfiring." Accessed February 23, 2021. https://www.sacbee.com/news/politics-government/capitol-alert/article153663779.html.

The Sacramento Bee. "Paris Climate Agreement More Popular than Trump or GOP Senators Opposing It." Accessed February 23, 2021. https://www.sacbee.com/news/politics-government/article153648794.html.

"Sacramento Historic City Cemetery." *Wikipedia*, November 16, 2020. https://en.wikipedia.org/w/index.php?title=Sacramento_Historic_City_Cemetery&oldid=989084588.

"Sacramento Kings Debut New Alternative Court Colorway With International Brand, Matching Global Uniform Design." Accessed February 23, 2021. https://www.nba.com/kings/news/kings-debut-new-alternative-court-global-uniform.

Sagan, Scott, D., and Kenneth N. Waltz. "The Spread of Nuclear Weapons: A Debate Renewed (Second Edition)." Stanford University. Accessed February 25, 2021. https://politicalscience.stanford.edu/publications/spread-nuclear-weapons-debate-renewed-second-edition.

Samuels, Brett. "Pope: Fear of Migration 'Makes Us Crazy.'" *Hill*, January 23, 2019. https://thehill.com/blogs/blog-briefing-room/426561-pope-fear-of-migration-is-making-us-crazy.

———. "Trump again Declines to Describe Mass Killings of Armenians as Genocide." *Hill*, April 24, 2018. https://thehill.com/homenews/administration/384644-trump-again-declines-to-describe-mass-killings-of-armenians-as.

Samuelson, Richard. "A Government of Laws, Not of Men." *Claremont Review of Books* (blog), Fall 2017. https://claremontreviewofbooks.com/a-government-of-laws-not-of-men/.

Sanchez, Ray, Mark Morales, and Sarah Jorgensen. "Lori Loughlin and Mossimo Giannulli Plead Guilty in College Admissions Scam." CNN, May 22, 2020. https://www.cnn.com/2020/05/22/us/lori-loughlin-guilty-plea/index.html.

Sanderson, Sertan. "From Ally to Scapegoat: Fethullah Gulen, the Man behind the Myth." Deutsche Welle, June 4, 2018. https://www.dw.com/en/from-ally-to-scapegoat-fethullah-gulen-the-man-behind-the-myth/a-37055485.

Sanger, David E. "Al-Baghdadi Raid Was a Victory Built on Factors Trump Derides." *New York Times*, October 27, 2019. https://www.nytimes.com/2019/10/27/us/politics/trump-baghdadi-raid-strategy.html.

Sanger, David E., and Maggie Haberman. "Trump Praises Duterte for Philippine Drug Crackdown in Call Transcript." *New York Times*, May 24, 2017, sec. U.S. https://www.nytimes.com/2017/05/23/us/politics/trump-duterte-phone-transcript-philippine-drug-crackdown.html.

Save the Children. "The Lottery of Birth: New Report Reveals World's Most Disadvantaged Children Are Being Left behind in Global Efforts to Improve Child Survival." Accessed February 23, 2021. https://www.savethechildren.org/us/about-us/media-and-news/2015-press-releases/the-lottery-of-birth--new-report-reveals-world---s-most-disadvan.

Schiavenza, Matt. "How Humiliation Drove Modern Chinese History." *Atlantic*, October 25, 2013. https://www.theatlantic.com/china/archive/2013/10/how-humiliation-drove-modern-chinese-history/280878/.

Schilling, Mary Kaye, Mary Kaye Schilling, and Mary Kaye Schilling. "How Pharrell and a Cast of Hundreds Got Happy for a 24-Hour Interactive Video." Fast Company, November 22, 2013. https://www.fastcompany.com/3022066/how-pharrell-and-a-cast-of-hundreds-got-happy-for-a-24-hour-interactive-video.

Schmemann, Serge. "End of the Soviet Union; The Soviet State, Born of a Dream, Dies." *New York Times*, December 26, 1991, sec. World. https://www.nytimes.com/1991/12/26/world/end-of-the-soviet-union-the-soviet-state-born-of-a-dream-dies.html.

Schow, Ashe. "Donald Trump." *Washington Examiner*. Accessed February 23, 2021. https://www.washingtonexaminer.com/tag/donald-trump.

Schwarz, Benjamin. "Dirty Hands." *Atlantic*, December 1, 1998. https://www.theatlantic.com/magazine/archive/1998/12/dirty-hands/377364/.

Segretariato generale della Presidenza della Repubblica. "The Quirinale Palace." Quirinale. Accessed February 24, 2021. http://palazzo.quirinale.it/palazzo_en.html.

Sevastopulo, Demetri, and Kathrin Hille. "US Warns China on Aggressive Acts by Fishing Boats and Coast Guard." Financial Times, April 28, 2019. https://www-ft-com.stanford.idm.oclc.org/content/ab4b1602-696a-11e9-80c7-60ee53e6681d.

ShareAmerica. "More than 50 Countries Support Venezuela's Juan Guaidó." *ShareAmerica* (blog), November 15, 2019. https://share.america.gov/support-for-venezuelas-juan-guaido-grows-infographic/.

Shattuck, Thomas J. "The Race to Zero? China's Poaching of Taiwan's Diplomatic Allies." *Orbis* 64, no. 2 (2020): 334–52. https://doi.org/10.1016/j.orbis.2020.02.003.

Shead, Sam. "Peter Thiel's New Zealand Estate Lies Neglected as Coronavirus Drives Preppers into Hiding." CNBC, May 15, 2020. https://www.cnbc.com/2020/05/15/peter-thiel-new-zealand-estate.html.

Sheffield, Rob. "Paul McCartney Is Dead: Bizarre Story of Music's Most Notorious Rumor." *Rolling Stone*, October 11, 2019. https://www.rollingstone.com/music/music-features/paul-mccartney-is-dead-conspiracy-897189/.

Sherwell, Philip. "The World According to Henry Kissinger." *The Telegraph*, May 21, 2011. https://www.telegraph.co.uk/news/worldnews/us-politics/8528270/The-world-according-to-Henry-Kissinger.html.

Shesgreen, Deirdre, and David Jackson. "'Military Action Is Possible' in Venezuela, Secretary of State Mike Pompeo Says." USA Today. Accessed February 24, 2021. https://www.usatoday.com/story/news/world/2019/05/01/venezuela-crisis-pompeo-raises-possibility-military-action-guaido-maduro/3631409002/.

Shi, Ting. "Xi's New Title Highlights China's Power Struggle." Bloomberg.Com, February 2, 2016. https://www.bloomberg.com/news/articles/2016-02-02/push-to-elevate-xi-s-party-status-could-shape-china-s-leadership.

Shultz, George P., and Ted Halstead. "The Business Case for the Paris Climate Accord." *New York Times*, May 9, 2017, sec. Opinion. https://www.nytimes.com/2017/05/09/opinion/the-business-case-for-the-paris-climate-accord.html.

Sigmund, Paul E. "Christianity and Violence: The Case of Liberation Theology: Terrorism and Political Violence." Vol 3, No 4, December 21, 2007. https://www-tandfonline-com.stanford.idm.oclc.org/doi/abs/10.1080/09546559108427127.

Silver, Nate. "How Popular Is Donald Trump?" FiveThirtyEight, March 2, 2017. https://projects.fivethirtyeight.com/trump-approval-ratings/.

Sisk, Richard. "Trump, Kim Commit to 'Immediate Repatriation' of Korean War Missing | Military.Com." Military.com, June 12, 2018. https://www.military.com/daily-news/2018/06/12/trump-kim-commit-immediate-repatriation-korean-war-missing.html.

Skelley, Geoffrey. "What If Trump Loses and Won't Leave?" *FiveThirtyEight*, September 14, 2020. https://fivethirtyeight.com/features/what-if-trump-loses-and-wont-leave/.

Sleuth Media. *Video Compilation: Azerbaijani Military Drones Destroys Armenian Armed Forces Tanks #NagornoKarabakh*, 2020. https://www.youtube.com/watch?v=HiSTvlBYx14&ab_channel=SleuthMedia.

Slodkowski, Antoni, and David Brunnstrom. "Suu Kyi Silence on Myanmar Ethnic Cleansing Charge Draws Cool Response." Reuters, September 20, 2017. https://www.reuters.com/article/us-myanmar-rohingya-suukyi-idUSKCN1BU0C5.

Smith, Helena. "How Greece Is Beating Coronavirus despite a Decade of Debt." *Guardian*, April 14, 2020, sec. World news. https://www.theguardian.com/world/2020/apr/14/how-greece-is-beating-coronavirus-despite-a-decade-of-debt.

———. "Tensions Flare as Greece Tells Turkey It Is Ready to Answer Any Provocation." *Guardian*, March 27, 2017. http://www.theguardian.com/world/2017/mar/27/tensions-flare-greece-turkey-answer-provocation-erdogan.

Smith, Michael Lane. "72 Years Ago, Former President George H.W. Bush Almost Died In World War II." *Task & Purpose* (blog), September 2, 2015. https://taskandpurpose.com/history/71-years-ago-former-president-george-h-w-bush-almost-died-in-world-war-ii/.

Smith, Patrick. "Boris Johnson's Conservatives Win Decisive Victory in Crucial Election." NBC News, December 12, 2019. https://www.nbcnews.com/news/world/boris-johnson-s-conservatives-win-decisive-victory-crucial-election-n1101326.

Smith, Sonia. "What Happened to Austin Tice?" *Texas Monthly*, October 2015. https://www.texasmonthly.com/articles/the-road-to-damascus/.

Smithsonian Institution. "Secretary Lonnie G. Bunch III." Accessed February 23, 2021. https://www.si.edu/about/secretary-lonnie-bunch.

Smithsonian Magazine. "Monster Invasive Tumbleweed Is Outgrowing Its Parent Species." Accessed February 25, 2021. https://www.smithsonianmag.com/smart-news/monster-hybrid-tumbleweed-out-growing-its-parent-species-180973072/.

Soderbergh, Steven. *Contagion*. Drama, Thriller. Warner Bros., Participant, Imagenation Abu Dhabi FZ, 2011.

Soergel, Matt. "Polar Adventurer Marks 100th Birthday, 81 Years after His First Expedition to Antarctica." Jacksonville.com, July 8, 2020. https://www.jacksonville.com/story/news/local/2020/07/08/polar-adventurer-marks-100th-birthday-81-years-after-his-first-expedition-to-antarctica/112286726/.

Southern Poverty Law Center. "EURO." Accessed February 23, 2021. https://www.splcenter.org/fighting-hate/extremist-files/group/euro.

Specia, Megan. "Who Is Sanna Marin, Finland's 34-Year-Old Prime Minister?" *New York Times*, December 10, 2019. https://www.nytimes.com/2019/12/10/world/europe/finland-sanna-marin.html.

Spetalnick, Matt, and Jonathan Saul. "Exclusive: U.S. Turns Screws on Maritime Industry to Cut Off Venezuela's Oil." Reuters, July 13, 2020. https://www.reuters.com/article/us-venezuela-oil-shipping-exclusive-idUSKCN24E0CD.

Staff. "Bill Clinton Regards Good Friday Agreement as His Greatest Foreign Policy Achievement Says Aide." IrishCentral.com, January 23, 2017. https://www.irishcentral.com/news/bill-clinton-regards-good-friday-agreement-as-his-greatest-foreign-policy-achievement-says-aide-187650671-237560151.

———. "Donald Trump Steps up Wild Attacks on Joe Biden as First Debate Looms." *Guardian*. Accessed February 25, 2021. https://www.theguardian.com/us-news/2020/sep/28/donald-trump-steps-up-wild-attacks-on-joe-biden-as-first-debate-looms.

———. "Nigerian President Likens Myanmar Crisis to Bosnia, Rwanda Genocides." Reuters, September 19, 2017. https://www.reuters.com/article/us-myanmar-rohingya-un-nigeria-idUSKCN1BU26Q.

———. "North Korea's Dear Respected Comrade Leader Gets a New Title." Reuters, June 30, 2016. https://www.reuters.com/article/us-northkorea-parliament-idUSKCN0ZF1R7.

———. "Tajikistan Leader's Son Named Senate Speaker." Reuters, April 20, 2020. https://www.reuters.com/article/us-tajikistan-president-son-senate-idUSKBN21Z1ZL.

Staff, Reuters. "China Denies Credentials to Wall Street Journal Reporter." Reuters, August 30, 2019. https://www.reuters.com/article/us-china-journalist-idUSKCN1VK15X.

———. "Chinese Frozen Food Firm Recalls Products Suspected of African Swine Fever Contamination." Reuters, February 19, 2019. https://www.reuters.com/article/us-china-swinefever-companies-idUSKCN1Q70EI.

———. "Russian, Turkish Foreign Ministers Back Libya Ceasefire in Call: Moscow." Reuters, May 21, 2020. https://www.reuters.com/article/us-libya-security-russia-turkey-idUSKBN22X0YC.

———. "Turkey Calls for International Investigation into Khashoggi Murder." Reuters, November 14, 2018. https://www.reuters.com/article/us-saudi-journalist-turkey-idUSKCN1NJ2KJ.

———. "Turkey Detains 300 People over Criticism of Syrian Offensive." Reuters, January 29, 2018. https://www.reuters.com/article/us-mideast-crisis-syria-turkey-security-idUSKBN1FI166.

Steger, Isabella. "China Ripped Off an Iconic Coke Ad for Its Belt and Road Theme Song." Quartz, September 7, 2018. https://qz.com/1382131/china-rips-id-like-to-buy-the-world-a-coke-for-belt-and-road-song/.

Stevis-Gridness, Matina, and Benjamin Novak. "E.U. Tries Gentle Diplomacy to Counter Hungary's Crackdown on Democracy." *New York Times*, March 31, 2020. https://www.nytimes.com/2020/03/31/world/europe/hungary-viktor-orban-eu.html.

Stewart, Will. "Edward Snowden Says U.S. Secret Service Are Trying to Kill Him." *Daily Mail*, January 26, 2014. https://www.dailymail.co.uk/news/article-2546389/Edward-Snowden-says-U-S-secret-service-trying-kill-him.html.

Stone, Mike, and Patricia Zengerle. "U.S. Pushes Arms Sales Surge to Taiwan, Needling China—Sources." Reuters, September 16, 2020. https://www.reuters.com/article/us-usa-taiwan-arms-exclusive-idUSKBN2671M4.

Strauss, Mark. "Though It Seems Crazy Now, the Neutron Bomb Was Intended to Be Humane." Gizmodo, September 19, 2014. https://io9.gizmodo.com/though-it-seems-crazy-now-the-neutron-bomb-was-intende-1636604514.

Stripes. "One Marine Dead, Five Missing after Jet and Tanker Collide off Japanese Coast." Accessed February 25, 2021. https://www.stripes.com/news/pacific/one-marine-dead-five-missing-after-jet-and-tanker-collide-off-japanese-coast-1.559418.

Strohm, Chris. "Barr Tells U.K. Islamic State Suspects Won't Face Death Penalty." Bloomberg. Accessed February 23, 2021. https://www.bloomberg.com/news/articles/2020-08-19/barr-tells-u-k-islamic-state-suspects-won-t-face-death-penalty.

Sturluson, Snorri. "How Iceland Flattened the Curve." MarketWatch, June 15, 2020. https://www.marketwatch.com/story/life-in-iceland-is-almost-back-to-normal-again-our-holy-trinity-fought-coronavirus-and-succeeded-where-others-failed-2020-06-09.

Sucato, Mea. "Enforcing the Ban on Chemical Weapons." *Sustainable Development Law & Policy* 6, no. 3 (January 1, 2006). https://digitalcommons.wcl.american.edu/sdlp/vol6/iss3/20.

Suciu, Peter. "Rumors and Hoaxes Continue to Spread Fast on Social Media, and Why It Is Unlikely to Stop." *Forbes*, December 10, 2019. Accessed February 25, 2021. https://www.forbes.com/sites/petersuciu/2019/12/10/rumors-and-hoaxes-conti nue-to-spread-fast-on-social-media-and-why-it-is-unlikely-to-stop/.

"Svartskalle." *Wiktionary*. Accessed February 23, 2021. https://en.wiktionary.org/wiki/svartskalle.

Swaine, Jon. "Osama Bin Laden: Code for Body Was 'Fedex Package.'" *Telegraph*, November 22, 2012. https://www.telegraph.co.uk/news/worldnews/al-qaeda/9694952/Osama-bin-Laden-US-Navy-emails-reveal-no-sailors-witnessed-secret-burial-at-sea.html.

Tagliabue, John. "A Nuclear Taint in Milk Sets Off German Dispute." *New York Times*, January 31, 1987, sec. World. https://www.nytimes.com/1987/01/31/world/a-nuclear-taint-in-milk-sets-off-german-dispute.html.

Takac, Balasz. "When David Černý Made a Tank Monument Interesting." Widewalls, May 6, 2020. https://www.widewalls.ch/magazine/monument-to-sov iet-tank-crews-david-cerny.

"Taliban." *Wikipedia*, February 21, 2021. https://en.wikipedia.org/w/index.php?title=Taliban&oldid=1008095596.

"Tansu Çiller." *Wikipedia*, February 17, 2021. https://en.wikipedia.org/w/index. php?title=Tansu_%C3%87iller&oldid=1007397787.

Tay, Shirley. "US Reportedly Warns China over Hostile Non-naval Vessels in South China Sea." CNBC, April 29, 2019. https://www.cnbc.com/2019/04/29/south-china-sea-us-warns-china-over-non-naval-vessels-ft.html.

Taylor, Adam. "'The Caliph Is Coming, Get Ready,' Pro-Erdogan Turkish Politician Tweets." *Washington Post*, March 19, 2015. Accessed February 22, 2021. http://www.washingtonpost.com/news/worldviews/wp/2015/03/19/the-caliph-is-coming-get-ready-pro-erdogan-turkish-politician-tweets/.

TEDx Talks. "TEDxDanubia 2011—Simonyi & Kounalakis—How Rock&Roll Saved the World," 2011. https://www.youtube.com/watch?v=8duy_vLfKcg&ab_chan nel=TEDxTalks.

The Telegraph. "France Nuclear Power by Numbers." September 12, 2011. Accessed February 23, 2021. https://www.telegraph.co.uk/news/worldnews/europe/france/8757834/France-nuclear-power-by-numbers.html.

Tharoor, Ishaan. "Hungary's Viktor Orban's New Coronavirus Law Is a Blow to the Country's Democracy." *Washington Post*, March 31, 2020. https://www-washing tonpost-com.stanford.idm.oclc.org/world/2020/03/31/coronavirus-kills-its-first-democracy/.

Thoburn, Hannah. "For Putin, for Stalin." Foreign Policy, January 25, 2016. Accessed February 23, 2021. https://foreignpolicy-com.stanford.idm.oclc.org/2016/01/25/for-putin-for-stalin-russia-propaganda/.

Tiffany, Kaitlyn. "The Hand-Sanitizer Hawkers Aren't Sorry." *Atlantic*, March 11, 2020. https://www.theatlantic.com/health/archive/2020/03/hand-sanitizer-online-sales-ebay-craigslist-price-surge/607750/.

"Tiger Penis Soup." *Wikipedia*, January 24, 2021. https://en.wikipedia.org/w/index. php?title=Tiger_penis_soup&oldid=1002440943.

Tisdall, Simon. "Love, Hate … Indifference: Is US-UK Relationship Still Special?" *Guardian*, April 28, 2019. http://www.theguardian.com/politics/2019/apr/28/brit ain-america-history-special-relationship-highs-and-lows-churchill-to-trump.

Tolliver, Sandy. "Turkey Weaponizes Refugees against Europe." *Hill*, March 10, 2020. https://thehill.com/opinion/international/486291-turkey-weaponizes-refugees-against-europe.

Travis, Alan. "Fear of Immigration Drove the Leave Victory—Not Immigration Itself." *Guardian*, June 24, 2016, sec. Politics. https://www.theguardian.com/politics/2016/ jun/24/voting-details-show-immigration-fears-were-paradoxical-but-decisive.

Treasury Department. "Treasury Targets Nicaraguan Vice President and Key Advisor over Violent Response to Protests." US Department of the Treasury, November 27, 2018. Accessed February 23, 2021. https://home.treasury.gov/news/press-releases/ sm554.

Triebert, Christiaan. "Russia 'Bombed Four Hospitals in Syria in Four Hours', Report Finds." *Independent*, October 13, 2019. https://www.independent.co.uk/news/ world/middle-east/russia-syria-bomb-hospitals-war-kurds-putin-assad-idlib-a9153 786.html.

Troy (2004). IMDb. Accessed February 22, 2021. http://www.imdb.com/title/tt0332 452/characters/nm0000093.

Trump, Donald. "Twitter/Tweet Deleted." Twitter. Accessed February 24, 2021. https:// twitter.com/realdonaldtrump/status/376329798588837888.

Trump, Donald J. "President Trump Says 'I Hereby Order' US Companies to Stop Doing Business with China." Twitter. Accessed February 24, 2021. https://twitter. com/i/events/1164965430143795200.

Tures, John A. "Is Erdogan 'Wagging the Dog' against the Kurds in Turkey?" *HuffPost*, August 24, 2015. https://www.huffpost.com/entry/is-erdogan-wagging-the-do_b_ 8033390.

Uberti, David. "Trump Is Congratulating Himself in Facebook Ads for Killing Soleimani." VICE News, January 7, 2020. https://www.vice.com/en/article/n7j v8w/trump-is-congratulating-himself-in-facebook-ads-for-killing-soleimani.

Understanding Uncertainty. "Florence Nightingale and the Crimean War." July 10, 2008. https://understandinguncertainty.org/node/204.

UNFPA—United Nations Population Fund. "Girls Are Saying No to FGM—and They Need Political Champions." October 9, 2018. Accessed February 23, 2021. https:// www.unfpa.org/news/girls-are-saying-no-fgm-and-they-need-political-champions.

UNICEF. "Clarke Gayford on the Little Milestones as a Parent." Accessed February 25, 2021. https://www.unicef.org/parenting/inspiration/clarke-gayford-little-mil estones.

UNICEF USA. "UNICEF Ambassador Pau Gasol Visits Syrian Refugees in Iraq." July 2013. Accessed February 23, 2021. https://www.unicefusa.org/press/releases/uni cef-ambassador-pau-gasol-visits-syrian-refugees-iraq/8270.

UNHCR. "More than One Million Refugees Travel to Greece since 2015." March 16, 2016. Accessed February 23, 2021. https://www.unhcr.org/news/latest/2016/3/ 56e9821b6/million-refugees-travel-greece-since-2015.html.

United Nations High Commissioner for Refugees. "The 1951 Convention Relating to the Status of Refugees and Its 1967 Protocol." UNHCR, September 2011. Accessed February 23, 2021. https://www.unhcr.org/1951-refugee-convention.html.

———. "Vietnamese Refugees Well Settled in China, Await Citizenship." UNHCR, May 10, 2007. Accessed February 23, 2021. https://www.unhcr.org/news/latest/2007/5/464302994/vietnamese-refugees-well-settled-china-await-citizenship.html.

"United Nations Office on Genocide Prevention and the Responsibility to Protect." United Nations. Accessed February 23, 2021. https://www.un.org/en/genocideprevention/about-responsibility-to-protect.shtml.

"United States Department of Defense (Defense.Gov)." Accessed February 23, 2021. https://archive.defense.gov/news/newsarticle.aspx?id=28976.

United States Department of State. "Department Press Briefing—February 3, 2021." February 3, 2021. https://www.state.gov/briefings/department-press-briefing-february-3-2021/.

University of California, Riverside. "The Good, the Bad and the Tumbleweed, 2016." https://www.youtube.com/watch?v=qxPAxD3pxIY&feature=emb_logo&ab_channel=Univ.ofCalifornia%2CRiverside.

US Government Publishing Office. "Empty Threat or Serious Danger: Assessing North Korea's Risk to the Homeland." Accessed February 25, 2021. https://www.govinfo.gov/content/pkg/CHRG-115hhrg28820/html/CHRG-115hhrg28820.htm.

USA TODAY. "Bolton on Venezuela: 'All Options on the Table.'" Accessed February 24, 2021. https://www.usatoday.com/videos/news/nation/2019/04/30/bolton-venezuela-all-options-table/3632339002/.

"U.S. Launches Missiles into Syria in Response to Chemical Attack, NBC Reports." Accessed February 23, 2021. https://www.sacbee.com/news/nation-world/national/article143235629.html.

US Department of Agriculture. "USDA APHIS | Feral Swine-Managing an Invasive Species." Accessed February 25, 2021. https://www.aphis.usda.gov/aphis/ourfocus/wildlifedamage/operational-activities/feral-swine.

US Department of State. "Milestones: 1977–1980—Office of the Historian." Accessed February 25, 2021. https://history.state.gov/milestones/1977-1980/soviet-invasion-afghanistan.

US News & World Report. "Editorial Cartoons on Donald Trump." Accessed February 25, 2021. https://www.usnews.com/cartoons/donald-trump-cartoons.

USNI News. "People's Liberation Army Navy Archives." Accessed February 25, 2021. https://news.usni.org/tag/peoples-liberation-army-navy.

Variety. "China Snubs Release of 'Christopher Robin.'" Accessed February 21, 2021. https://variety.com/2018/film/news/christopher-robin-china-winnie-the-pooh-ban-1202895071/.

Vazquez, Marietta. "Calling COVID-19 the 'Wuhan Virus' or 'China Virus' Is Inaccurate and Xenophobic." Yale School of Medicine, March 12, 2020. https://medicine.yale.edu/news-article/23074/.

Vettese, Troy, and Alex Blanchette. "Covid-19 Shows Factory Food Production Is Dangerous for Animals and Humans Alike | Troy Vettese and Alex Blanchette." *Guardian*, September 8, 2020. http://www.theguardian.com/commentisfree/2020/sep/08/meat-production-animals-humans-covid-19-slaughterhouses-workers.

Vimeo. "Architects of Denial." Accessed February 22, 2021. https://vimeo.com/ondem and/architectsofdenial?fbclid=IwAR3hy8o6WxNAYFJMqpCpl6ijD6JklBqnlq2P 1y_HBQrslSPMvnP5D_kjYTM.

Vinocur, John, and Special to the *New York Times*. "France to Produce Neutron Bomb with U.S. Help, Allied Aide Says." *New York Times*, October 15, 1982, sec. World. https://www.nytimes.com/1982/10/15/world/france-to-produce-neutron-bomb-with-us-help-allied-aide-says.html.

Volokh, Eugene. " 'Shouting Fire in a Crowded Theater.' " *Washington Post*. Accessed February 20, 2021. http://www.washingtonpost.com/news/volokh-conspiracy/wp/2015/05/11/shouting-fire-in-a-crowded-theater/.

Volz, Dustin. "Trump Signs into Law U.S. Government Ban on Kaspersky Lab Software | Reuters." Reuters, December 12, 2017. https://www.reuters.com/article/us-usa-cyber-kaspersky/trump-signs-into-law-u-s-government-ban-on-kaspersky-lab-softw are-idUSKBN1E62V4.

Vote Smart. "Sen. Feinstein S. Con. Res. 79." Accessed January 29, 2021. http://votesm art.org.

———. "The Voter's Self Defense System." Accessed February 23, 2021. http://votesm art.org.

Voytko, Lisette. "Trump: 'Iran Appears to Be Standing Down.' " Forbes. Accessed February 24, 2021. https://www.forbes.com/sites/lisettevoytko/2020/01/08/trump-iran-appears-to-be-standing-down/.

Waddell, Benjamin. "Venezuelan Oil Fueled the Rise and Fall of Nicaragua's Ortega Regime." The Conversation. Accessed February 23, 2021. http://theconversat ion.com/venezuelan-oil-fueled-the-rise-and-fall-of-nicaraguas-ortega-regime-100507.

Walker, Peter. "Clive Lewis Says Labour Should Consider Referendum on the Royal Family." *Guardian*, January 10, 2020, sec. Politics. https://www.theguardian.com/politics/2020/jan/10/clive-lewis-labour-leadership-must-push-proportional-rep resentation.

Walker, Shaun. "No Entry: Hungary's Crackdown on Helping Refugees." *Guardian*, June 4, 2018, sec. World news. https://www.theguardian.com/world/2018/jun/04/no-entry-hungarys-crackdown-on-helping-refugees.

Wallis, Jim. "America's Original Sin | Racism, White Privilege, and the Bridge to a New America." Accessed February 23, 2021. http://americasoriginalsin.com/.

Wallström, Margot. "Margot Wallström on Twitter." Twitter. Accessed February 23, 2021. https://twitter.com/margotwallstrom/status/1034823042395000842.

Walsh, Kenneth T. "Ronald Reagan and John Paul II: A Primer on Papal Diplomacy." US News & World Report, March 27, 2014. https://www.usnews.com/news/blogs/ken-walshs-washington/2014/03/27/ronald-reagan-and-john-paul-ii-a-primer-on-papal-diplomacy.

Waltz, Kenneth. " 'The Spread of Nuclear Weapons: More May Better,' Adelphi Papers, Number 171." International Institute for Strategic Studies, 1981. https://www.mtholyoke.edu/acad/intrel/waltz1.htm.

Wang, Jin. "Why Do Chinese Reject Middle Eastern Refugees?" *Diplomat*, June 23, 2017. https://thediplomat.com/2017/06/why-do-chinese-reject-middle-eastern-refugees/.

Warner, Gregory, and Tina Antolini. "As New Zealand Police Pledge to Stay Unarmed, Maori Activists Credit U.S. Protests." NPR.org, June 11, 2020. https://www.npr.org/sections/live-updates-protests-for-racial-justice/2020/06/11/874851593/as-new-zealand-police-pledge-to-stay-unarmed-maori-activists-credit-u-s-protests.

Washington Examiner. "The Sovereignty Doctrine." September 25, 2018. https://www.washingtonexaminer.com/tag/donald-trump?source=%2Fopinion%2Feditorials%2Ftrumps-sovereignty-doctrine.

Washington Post. "The 'Ethnic Cleansing' of the Rohingya." Accessed February 24, 2021. http://www.washingtonpost.com/graphics/2017/world/rohingya/.

Water Encyclopedia. "Ocean Basins—Sea, Depth, Oceans, Temperature, Important, Largest, System, Marine, Pacific." Accessed February 23, 2021. http://www.waterencyclopedia.com/Mi-Oc/Ocean-Basins.html.

Weber, Tad. "Armenian Genocide | Rep. Devin Nunes | President Trump." *Fresno Bee*, April 24, 2018. https://www.fresnobee.com/news/local/article209737409.html.

The Week. "Germany Gets 50 Percent of Its Electricity from Solar for the First Time." Accessed February 23, 2021. https://theweek.com/speedreads/451299/germany-gets-50-percent-electricity-from-solar-first-time.

Weinberg, Tessa. "Abbott, Paxton Defend Dallas Salon Owner Jailed after Opening." *Fort Worth Star-Telegram*, May 6, 2020. https://www.star-telegram.com/news/politics-government/article242540886.html.

Weiser, Benjamin. "Michael Cohen, Broken and Humiliated, Asks for Leniency from Prison." *New York Times*, December 12, 2019, sec. New York. https://www.nytimes.com/2019/12/11/nyregion/michael-cohen-trump-jail.html.

Weldon, Curt. "Washington Absolutely Must Save the EMP Commission." *Hill.* Accessed February 25, 2021. https://thehill.com/opinion/national-security/351174-washington-absolutely-must-save-the-emp-commission.

Westcott, Ben, and Carvajal. "US President Trump Says He Called Xi Jinping the 'King' of China." CNN, April 2, 2019. https://www.cnn.com/2019/04/02/politics/trump-xi-king-of-china-intl/index.html.

Whalen, Bill, and Markos Kounalakis. "Area 45: Foreign to This Election." Hoover Institution. Accessed February 25, 2021. https://www.hoover.org/research/area-45-foreign-election.

"Why Are Teens Snorting Condoms? Here Are Five Things to Know about Latest Online Fad." *Sacramento Bee.* Accessed February 23, 2021. https://www.sacbee.com/news/nation-world/national/article207645134.html.

Wike, Richard, Jacob Poushter, Jannell Fetterolf, and Shannon Schumacher. "Trump Ratings Remain Low Around the World, While Views of U.S. Stay Mostly Favorable." Pew Research Center, January 8, 2020. https://www.pewresearch.org/global/2020/01/08/trump-ratings-remain-low-around-globe-while-views-of-u-s-stay-mostly-favorable/#more-negative-ratings-for-trump-than-for-other-world-leaders.

Williamson, Kevin D. "Burning Books and Children." National Review, July 9, 2013. https://www.nationalreview.com/2013/07/burning-books-and-children-kevin-d-williamson/.

Williams, Pete, and David K. Li. "Derek Chauvin, Three Other Ex-Minneapolis Police Officers Indicted by Federal Grand Jury." NBC News, May 7, 2021. https://www.nbcnews.com/news/us-news/derek-chauvin-three-other-ex-minneapolis-police-officers-indicted-federal-n1266671.

Wilson, Chris. "The U.S. Has Flattened the Curve. Next Up Is 'Squashing' It." *Time*, August 22, 2020. https://time.com/5827156/squashing-squash-curve-coronavirus-covid19/.

The Wire. "In Russia, Anti-Putin Protests Thrive with a Little Help from the Internet." Accessed February 23, 2021. https://thewire.in/world/coronavirus-in-russia-anti-government-protests.

Witte, Griff, and Michael Birnbaum. "Putin Implicated in Fatal Poisoning of Former KGB Officer at London Hotel." *Washington Post*, January 21, 2016. https://www-washingtonpost-com.stanford.idm.oclc.org/world/putin-implicated-in-fatal-poisoning-of-former-kgb-spy-at-posh-london-hotel/2016/01/21/2c0c5052-bf92-11e5-98c8-7fab78677d51_story.html.

Wittenberg-Cox, Avivah. "What Do Countries with the Best Coronavirus Responses Have in Common? Women Leaders." *Forbes*. Accessed February 23, 2021. https://www.forbes.com/sites/avivahwittenbergcox/2020/04/13/what-do-countries-with-the-best-coronavirus-reponses-have-in-common-women-leaders/.

Wong, Julia Carrie, and Lauren Gambino. "Donald Trump Pardons Joe Arpaio, Former Sheriff Convicted in Racial Profiling Case." *Guardian*, August 26, 2017. https://www.theguardian.com/us-news/2017/aug/25/donald-trump-joe-arpaio-pardon-arizona-sheriff.

World Affairs Council. "The Decline of Western News." Accessed February 25, 2021. https://www.worldaffairs.org/video-library/event/1876.

World Bank. "Poverty Reduction in Belarus." Accessed February 25, 2021. https://doi.org/10/17/poverty-reduction-in-belarus.

World Trade Organization. "WTO | Anti-Dumping—Gateway." Accessed February 25, 2021. https://www.wto.org/english/tratop_e/adp_e/adp_e.htm.

"World War I Casualties." *Wikipedia*, February 20, 2021. https://en.wikipedia.org/w/index.php?title=World_War_I_casualties&oldid=1007872472.

XinhuaNet. "Xinhua—China, World, Business, Sports, Photos and Video | English. News.Cn." Accessed February 25, 2021. http://www.chinaview.cn/.

Xiong, Chao. "Court of Appeals Will Hear Arguments to Add Third-Degree Murder in George Floyd Case." *Star Tribune*, February 23, 2021. https://www.startribune.com/court-of-appeals-will-hear-arguments-to-add-third-degree-murder-charge-in-george-floyd-case/600026545/.

Yacoubian, Mona. "Syria Timeline: Since the Uprising against Assad." United States Institute of Peace, January 1, 2021. https://www.usip.org/syria-timeline-uprising-against-assad.

Yaqoob, Tahira, and Amanda Fisher. "American Grandfather Faces Five Years Jail in Arab Emirates for Taking Picture of 'No Photography' Sign." *Daily Mail* Online, November 4, 2014. https://www.dailymail.co.uk/news/article-2820753/American-grandfather-70-faces-five-years-jail-Arab-Emirates-taking-picture-no-photography-sign-held-secret-week-police-jail-diabetic-s-health-risk.html.

Yeung, Peter. "Ai Weiwei: A Tumultuous Timeline." *Telegraph*, April 13, 2015. https://www.telegraph.co.uk/culture/art/11522659/Ai-Weiwei-a-tumultuous-timeline.html.

Yilek, Caitlin. "'America Is Very Rude': Philippines to End Major Security Pact with US." *Washington Examiner*, February 11, 2020. https://www.washingtonexaminer. com/news/america-is-very-rude-philippines-to-end-major-security-pact-with-us.

Ying, Guo, and Mi Li. "China Focus: Smart Tech Helps Whole-Hog Reshaping of China's Pig-Raising Industry." XinhuaNet, November 14, 2019. http://www.xinhua net.com/english/2019-11/14/c_138554901.htm.

YouTube. "Страна Для Жизни." Accessed February 25, 2021. https://www.youtube. com/channel/UCFPC7r3tWWXWzUIROLx46mg.

Yuan, Shawn. "'Political Show': Xi Visits Wuhan as China Coronavirus Cases Slow." Accessed February 23, 2021. https://www.aljazeera.com/news/2020/3/10/politi cal-show-xi-visits-wuhan-as-china-coronavirus-cases-slow.

Yuen, Chantal. "Yellow Umbrella Protesters in Tense Standoff with Police in Mong Kok." Hong Kong Free Press HKFP, February 12, 2016. https://hongkongfp. com/2016/02/12/yellow-umbrella-protesters-in-tense-standoff-with-police-in- mong-kok/.

Zeitung, Süddeutsche. "All You Need to Know about the Panama Papers." Süddeutsche. de. Accessed February 23, 2021. https://panamapapers.sueddeutsche.de/articles/ 56febff0a1bb8d3c3495adf4/.

Zerkal, Olena. "Russo-Ukrainian War: Putin Must Be Held Accountable." Atlantic Council, March 26, 2010. https://www.atlanticcouncil.org/blogs/ukrainealert/ russo-ukrainian-war-putin-must-be-held-accountable/.

Zernike, Kate. "Nancy Pelosi: Demonized or Celebrated, She Refuses to Agonize." *New York Times*, November 4, 2018, sec. U.S. https://www.nytimes.com/2018/11/ 04/us/politics/nancy-pelosi-house-leader-women.html.

Zill de Granados, Oriana. "Did Jeffrey Epstein Kill Himself? '60 Minutes' Investigates." CBS News, January 5, 2020. https://www.cbsnews.com/news/did-jeffrey-epstein- kill-himself-60-minutes-investigates-2020-01-05/.

Zotigh, Dennis. "Introduction & 1st Question: American Indian or Native American?" Smithsonian Institution, January 2011. https://blog.nmai.si.edu/main/2011/01/ introduction-1st-question-american-indian-or-native-american.html.

INDEX

CPSIA information can be obtained
at www.ICGtesting.com
Printed in the USA
LVHW091500220222
711728LV00004B/56